AIDAN HIGGINS:
THE FRAGILITY OF FORM

D1329008

ALSO BY NEIL MURPHY

Irish Fiction and Postmodern Doubt:
An Analysis of the Epistemological Crisis in Modern Irish Fiction (2004)

British Asian Fiction:
Framing the Contemporary (co-edited, 2008)

Literature and Ethics:
Questions of Responsibility in Literary Studies (co-edited, 2009)

AIDAN HIGGINS: THE FRAGILITY OF FORM

edited by Neil Murphy
with essays from

ANNIE PROULX

JOHN BANVILLE

DERMOT HEALY

DEREK MAHON

GERRY DUKES

KEITH HOPPER

GEORGE O'BRIEN

PETER VAN DE KAMP

& AIDAN HIGGINS

Dalkey Archive Press
Champaign and London

Copyright © 2010 by Dalkey Archive Press
Introduction © 2010 by Neil Murphy
First Edition, 2010
All rights reserved

Library of Congress Cataloging-in-Publication Data

Aidan Higgins: the fragility of form / edited by Neil Murphy ; with essays from
Annie Proulx ... [et al.]. -- 1st ed.
p. cm.
Includes bibliographical references.
ISBN 978-1-56478-562-6 (pbk. : alk. paper)
1. Higgins, Aidan, 1927---Criticism and interpretation. I. Murphy, Neil. II.
Proulx, Annie.
PR6058.I34Z53 2010
823'.914--dc22
                              2009043920

All individual essays collected in this volume are copyrighted by
the respective authors and cannot be reproduced without permission.
For individual credits, please see acknowledgments.

Partially funded by the University of Illinois at Urbana-Champaign
and by a grant from the Illinois Arts Council, a state agency

www.dalkeyarchive.com

Cover: design by Danielle Dutton
Printed on permanent/durable acid-free paper
and bound in the United States of America

CONTENTS

Acknowledgments   11

Introduction   13
NEIL MURPHY

Section I: Writers on the Writer

Aidan Higgins's *Flotsam & Jetsam*   23
ANNIE PROULX

The Missing Link   42
JOHN BANVILLE

Auld Lang Rish and After   54
BERNARD SHARE

A Chance Meeting Outside the Irish Tourist Board   68
DERMOT HEALY

The Blithely Subversive Aidan Higgins   72
DEREK MAHON

Aidan Higgins in Berlin: 79
The Great Walker—A Personal Omnium Gatherum
MARTIN KLUGER

Balcony of Europe: 87
Difficulties for Dramatists
NEIL DONNELLY

Aidan Higgins in Conversation with Neil Donnelly   91

Prose Familiars   96
    AIDAN HIGGINS

Section II: Critical Responses

For the Record: 105
Aidan Higgins's Autobiographies
    PETER VAN DE KAMP

Aidan Higgins's Ear Plays: 130
Narrative as the Sport of History
    DANIEL JERNIGAN

A Glimpse of Aidan Higgins through his Critical Work   152
    ANGELA FRATTAROLA

Windy Arbours: 173
Reading the Runes
    ROBERT LUMSDEN

Aidan Higgins: 189
Forging Fictions and Memoirs
    GERRY DUKES

"Romance and Pathos among Four Human Derelicts":   199
Harold Pinter's Adaptation of Langrishe, Go Down
    KEITH HOPPER

Aidan Higgins   233
    PATRICK O'NEILL

Felons of Our Selves: 258
The Fiction of Aidan Higgins
    MORRIS BEJA

Questions of Travel: 282
Writing and Travel in the Work of Aidan Higgins
    GEORGE O'BRIEN

Despair and Desire: 302
Langrishe, Go Down and a Poetics of the Body
    ROBERTA GEFTER WONDRICH

"The Other Day I Was Thinking of You":   326
Love Remembered in *Bornholm Night-Ferry* and
Lions of the Grunewald
    NEIL MURPHY

Select Bibliography   345

Contributors' Notes   353

Acknowledgments

Initially, special mention must be made of Alannah Hopkin, for her endless assistance in numerous ways over the past few years, for her extraordinary graciousness when responding to every request, and for connecting Rory via e-mail to many of us.

Thanks too are due to Neil Donnelly for organising the Aidan Higgins 80th birthday celebrations in Celbridge in 2007, an enormously successful event that convinced me that the time was right to proceed with this volume, planned for several years. Neil's assistance with making connection with some of the contributors is warmly appreciated.

Colleagues near and far have been valuable sounding-boards over the past couple of years, most notably Angela Frattarola, Keith Hopper, Daniel Jernigan, and Peter van de Kamp, all of whom offered much needed assistance without hesitation. Thank you all.

Many thanks too are due to John O'Brien, and everyone at Dalkey not just for their perpetual willingness to promote the kind of literature that matters, but for ensuring that most of Higgins's works are now back in print.

Many exchanges with the students of my contemporary literature and Irish literature courses inadvertently echo through the pages that I have written for this volume, for which I say *Terima Kasih—Xie Xie—Nandri*. And extra special thanks to Adibah Mustafa's sharp eye, and invaluable help with preparing the manuscript, and to Emma Yuana binte Muhamad for her graciousness and greatly-appreciated contributions. Finally, deepest gratitude is offered to our research student, Michelle Wang, for her expert assistance, and endless patience, in working on the final proofs.

And, as always, to Su, mo chroi—and to my trio of angels whose smiles shimmer in all that I do. *Go raibh maith agaibh.*

And to Rory of the endlessly echoing hills, I say *gratias*, for the gleaming words.

■

Thanks are offered, on behalf of several contributors, to the McPherson Library Special Collections at the University of Victoria, Canada, which houses a collection of Higgins's first drafts, unpublished work, and letters.

Thanks too Morris Beja, and to the editors of the *Irish University Review* for permission to reprint his essay, "Felons of Our Selves: The Fiction of Aidan Higgins." *Irish University Review* 3.2 (Autumn 1973): 163–178.

Thanks to Patrick O'Neill for permission to reprint his essay— due acknowledgment is also offered with thanks to Gunter Narr, who originally published O'Neill's essay: "Aidan Higgins" in Rüdiger Imhof, ed., *Contemporary Irish Novelists* (Tübingen: Gunter Narr Verlag 1990): 93–107.

Thanks to John Banville (and publisher), for permission to reprint his essay, "The Missing Link," originally published in the *Times Literary Supplement* Vol. 51 No. 19, December 2nd, 2004.

Thanks also to Derek Mahon (and publisher) for permission to reprint his essay, "The Blithely Subversive Aidan Higgins," originally published in the *Times Literary Supplement*, May 9th, 2007.

Thanks to NTU's (Singapore) School of Humanities & Social Sciences for contributing valuable financial support to this venture.

Introduction

Neil Murphy

> That time, that place, was it all your
> own invention, that you shared with me?
> And I too perhaps was your invention.
> —*Helsingør Station & Other Departures*

The publication of a volume of essays that offers critical response, artistic (re-)evaluation, personal literary recollections, and various attempts to contextualize its subject's work in the complex streams of twentieth-century literature, will inevitably have more than a whiff of the *festschrift* about it. The very act of assembling a collection of this kind infers a kind of acknowledgment of its subject having *arrived*, of being a worthy recipient of the critical gesture that such an act entails. While this is true of the present volume in many respects, the subject in this instance, Aidan Higgins, predictably poses problems for such easy assumptions. Despite having received numerous literary awards, having published more than a dozen major works (of fiction, travel-writing, autobiography), and having received plaudits from major authors like Beckett, Banville, Proulx, and Pinter (and several others in the present volume), and from most major Irish literary critics, there remains the niggling sense that Aidan Higgins's work still requires some justification when one makes claims for its significance—so much so that several of the contributors in the present collection make explicit reference to Higgins's relative obscurity: Proulx attempts to explain the "puzzle" of why his work remains obscure by arguing that his erudition may have worked against him, claiming that Higgins's work represents an "incomprehensible codex from an ancient civilization" to poor contemporary readers who simply do not possess the necessary learning to recognize the abundance of rich textual treasures in Higgins's fictional universes. Similarly, John Banville suggests that Higgins is the "missing link" between high modernism and contemporary fiction, his work being highly subjective and allusive, fare for a different world perhaps; a point echoed by Mahon, who in suggesting that the "unfashionable literary" quality of the work accounts for its relative lack of popularity, implicitly indicts the reading public in the process. It is also probable that the non-Irish canvases that characterize most of Higgins's work, after *Langrishe, Go Down*, ensure that the work doesn't fit the easy categories employed by the reading public, reviewers and academics. Furthermore, as Irish academia has increasingly foregrounded identity politics, postcolonial studies, and the centrality of national history over the past few decades, fiction by an Irish writer that is variously located in Copenhagen, Berlin, Nerja, London, among colonies of expatriates, simply doesn't fit. Quite simply, certain writers do not facilitate ideological agendas, and Higgins is one such writer, being no fan of politics himself, as indicated in his review of Günter Grass's *Headbirths, or, the Germans Are Dying Out*: "I was invited to participate, discuss the equation Literature and Politics. I said there was no connection. Ah, but that's a political comment, they said. Not my cup of tea, I said, thanks all the same" (*Windy Arbours* 303). One can only hope, of course, that Higgins's time may yet come, when literary fashions change and readerly viewfinders retrain their focus on texts rather than almost exclusively on contexts.

Thus, this volume is not simply an act of critical acknowledgment (though it is certainly that); it also seeks to assist new readers of Higgins to find worthwhile ways to enter the work, to offer signposts to a body of work that always resists classification and oftentimes poses interpretive challenges for the uninitiated reader. This then represents, in its way, a code to the codex that is the Higgins universe. Other valuable critical responses have been contributed over the years since the first publication of *Felo de Se*, most notably in the *Review of Contemporary Fiction* Aidan Higgins Special (3.1 1983) which made a major contribution to Higgins scholarship. In addition, several of the authors in the current collection have written previously about Higgins (Banville, Donnelly, Dukes, Healy, Mahon, O'Brien, Proulx, Share, van de Kamp, myself). Essays by authors who are relatively new to Higgins (Frattarola, Hopper, Jernigan, Lumsden, Gefter) feature too, indicating that this "obscure" author is still attracting readers who bring fresh perspectives and offer critical reactions to aspects of Higgins's work that have not previously been offered close analysis. I have also reprinted two extremely important essays by Morris Beja (1973) and Patrick O'Neill (1990), quite simply because they represent two of the more significant contributions to the body of critical work on Higgins over the past four decades, and offer useful critical contextualization. Other important essays were written during this period by Imhof, Kreilkamp, Lubbers, Rauchbauer, and Skelton, all of which are listed in the *Select Bibliography* at the rear of this volume.

One of the qualities of Higgins's work that has always intrigued, and irritated at times it must be acknowledged, is the way in which earlier fugitive Ur-fiction, as he puts it (*Lions*, Apologia), is recycled to such a degree that many of the texts echo each other; variants of *Langrishe* appear in the earlier "Killachter Meadow" (later reprinted as "North Salt Holdings" in *Flotsam & Jetsam*) while the fictional sisters re-appear (re*invented* as Higgins's brothers) throughout the autobiographies; parts of *Lions of the Grunewald* and *Bornholm Night-Ferry* are echoed in *Helsingør Station & Other Departures*, in *Ronda Gorge & Other Precipices*, and again in the autobiographies, and in

Flotsam & Jetsam. Fiction is frequently reinvented as autobiography, and vice-versa, until it becomes apparent that Higgins sees little difference between the two. Almost forty years ago, he indicated that all of his work followed his life, "like slug trails . . . all the fiction happened" ("Writer in Profile" 13) and, more recently, the trilogy of autobiographies opens with the assurance that he is still "consumed by memories, and they form the life of me; stories that make up my life and lend it whatever veracity and purpose it may have" (*Dog Days* 3). When Higgins uses the words veracity, stories, and life in such a fashion, one needs to be alert to the inevitable conflation of all three that soon after occurs. Everywhere in his work, the life finds expression, but in such a way that the distinction between autobiography and fiction gradually grows to mean less and less. This is because the traditional demarcations between fiction and reality are constantly confronted in Higgins's work, and much of the significance of his writing finally rests on the author's deeply troubled response to the way one grapples with a life that frequently struggles to be named in the stories one writes. Thus, when Higgins's work constantly echoes itself, sometimes even within the text itself, there is more than mere slippage, and recycling, at work. In the present collection, Dukes refers to the "repetitions with variations" as narrative strategy in the autobiographies, and van de Kamp refers, similarly, to Higgins's "multidimensionality" in an effort to explain the peculiarities of his curiously circular technique where scraps of living are energized, and later re-visited with a different eye. This is especially apparent in the autobiographies but when this idea is reflected back onto a consideration of the fiction, certain characters and thematic patterns repeatedly re-emerge, revised, always circling the same obsessions.

This collection, one hopes, echoes something of the Higginsian circularity, with many contributors fixing their gaze on similar landscapes that appear to send back different echoes. So while Angela Frattarola illustrates how Higgins's review of Faulkner gains

Somewhat inevitably, many of the contributors repeatedly circle back to the first novel, *Langrishe, Go Down*, with Banville unequivocal in his praise of the "masterpiece," and Mahon referring to it as "an outstanding work of the time and a modern classic." Keith Hopper, in his examination of the film that grew out of *Langrishe, Go Down*, continually cuts back to consider the commanding presence of the original literary work on all aspects of the film. Hopper's approach offers a new trajectory for readers of Higgins, as does Daniel Jernigan who also ploughs relatively untouched ground in his consideration of Higgins's playfully experimental ear plays, and considers some of the implications of Higgins's subversions in the context of Lyotard.

George O'Brien has previously written about Higgins's work but here he considers the author's travel writing, in the context of the absence of structured experience in the landscapes. During a sustained examination of the figure of travel, and the traveler, a sense of Higgins, the artist-in-perpetual-transit emerges, suggesting that O'Brien sees Higgins's work as extraordinary and highly nuanced. Similarly, Morris Beja's essay, first published in 1973, describes Higgins as "one of the most important Irish novelists writing today," a diagnosis that reminds one of the esteem in which his work was held during the 1960s and early 1970s. Beja's assessment, filtered in part through R. D. Laing's *The Divided Self*, was based on his sense that Higgins's heroes were unique in their evocation of a disembodied self. Peter van de Kamp too is acutely aware of multiple versions of Higgins in his autobiographies and beyond, forever slipping in and out of view, while penning "acts of commemoration." Alternatively, Angela Frattarola focuses on the notion of the "faceless creator" in Higgins, through her reading of *Windy Arbours*, and concludes that there are many faces, hidden and otherwise, in the Higgins pantheon. Of course, the same can be said of the account of Higgins that emerges from years of correspondence with Bernard Share; several visages show themselves

as author and Share both journey through the years. The significance of the personal literary memoir lies in part in the nature of
the exchange between Higgins and the author of the remembered
events, and Martin Kluger's highly personal recollections also offer us a glimpse of Higgins's curiously distant persona during his
Berlin years. These recollections are primarily characterized by
the admiration of a young apprentice-of-sorts but in the process,
a curiously memorable image of Higgins, the great walker, the
perpetual outsider, also emerges. So too does a sense of the great
difficulties that accompanied the writing of *Balcony of Europe*, a
theme revisited both by Gerry Dukes and Neil Donnelly in their
respective essays. In his conversation with Higgins, Donnelly also
directs several questions at the author about *Balcony of Europe*,
and in Higgins's answers a greater understanding of the difficulty
of writing this, his second novel, becomes evident. But his fiction
has always, almost by definition, been a struggle because it has
always sought new directions, has always searched for a way to
perceive and say the living world, and it is a deep awareness of the
complex nature of that seeing and saying that has always marked
the work, and the man. Throughout his work there are certain
key moments, in the midst of the rigmarole of living, in which a
deeply self-conscious voice emerges, even as the world swirls in
wild patterns all around him. In such moments, the curtains are
drawn back and we are offered a glimpse of the perennial Higgins
question, a question of being, of knowing. And the answer is embedded in the utterance:

> Who am I? Am I or am I not the same person I have
> always taken myself to be? In that case, who am I? Is the
> silence significant or just lack or something to say? Is that
> significant? Speak up, but kindly confine yourself to es-
> sentials; write on one side of the paper only.

Where am I? Where was I then? What do you do when memory begins to go? I spend much of the time looking back into the past. It is no longer there. It has moved. Where to? ("Sodden Fields," in *Flotsam & Jetsam* 257)

Readers of Higgins will be all too familiar with the endlessly critical and ironic eye that he directs, with deadly precision, at his own life and work. Lest one forgets that this eye also frequently casts a withering glare on critics and "critical appreciators," Higgins's essay, "Prose Familiars," has also been reprinted here, rescued from the early 1950s, in partial hope that we may have changed its author's mind, ever so slightly.

WORKS CITED

Higgins, Aidan. *Dog Days: A Sequel to Donkey's Years*. London: Secker & Warburg, 1998.

—. *Donkey's Years: Memories of a Life as Story Told*. London: Secker & Warburg, 1995.

—. *Flotsam & Jetsam*. Champaign, IL: Dalkey Archive Press, 2002.

—. *Lions of the Grunewald*. London: Secker & Warburg, 1993.

—. *Windy Arbours*. Champaign, IL: Dalkey Archive Press, 2006.

—. "Writer in Profile: Aidan Higgins." Interview with Aidan Higgins. *RTE Guide* 5 February 1971: 13.

NOTES

1. Higgins's plays are published in 2010 for the first time as follows: *Darkling Plain: Texts for the Air*. Ed. Daniel Jernigan. Champaign, IL: Dalkey Archive Press, 2010.

Section I: Writers on the Writer

Aidan Higgins's *Flotsam & Jetsam*

ANNIE PROULX

Aidan Higgins's *Flotsam & Jetsam* is a good sampler of his literary range. Rather than reading the selections as conventional
stories, most should be appreciated as fine, small paintings, as examples of how this powerful writer arranges experience and personal dreamtimes through exploration of a past which exists only
through memory. Both the historical past and its cousin, myth, are
formed through accumulated and recorded memories into public
consciousness of nation and universe. The process begins with individual lives, and Higgins has fixed the core decades of the twentieth century in literature's amber.

Born March 3, 1927, Aidan Higgins was the third of four sons
of "Batty" Higgins and Lilly Boyd. The father had money inherited
from the grandfather's shares of a copper mine in Bisbee, Arizona.
"Batty" Higgins, "quiff parted in the middle like Mandrake the
Magician," bought "Springfield House" in Celbridge after the First
World War. The family lived high on the hog until the money ran
out, and Aidan Higgins's childhood on the 75-acre estate marked
him for life.[1]

Higgins tells us again and again that all his fictions derive from
his personal past, from memory, from the history of the Higgins
family. Underneath the surfaces of *Langrishe, Go Down* and Higgins's tripartite autobiography, *A Bestiary*, there seems to lie a sim-
mering rage at "Batty" Higgins who used up all the money and lost
the house.[2] After the money was gone the parents lived out their

lives in increasingly squalid digs while the four sons, like characters in a fairy tale, went into the world to seek their fortunes.

One of the puzzles of Aidan Higgins is why, after the great critical success of his first novel, the classic *Langrishe, Go Down,* this prince of stylists has remained relatively obscure. Some reasons are discussed in Neil Murphy's essay "Dreams, Departures, Destinations."[3]

Higgins wrote *Langrishe,* Murphy said, at a time when "he had not yet fully dispensed with the formal devices of plot and characterisation in the traditional sense." The fact that it was a big house novel and apparently told a love story as well as the collapse of the landed Langrishe family "deceives its readers" into taking it for a novel in traditional form. But it was more than that according to Murphy; it was "a profound meditation on the meaning of the past and how memory invents its own past." And after *Langrishe,* Murphy continued, Higgins forever rejected formal literary structures.[4]

But in fact he had already spurned the templates of traditional literature with the short "story" collection *Felo de Se* before he wrote *Langrishe, Go Down.* (Higgins, like Robbe-Grillet, called the pieces "fictions.") Five of those early stories are included in *Flotsam & Jetsam* and they are idiosyncratic, original and still fresh.[5] They contain some of the richest sentences and paragraphs to come from a writer's pen in the 20th century, and show Higgins's fascination with the deceitful shapes of the past.[6]

In the *Flotsam & Jetsam* collection—the fictions were written over a 30-year period, some of them belonging originally to larger works—Higgins is concerned with human perceptions of others, personal and historical events, memory and its distortions. The pieces are usually focused around love, erotic bonds and physical sensations, heightened by his frequent address, especially in sexual or love passages, to "You" which intimately pulls the reader into the fiction. He gives us worlds that seem to quiver with impermanence and fragmentation, that indicate subterranean rifts like those invisibly tearing continents apart deep below. His work implies that certain massive, unseen and shifting forces support human experience—Piscean astrology? Memory is the ill-made key that allows access to whatever is there.

One can make a stab at classifying Higgins's work, but perhaps "experimental" (as Beckett and Joyce were experimental) comes close. Higgins himself sees his work as modern.[7] Although Beckett and Joyce are often named as great influences on Higgins, they are perhaps more accurately seen as fellow travelers in modernist literature than Virgil's. Other streams feed into the river of Higgins's work. But the great thing was probably his privileged boyhood in a grand house with stables, horses, servants and exclusive schools, a halcyon time followed by the short, sharp shock of poverty.

There are in Higgins's work Dadaist and Surrealist moments, both painterly and intellectual. The many discursive passages that veer away from apparent storylines were likely meant to unsettle the reader. Higgins's knowledge of (European) painting lets him use art in the same way he uses lists, billboards and graffiti, as temporal referents, as evocations of particular times and places, colors and poses, expressions. And in the years when he was moving around Europe there was still some vigor in the realist art of the New Objectivity of the 1920s and early 1930s (many of these artists were featured in the infamous Nazi 1937 exhibition of "degenerate art") and Higgins, swimming in a sea of influential and experimental ideas, may have felt some comradeship with the *geist*.[8]

Higgins began to write seriously in the 1950s. Although we now think of the 1950s (at least in the United States, Australia and New Zealand) as a period of stasis and creeping suburban conformism, in Europe, especially in France, a rebellious impetus for change erupted here and there, some of it metamorphosed from the *Neue Sachlichkeit* of the 1920s.[9] Anglo-Irish Beckett's *En attendant Godot* opened in Paris in 1953. Robbe-Grillet's *Les Gommes* appeared, apparently shorn of plot and most adjectives, limiting itself to realist presence and opening the literary door to the "new novel" and the "new objectivity" which rejected the psychological analysis of the traditional novel form. When Robbe-Grillet's masterpiece, *Jalousie*, arrived in 1957 the critics, who simply did not get it, had a hey-day making fun of it, calling the then-infamous passage "counting the banana trees" the "cadastre style" for its presumed resemblance to surveyors' plotted lines. Higgins's lists are not Robbe-Grillet's banana trees, but hyper-rich series of varied yet connected images. This stylistic device works brilliantly when the passages are read aloud as in "Lengthening Shadows," one of Higgins's pieces for the BBC 4's "Texts of the Air."[10]

Higgins, comfortable with languages, with a massive body of literature, art, mythology and various sciences, traveled far and intimately knew many places. He moved himself out of the "Irish writer" slot into that of an apparent chronicler of slippery, amorphous love in awkward places—South Africa, Germany, Scandinavia. He seemed something of a wandering literary man who defied the oppressions of regional literature, yet the Ireland he knew as a child is never out of sight.

In terms of reader popularity, his erudition worked against him. Readers (especially ill-educated Americans) may be dazzled by the beauty of his prose, the breath-catching similes, but are confounded by references to Zöllner's Patterns, Pistrucci and Briot, the wizard of Ferney, Lippershay, lammergieres, lesser-known artists and literary characters, his handiness with Latin and German. His fictions, with their abrupt partitions, layers of collage and interlocked allusions make it likely that some duller readers put aside his books as they would a maddeningly incomprehensible codex from an ancient civilization.

The self and, by extension, the family, is Higgins's tool to open up a time and place both beloved and hateful, the same tool Giuseppe

Lampedusa used to pry the Prince of Salinas and his time from the foxed pages of history. There is nothing simple about this; readers may mistake the tool for the whole (as in *Langrishe, Go Down*) but such a use of the family is as if one pulled up a single clump of grass and discovered the subterranean network of roots, the web of life below—vast and intricate, nodes and hairs, rootlets branching endlessly, connected to the far past, some broken in the uprooting, and, though unseen, the pale snouts of new growth aggressively thrusting into the future.

The maverick American anthropologist, Loren Eiseley (1907–1977), wrote: "Everything in the mind is in rat's country. . . . Nothing is lost, but it can never be again as it was. You will only find the bits and cry out because they were yourself. Nothing can begin again and go right, but it still is you, your mind, picking endlessly over the splintered glass of a mirror dropped and broken long ago."[11]

In *Flotsam & Jetsam* some particulars of Higgins's style show themselves. In these fictions one butts up against disconcertingly abrupt shifts.[12] The fictions are not linear, but like blocks of events arranged provocatively on the page. New characters and places leap from the page, yet only slowly reveal a relationship to the whole. Mistaken identities and look-alike characters (usually men), including William Trevor, Charlie Chaplin, Von Stroheim, James Joyce, impart a wavering, illusory texture to the fictions. Characters' motives and salient behaviors often do not enter until late in the piece, and then through a side door. A caustic humour and a taste for juxtaposing the ineffable and repulsive add alkaline sharpness. A cascade of events and periods may be telescoped into a few sentences, often partitioned and framed by plangent titles.[13] There are many full-throated and gorgeous sentences like rivers gathering the most remote tributaries from vast watersheds. Some of the fiction is addressed to the intimate, yet unknowable and mysterious "You." A rancorous dislike of homosexuals, transvestites and lesbians runs throughout—"Last up the fire escape is a lesbian!" a child cries. The weather is almost always freezing cold. And Higgins favors brief, powerful but enigmatic final sentences like tough punches.

There are recurring themes. His great theme is love—love's beginning, love broken, betrayed, separation of the lovers, love degraded, unrequited, lost, regained, and, above all, made real because it is remembered. Then there is "the continuing event," an unpleasant situation that seems to have no exit and that often afflicts the protagonist with aecidia and self-doubt. Privation, hunger and cold give the fictions the undercurrent of a struggle to live. The fall from ease to the discomforts of poverty shapes several of the stories. The Catholic Church and its ceremonies run as a thready stream throughout his writing.

The title story, "Flotsam & Jetsam," (originally "Nightfall on Cape Piscator") is set in a seaside resort in South Africa during the Apartheid period. It is a story of racist sexual aggression by a mild-mannered antique dealer, Mr. Vaschel, on his mother-in-law's black servant, Amalinda. Throughout, the sexual imagery is of red-eyed donkeys with monstrous erections. The last sentence, "The sun was up," dashes a shot glass of irony over all that has preceded it. The fiction is an example of the "continuing event," for the reader knows the emboldened Mr. Vaschel will again indulge in the custom of the country.

"In Old Heidelberg" (originally "Tower and Angels") is set in that romantic city in December 1949. It is bone-chillingly cold outside, but in the hot cafés American tourists mingle with ex-Luftwaffe officers. A woman, Ellen Rossa-Stowe, enters a narrow door and climbs steep stairs to a tower for an assignation with Irwin Pastern, a modernist painter who favors the deceitful converging lines of Zöllner's optical illusions. They often walk through sharp cold "into the municipal wilderness" illuminated by bonfires of burning rags. Abruptly Ellen Rossa-Stowe is gone. Another woman appears,

Annelise von Fromar, with her "sad and elongated face" and her skin texture recalling "canopic jars." Together they take a train to Mossback, make love, depart. Alone and in his tower Irwin notices the shadows of the rearing walls. They seem like gigantic hawsers and "parted already by the prodigious strain exerted against them they had begun to fall away in terrific slow motion . . . watched by a person who had become paralyzed, incapable of lifting a hand."[14] Again it is the continuous event; again the protagonist falls back weakly.

"Berlin After Dark" (originally "Winter Offensive") features the bulky, bullet-headed Herr Bausch, a cement entrepreneur who expresses a "rufous virility" and walks as though "adjusting his stride to the inconveniences of a cavalry sabre." Bausch might have stepped out of the studios of George Grosz, Otto Dix or photographer August Sander, whose full-length portrait subject, "The Pastry Cook," lacks only the cement block and prone position.

This sexually motivated hero goes from lowly concrete worker in the 1930s to partner in a trucking firm after he joins the *National-Sozialistische Reicharbeitsdienst* party. Part of the opportunistic scum that floats atop every greasy money wave he becomes rich and indulges his taste for the wives of wealthy men. When we meet him he is taking his "summer pleasure" on the Isle of Sylt in the North Sea with the "countess" Gerta Kroll (a.k.a. "the puma"). He goes for a dip, then rests on a concrete block. In a haunting image, Higgins describes him thus:

> His own gross bulk and the purposeful arrangements of spine and buttock (free of bathing drawers) created in conjunction with the block a truncated and obscene effect. Fixed and stern, it seemed as though his member was embedded in the cement, which took on the property of a prodigious root or membrane doubled under him and upon which he lay passive—something by which he could

be immediately recognized, as the monsters of antiquity are recognized by a particular vice or the unicorn by its extravagant horn.[15]

Back in Berlin he resumes his chase after luxury women and ends up marrying one—Annelise von Fromar, who later becomes one of painter Irwin Pastern's lovers. This reappearance has the effect of transmuting the Annelise character into an interchangeable piece that might be used in any number of fictions. She is not permanently fixed in any character or situation, but like certain lizards and moths takes on the color of the fiction in which she appears. It is an indication of Higgins's regard for the past as malleable, even fluid. As for Herr Bausch, he loses everything, gets into the black market and ends up on the sidewalk bragging about his Venezuelan deals in flints for cigarette lighters and "razors that cut both ways."

"*Lebensraum*" is not so much a backhand reflection on Nazi Germany's perceived need for more land as it is a sad three-part intermezzo in two sad, vague lives. It has a surreal flavor and suggests the "continuing event." In 1949 Fraulein Sevi Klein, a 39-year old whore, moves to London. In a pub she meets Michael Alpin, age 27, from Dublin, who has thrown up his legal profession, to drift around London. They move in together, he furtive and gloomy, she half whore, half wife.

In the summer they go Ireland, to a beach littered with cigarette tins and populated with hordes from "the sloblands . . . the shape of the common plural." On the beach they see a deformed man in his 20s. Nobody can bear to look at him. "Look here! Look there! Unkind life is roaring by in its topmost branches."

At last is it late summer. The affair is over. Alpin sits on a sea wall. Sevi comes onto the beach. She writes in the sand "Das ist der Pudel Kern" ("so that's the gist of it") and walks away, retreating into her background, into the twilight sea line. "There is no commencement or halfway to that fall: only its continuing."

The much-acclaimed story "North Salt Holdings" (originally "Killachter Meadow") is the skeleton shape of *Langrishe, Go Down*. The half-dozen sections end with lines that seem dark and aching poetry. The Kervicks have owned Springfield House in old Killachter since the 1880s. After they die the four spinster daughters continue to live there. A German student, Klaefisch, lives in a hut on the property for a summer. Imogen writhes with lascivious dreams featuring Klaefisch. Emily-May is fat, bald, cannot swim, but loves to float naked in the river. Helen likes to watch the hens that "seemed to live in a lifelong coma." The servant, Joseph, who stinks and knows his place, kills the hens. At last Emily-May strips and gets into the cold river. She floats away under the roaring trees toward "extinction and forgetting . . . until all, prostrate and rank, sank from human sight."

Enigmatically titled, "Asylum" is a tragic-comic novella more reminiscent of Nathanael West than Joyce or Beckett. Eddie Brazill is the oldest son of a lodge-keeper on an estate. When the mother dies the family breaks up and, after working as a blacksmith's helper, Eddie goes to London, "bathed in a pale sourceless light neither of morning nor evening, which came neither from the earth nor from the sky" where his identity is Irish day laborer. Job follows job, but gradually he sees no possibilities for him in London. Wandering, starving, laughing, fainting, he walks endlessly through the city.

Ben Boucher, deaf, a keen golfer, a heavy drinker, is the victim of an eccentric will. He inherits nothing unless he stays sober for a year. He is in the clutches of a faith healer, Dr. M. A. Vergiff, "ringmaster, rather than doctor." Vergiff outlines a ten-week cure and advises a golfing companion. Boucher hires Eddie Brazill (with whom he played golf in long-ago days) to keep Boucher away from drink and be his golfing companion while he undergoes Vergiff's regimen.

Eddie has a pleasant room in the Bon Accord Hotel, but there is an oil painting above his bed. "Brazill did not care for the look of it." It shows a half-naked woman reclining on blue satin "in a bedchamber full of drooping stuffs . . . which gave a suggestion of the 'continuous event' to what was happening in the foreground—as a wall of water falling sheer from a reservoir will lead the eye . . . forward." The woman's arm rests on a "blazing turkeycock, big as a buzzard, blue-black, its scarlet comb tumescent, its claw fastened on the lady's thigh." Satanic, unsigned and awful, this painting dominates the room. Although it seems of central importance to the fiction, it is never mentioned again.

After a week they move out of the hotel and into a boarding house run by Mr. and Mrs. Crowe, closer to the sanatorium. They play a daily round of golf, no matter what the weather. The links are cold and windy, then "frozen and detested." In the evenings they read, Boucher La Rochefoucauld's *Maxims*, Brazill *Clubfoot the Avenger*.

At the Empress Theatre Brazill is smitten by actress Elizabeth Sted. They begin a love affair. Meanwhile, night after night, Boucher, like Scheherazade, talks and tells stories, gives accounts, lectures, speaks. Brazill listens with half an ear. In courting Elizabeth Sted he spends much time in her mother's "rug-infested drawing room." And through it all, with Brazill increasingly absent, Mr. Boucher talks on excitedly, whinnies and drones, fastening at last on his father and calling the dead man "by every opprobrious name in the gutter vocabulary." Brazill is rarely there to notice, but the landlord, Tom Crowe, hears the strident voice uncoiling for hours and shudders. He asks Brazill if Mr. Boucher is all right, and when reassured, says "He counts to himself in French." As if this is not proof enough that something is awry with Boucher, Brazill awakes one night to a terrific noise, the gate shaking, the door slamming. Mr. Boucher is drunk.

In the seventh week of the treatment Dr. Vergiff gives a Rosicrucian talk: ". . . an evening of snow and craziness." Afterwards Boucher sets fire to the curtains and throws objects out of the windows. He is brought to the asylum while Brazill finds a church, his own asylum.

"Catchpole" is a long selection from *Balcony of Europe*, the book Higgins eventually withdrew from circulation. He had great difficulty with the characters that remained nebulous and stunted. "I could not grasp them, to draw them into life. Their common fate—doomed for ever to be stunted beings—worried them, and me. They began to retire again whence they had come, still hardly human, apparitions frowning with displeasure, not speaking much. They were my despair."[16] Catchpole himself is a detestable, inhuman "London pansy," lewd and indiscreet, "permanently horny" and given to unsavory misadventures. Higgins's dislike of the character gleams from every sentence.

"Helsingør Station" prefigures "The Other Day I Was Thinking of You" in its tenth sentence. It is the most Dada-like story, the most collaged in form with constant abrupt switches in tone and place.

"You" is a woman who lived in a Copenhagen cellar "like a rat wife with good old Psycho" before the narrator knew her. She writes poetry and radio plays. Her husband is Kaare, a tall transvestite, father of their child Petrusjka. Kaare and "You" move to Sweden on his motorbike. Starving, he returns to Copenhagen but "You" stays, walks in the forest and comes face to face with a grey elk. The authorial voice enters: "perhaps the best idea is to imagine a country, never going there."

There is an abrupt break and we are in the mountains of Spain. "You" describes the flat she shared with Psycho and earlier loves, her attempt at suicide by pencil. And at the hotel in Málaga the narrator asks, "Whatever happened to those far-off happy days?

Were they happy days?" "You" books a flight as she feels it is beginning to end.

Again a sharp break and we are in Copenhagen's freezing streets. Old friends reappear. It is bitterly cold. Drinking, walking, remembering—then back to Spain in an olive grove, a band of sheep passing, and again another rapid switch to Denmark and freezing air.

"Sodden Fields," addressed to the mysterious "You," is an ebullient, rolling review of the year 1927, the year of Higgins's birth. He was expelled from the womb into intense cold. But there is no orderly progression of events. He leaps from his shivering birth to the moment fifty years later when he receives the "most welcome" $7,000 Irish-American Foundation award—"Kennedy bad-conscience money paid out on sole condition that I reside for ten months in my erstwhile homeland, which I had not been in a position to afford since leaving it twenty-five years before."

And then back to 1927 again—what a year! Sacco and Vanzetti electrocuted, Lindbergh feted, empress, diplomat, countess, king, all dying strange deaths, Orson Welles's older brother committed to the asylum, Sean O'Casey marrying a very young actress. Books are written. George Bernard Shaw eats boiled eggs and raw vegetables. V. S. Pritchett walks across western Spain, Gunter Grass is born, there is an eclipse of the sun and Malcolm Lowry sails with a cargo of wild animals for the Dublin Zoo. Later Higgins sees those animals: "Cracked semi-human voices spoke out from the fidgety macaws in the parrot house, their plumage the color of fire and blood, of red rage trapped in a hothouse, humming, lurid, obscene."

And on he leads us into the future sixty years from that cold March birth day to a kaleidoscope run of the 1601 Battle of Kinsale and a description of the Beast of Ballynagrumoolia, a frightful beast that puts Medusa in the shade. On from the Beast to free range eggs, all the things that can be eaten, to illegal monofilament salmon nets, drunks and pubs, the adventures of Paddy Locke.

The brilliant, feverish sentences rocket off the page. The final paragraph, addressed to "You," smoothes out and flows, and it all ends. "From southern Europe in May, flying over the Brenner, came the red admirals to breed in the nettles." What great pleasure one receives from this half hour of reading.

"The Bird I Fancied," an account of rugby and fate is one of Higgins's best fictions: lyrical, lubricious, full of heartaches and longing, going down into loss and rain.

The narrator, Brian, mistakes a gingery man in a pub for William Trevor, but he turns out to be Beamish, who has a girlfriend, Mitzi. Gradually Brian and Beamish solidify a friendship over Beamish's drink specialty, the silver bullet. Mitzi has a friend, Sally (who becomes "You") who tells a wretched tale of her father's sexual abuse. Everyone has a spouse. Brian has Margaret, Sally has Moose, a rugby-player, Beamish has Gerda. Pub-crawls, unbridled drinking, sex games, children and friends make up their days. There are long, long silences between Brian and Sally, then her summoning phone call. The affair jolts along over the years, a kind of half-life punctuated by anguished separations and postcard messages.

Higgins's asides in this fiction are rich and coiling. He and Sally notice a black transvestite wearing a Napoleonic hat boarding a bus which leads Higgins, in the voice of Brian, to nearly two pages on Napoleon, canopied bed, sarcophagus, Japanese tourists and spy holes, the battlefield at Eylau littered with 30,000 dead, Napoleon walking over the field, turning a corpse over with his toe and commenting "'*de la petite monnaie.*'" And, says Brian, "*We* were love's small change." But Higgins packs all of the pain, longing and passion of an intense love affair into one superb sentence:

> Bugger my old boots, but of all the birds in the air that ever floated on dark water, twittered, hid in reeds, flew in the night, skidded on ice, sang from treetop, perched

in impossible places, lamented, rose early, retired late, had young, choked on chicken, reappeared next morning, drank to excess, went on the wagon, regretted nothing, died on the wing, struck against lighthouses, were incapable of restraint, I surely fancied you.

"Frère Jacques, Bruder Hans" is a small and poignant memoir of the narrator's father as a "small bully" and as an old, dying man that segues into a description of his own three sons upstairs in the bathtub, laughing as their mother converts the nursery song "Frère Jacques" into German—"Bruder Hans." The generations are the "continuing event."

"The Other Day I Was Thinking of You" is composed of eight exquisite and brief prose poems of love and the ineffable "You" in different times and places, from a giddy time in the Bavarian spring to the Playa de Burriana in Spain to Rijeka Harbour. The title and the memories of "You" hold the abrupt shifts of scene together.

"Under the Ice Shelf" is in the form of a letter to a friend, the writer emerging from a winter in the Pennines after a "whoreson year." It is a caustic review of the times listing shaved-head yahoos, mildewed prayer books and smog in the valleys as modern evils.

"Ronda Gorge" is from *Ronda Gorge & Other Precipices.* This gorgeous piece of writing, full of wild beauty and its own hard-boned grace, is something of a travel diary through Spain. The writer is in Málaga in post-Franco days and the port cities roil with excess. Málaga teems with stinks, transvestite whores, bars, foreign sailors, wind, rumps, Bob Dylan's voice sounding "like an unhinged aunt," restaurants and Frenchmen, leather jackets and nuns, the New Town a "sort of Arab shanty town"—and all this tangle of life and vice, food and smells, cat fur and local wine pours into the reader's senses. Higgins says, "Over Ronda hangs a most Moorish moon and I never wish to leave it." Nor does the besotted reader as we travel with him along the southwest coast to Torremolinos, filled with shifty characters who resemble what he sees in the slaughterhouse, "the hung things, the carcasses . . . bleeding away, bleeding away, bleeding away."

"Black September" is a disturbing piece. It is September 4, 1972 with the infamous "*Föhn*" blowing in from Italy and the writer arriving in Munich. The Olympic games are in progress. He leaves the airport, somewhat mixed up on directions. "My taxi was driven by a woman. I offered Prinzregenten-Strasse Fünf as my address, a Freudian slip if ever there was one, and was smartly driven up to Adolf Hitler's old address." He redirects the taxi to Schwabing, and sees a limousine full of men he takes for Italian gangsters. They turn out to be visiting Irish government VIPs. The same day he arrives so does another person. "Terrorism, late-twentieth-century style, entered Germany from the Middle East . . . in the person of Muhammad Daoud Odeh (code name Abu Daoud), probably traveling on a forged Iraqi passport." This man later acknowledged being the mastermind of the hostage taking in the early morning hours of September 5 when Palestinian terrorists captured and killed Israeli athletes. Seventeen people died.

In Schwabing all was peaceful although "the sirens never stopped wailing" at the distant Olympic Village. Then came the newspaper headlines accompanied by crass advertisements, the world of business rolling on without pause. "On Saturday the Süddentsche Zeitung obituary notices faced pages of movie advertising of unrestrained lewdness. . . . It was time for MacBaren's Golden Blend. It was time for Volksbier." The narrator himself plays golf in the Alps for the day, then returns to Munich. City life continues. "We cannot stop even if we wanted to, have become voyeurs watching atrocious acts. The lies are without end because the hypotheses are without end . . . all adults occupy the thrilling realm of moral dilemmas (civic inertia), political drama . . ." After a day of mourning the Games continue. The moiling street clotted with humans, Manson headlines, graffiti, hedonism, statistic and facts, tight jeans, *schlagermusik* and hallucinations—on it all goes. Higgins closes the piece "Abu Daoud, where are you now?" Metaphorically this question continues to be potent today.

"The Opposite Land" is the England of Margaret Thatcher, she depicted here as a monster. Out slides a long list of frightful types: the Spanking Colonel, the Sheep in Wolf's Clothing, William Faulkner's Double, the Cad with the Pipe. The pressure to get away is enormous, and the narrator tries fruitlessly to telephone "You" in Copenhagen to say he is catching a plane. He arrives in Copenhagen and she is not home. "Time passes." At last "You" arrives from an outing to Elsinore Castle. They have four good days to enjoy food and wine under the trees, then the idyll ends as it must. The train, the boat, the disco, the bar, sleep and he is once more in England, "come full circle."

"Lengthening Shadows (An Elegy for England)" is an adaptation of a script for the BBC 4's "Texts for the Air." It is a series of tiny but vigorous essays: the somber, overcast day; Lady Genevieve and Sir Wilf from the cresting days of Empire; Hoyle Rules deploring the seafarers of the past reduced to fishing for minnows in sewage ponds with lewd graffiti for their literature; a celebration of cricket for Harold Pinter; the closing note on A Pearl of Days, "Blown spume, ruddy faces, thick ears, jug ears nothing daunted, briny smells, kippers and herrings, shelly seafood of Skegness, stinking tides, tidal motions, semen-stench of the great heaving ocean. Tar-pots and fish-heads of Deal, nets drying."

The final piece in the collection, "*Rückblick*," is an unquiet and mysterious mélange. The reader is dropped directly *in media res*. A Miss Esther Vanhomrigh writes letters from Dublin and Cellbridge

[sic] in 1714 and 1720 to someone—her warden, "the sour Dean of St Patrick's"? The unknown one is sometimes addressed as "Cad." But who is Jonathan? Who is Stella? Who is "poor Molkin"? A cat?

The letters beseech and rail and we learn that Miss Vanhomrigh thinks constantly of _____ who does not reciprocate her love. She and another (poor Molkin?) are the Dean's wards. The Dean secretly loves Miss Vanhomrigh, but she has mightily displeased him. "His two pure angels had grown to be not dolts but worse, Odious Animals, lusty and breedy animals prone to squat and release stinks; their soiled underclothes and unseen dishonorable parts inspired a kind of horror in his bosom, as did their courses, their discharging of the necessities of nature."

With characteristic abruptness Higgins switches to an account of two auctions he has attended, one in 1937, another in 1952. The piece ends with a dip in a tank of cold water and four very fine paragraphs on odors, then a few lines that apply to all of Higgins's work: "That which is past is past; that which is wished for may not come again, cannot come again. Certain scents even imply: the longing for that which cannot come again. The exuberance of the eternal lymph."

NOTES

1. *A Bestiary*, "Donkey's Years," Dalkey Archive Press, n.p., 2004, 12. Dalkey Archive Press with support from the Lannan Institute of New Mexico has kept most of his works in print.

2. Although *A Bestiary* is usually termed a memoir, one looking for cold facts should approach it with suspicion. Higgins's personal history is his literary mine, marbled with rich veins of ore which he smelts into fiction. He himself says "Perhaps one's history could be written in no other way. All history is to some extent

man's invention and much of it untrue. . . ." Aidan Higgins, "The Hollow and the Bitter and the Mirthless in Irish Writing," *Force 10 Magazine*, No. 13, June, 2008, 21–27. (Hereafter "Hollow and Bitter.")

3. Neil Murphy, "Dreams, Departures, Destinations," *Graph*, 2.1, 1995, Irish Writers' Centre.

4. One could argue that his brilliant critical essays, collected in *Windy Arbours*, take more of a traditional form than his fiction.

5. "In Old Heidelberg," "Berlin After Dark," "North Salt Holdings," "Lebensraum" and "Asylum," the first three with different titles. "North Salt Holdings" (originally "Killachter Meadow") can be read as an early form of *Langrishe, Go Down*.

6. "I tell you a thing. I could tell it otherwise. A few pictures emerge into the light from the shadows within me. I consider them. Quite often they fail to please me. I call them 'pictures' but you, kind readers, ideal readers suffering from ideal insomnia, must know otherwise. What I mean to convey is: *movements from the past*." "Sodden Fields," *Helsingør Station & Other Departures*, Secker and Warburg, 1989, 250–1.

7. Aidan Higgins, "The Hollow and the Bitter . . ." Higgins here says that the modernist movement failed in Ireland, "hardly making a ripple." He lists, as exceptions, the following: *Sailing, Sailing Swiftly*, Jack B. Yeats; *Murphy*, Samuel Beckett; *The Ginger Man*, J. P. Donleavy; *Felo de Se*, Aidan Higgins; *Night in Tunisia*, Neil Jordan; *In Night's City*, Dorothy Nelson; *Banished Misfortune*, Dermot Healy; *Cadenza*, Ralph Cusak; *The Engine of Owl-Light*, Sebastian Barry.

8. "Realism" is perhaps as trustworthy as memory.

9. In the United States the "new objectivity" tinged the 1930s New Deal propaganda photographs of dispossessed sharecroppers and destitute rural Americans. In the 1970s it contributed to the attitude of the "new photographers" who disdained Ansel Adams's

romantic images of pure landscape, instead photographing pipe-
lines, discarded mechanical junk, polluted waterways, highways
and boring look-alike suburbs.

10. One wishes these pieces would be aired again.

11. Loren Eiseley, *All the Strange Hour, the Excavation of a Life*,
Scribner's, N. Y., 1975, 3.

12. Many of Higgins's fictions have appeared in different collections under different titles. In *Flotsam & Jetsam* there are five stories
from the 1960 *Felo de Se* (the title is the English legal term meaning "felon of the self" or self-murderer); the Catchpole sections are
from the 1972 *Balcony of Europe*. From the 1989 *Helsingør Station
& Other Departures* come "Helsingør Station," "Sodden Fields,"
"The Bird I Fancied," "Frère Jacques, Bruder Hans," "The Other
Day I Was Thinking of You" and "Under the Ice Shelf." "Ronda
Gorge," "Black September" and "The Opposite Land" are from the
1989 *Ronda Gorge & Other Precipices*. "Lengthening Shadows (An
Elegy for England)" was a commissioned piece for BBC Radio 4.

13. Devin Johnson in *Reading Aidan Higgins*, cites a paragraph
from "The Other Day I Was Thinking of You": "An autumn of acorns
in Highgate Wood and Queens Wood, where the mass graves for
the Plague dead were dug; archeologists unearth pottery made by
Roman slaves. An autumn of conkers and red berries and an oldish
man saying to his wheezing, waddling old dog: 'You're only a big
overgrown puppy, that's all you are.'" The collection is illuminated
by hundreds of similar examples.

14. "In Old Heidelberg," *Flotsam & Jetsam*, Minerva, London,
1997, 42.

15. "Berlin After Dark," *Flotsam & Jetsam*, Minerva, London,
1997, 36–7.

16. "Catchpole," *Flotsam & Jetsam*, Minerva, London, 1997, 177.

The Missing Link

JOHN BANVILLE

The American publication of Aidan Higgins's *Langrishe, Go Down* is, or should be, a cause for celebration. The novel, Higgins's first, appeared in Britain in 1966 to wide critical acclaim, and was awarded the James Tait Black Memorial Prize, which still counted for something in those days. Although Higgins went on to produce further novels—notably *Balcony of Europe*, a big, ambitious tale of a mixed group of expatriates living in Spain in the 1960s—*Langrishe* is without doubt his masterpiece. It is a bitter fate for a novelist to be best known for his first work. However, Higgins should keep in mind the response Joseph Heller gave to an interviewer who was crass enough to remark the fact that Heller had not managed to write anything better than his first book, *Catch-22*: "Who has?" Heller asked.

It is hard to account for the decline of Higgins's reputation from the early highs of *Langrishe, Go Down* and *Balcony of Europe*. He was perhaps not as fortunate as he might have been in his early publishers, although in his autobiographical trilogy *A Bestiary* he acknowledges, albeit coolly, the editorial skills of John Calder, who was also, of course, the publisher of Samuel Beckett's novels and poetry. In *A Bestiary* Higgins notes, with what seems admirable resignation, that both *Balcony of Europe* and the quasi-fictional *Scenes from a Receding Past* (1977) are out of print "and will remain so in my lifetime." "I have freely pillaged from both [books] for sections of this present work," he insouciantly admits, and adds a characteristically elegant and caustic metaphor: "bold Robin Crusoe ferrying booty from the two wrecks." With writers such as Higgins—if, indeed, there be other such—nothing is lost, nothing wasted, and his own work is precisely that—his own—the components of it his to revise, recycle, reuse.

An admiring reviewer in the *Times Literary Supplement*, quoted on the jacket of *Flotsam & Jetsam*—a representative selection of Higgins's "fiction and prose" first published in Europe in 1996 and now republished, along with *Langrishe* and *A Bestiary*, by the admirably enterprising Dalkey Archive Press, with the support of the Lannan Foundation—may inadvertently have hit on at least part of an explanation for the withholding of the literary fame Higgins deserves. Writing of Higgins's exalted place in the history of twentieth-century Irish literature, the *TLS* reviewer saw him as "a missing link between the modernist period and contemporary writing."

Certainly Higgins's abiding characteristics as an artist are of a High Modernist order: obsessive subjectivity, a broad range of allusive references, insistence on formal freedom, a plethora of polyglottal quotations, aristocratic disdain of the audience. His influences, or at least the ones he is willing to acknowledge, are unusual for a twentieth-century Irish writer: less Joyce and Beckett than Djuna Barnes and Paul Bowles. Like Bowles and Barnes, Higgins is a cosmopolitan wanderer, an exile everywhere and nowhere at home. He writes continually of Ireland, but also of London, Berlin, Spain, Scandinavia, South Africa. His subjects are the past, family, loves found and lost, the pleasures of sex, the pleasures of drink, the self as artist, and, just the self—has there ever been a more introspective oeuvre than this?

Higgins is that rare, perhaps unique, phenomenon, a writer to whose fiction one goes in search of illumination of the life, and not vice versa, the more usual direction. In a sense, indeed, life and fiction are one for Higgins, since as far as can be ascertained he has never written of anything that did not originate in his own experience. For anyone who knows Higgins's novels and short stories, *A Bestiary*—"this bogus autobiography"—will be haunted territory, abounding in echoes from the fiction, most of them resonant, but some, it must be said, that strike the ear with a dull thud. Autobiography and fiction alike are a recuperative endeavour:

> What I would hope to convey, reader, is movements from the past (movements of the hidden heart), clear as sand in running water; the strange phosphorous of a lost life nameless under the old misappellations.

Yet feed though he does on his own life, the precise facts of that life remain conjectural. As in the case of Beckett, even the date of his birth, March 3, 1927, is a matter of doubt: in the closing lines of *A Bestiary* an old flame demands to know, "How can you be seventy-one in the year 2000 when you were born in 1927?" How indeed. We must be content with approximations. Aidan Higgins was born sometime in the late 1920s, in Springfield House, a fine Georgian mansion near Celbridge, County Kildare, a score of miles due west of Dublin. The Higginses were minor rural gentry, not Protestant, however, but Catholic—landed Catholics were a rare species until more recent times. His father, Bart, known as Dado, lived the life of a hard-riding country gentleman on the rents from properties in America that eventually had to be sold because of "increasing rural dilapidation," leaving him financially broke and spiritually broken.

Higgins's mother, Lil, or Mumu, had pretensions to the cultured world. She knew a number of literary figures including Oliver St.

John Gogarty, the model for Buck Mulligan in *Ulysses*, and claimed familiarity with numerous others; Higgins reports her brazenly introducing herself to Noël Coward when she spied him one afternoon taking tea with the handsome young Beverly Nichols in the lounge of the Shelbourne Hotel in Dublin—"Mumu referred thereafter to dear Noel [*sic*] and dear dear Beverley [*sic*]."

Life was good at Springfield *avant le déluge*:

> With us who lacked nothing in the way of home comforts, 'want' was a dirty word; servants and nannies were always there, dancing attendance. We lived, as Mumu put it, in the very lap of luxury, and servants attentive to our every wish were at the end of every bellpull, five or six of which were situated strategically about the house, in the upper rooms set into the wall by the fireplaces of white marble, the roaring coal fires.

It is an old story in the annals of the landed Irish: the dog days are sweet but eventually all goes to the dogs.

There were four Higgins brothers, two older than Aidan and one younger. In *A Bestiary* Higgins cheerfully admits that although a real pair of Langrishe sisters had lived at Springfield before the Higginses, the "four apathetic spinsters" at the center of *Langrishe, Go Down* "were my brothers and myself in drag, subjected to a sea-change and all the names altered except the dog's."

Langrishe, Go Down, the very core of Higgins's life work and the repository of his and his family's history,

> was about the death of a house and the break-up of a family. It took me two years to write, two more for a dilatory publisher to bring it to the public eye; the final editing took twenty-four hours non-stop (but for dinner in Jammet's

[a then-fashionable Dublin restaurant]) and I stayed up all night, wearing out two copy-editors. *Langrishe* sold just over 2,000 cloth copies in the first fortnight after publication in September 1966, after which sales sank to a dribble. And it has consistently sold in a dribble ever since, in five or six European languages. Beckett called it 'literary shit.'

Beckett and Higgins were friends in Paris in the 1950s, and despite that harsh judgment on *Langrishe* the older writer gave the younger a handsome compliment, declaring that "in you, together with the beginner, is the old hand." Although the shadows of Beckett and, of course, of Joyce fall darkly in places upon his style, Higgins has always been very much his own man, as he showed in his first book, the remarkably poised and confident story collection *Felo de Se* (1960). In these stories a voice was heard that was new in Irish writing. We were used to the Protestant tones of the likes of Synge and Yeats and Beckett and, among the Catholics, the petit-bourgeois accents of Frank O'Connor and Sean O'Faolain at one end of the scale and the Jesuitical strains of James Joyce at the other. Higgins's work, however, spoke in a wholly original manner that sounded to Irish ears at once foreign and familiar: mordant, dandified, waspishly comic, cosmopolitan to the point of world-weariness, and steeped in history, the history of a continent, a country, and a family.

Home and away: these are the two poles between which all of Higgins's writing is strung. Much of the melancholy beauty of his work derives from a pervading sense of displacement, whether it is that of his Hemingwayesque expatriates loving and squabbling among themselves in Berlin, Alicante, Cape Town, or the Langrishe sisters marooned in a decaying house in the plains of Kildare. Baudelaire remarks somewhere that literary genius consists in the ability to summon up childhood at will, and at times it seems that Higgins never quite left the scenes of his own receding past:

> Were I a painter of the stamp of Magritte, I might have suggested the decline of the Higgins family in one significant image: Virginia—creeper leaves from above my father's room now blown into a gutter of the small balcony above the long windows, one opened about a foot at the bottom for fresh air. The leaves would change colour from spring into autumn, first green, then scarlet, then orange, then purple, then dark plum-coloured, blown about the little balcony by various winds, then clenched together in a ball by frost, reduced to the size of a clenched fist, now the teak colour of Tollund Man dug out of the Danish earth.

As so often with Higgins, *Langrishe, Go Down* grew out of something else. "Killachter Meadow," the first story in his collection *Felo de Se*, contains all of the later novel in embryo. In the story, the four "unprepossessing and unmarriageable" Kervick sisters, Emily-May, Tess, Helen, and Imogen, after the death of their parents live on at Springfield House, "a freehold premises in the barony of old Killachter, situated one mile from Celbridge village and the ramparts of Marlay Abbey, whilom home of Hester Vanhomrigh." "Killachter Meadow" ends in March 1927 with the suicide by drowning of Emily-May; in *Langrishe, Go Down*, Emily Langrishe, as she is called now, has been dead a long time, and figures only as an unsettling memory for her three surviving sisters. As the novel opens it is 1937, and Helen, the eldest of the sisters, who is herself dying of an unspecified illness, is returning to Springfield after a fruit-less foray into the city to see if something might be salvaged of the family's fortunes:

> They would have to talk . . . talk together, discuss what was best to be done, and make some arrangements to change their ways, for the old impossible life was ending. They would have to sell the house, that was all there was to it. Solicitors, land-agents, undertakers—as they came tramping in, the Langrishe world was falling down.

For all its originality, the book in this early section is quick with hints and echoes of earlier Irish masters. Helen's night journey is a tour de force of writing reminiscent of the Joyce of *Dubliners*:

> The lights in the bus burned dim, orange-hued behind opaque bevelled glass; ranged below the luggage racks they lit up the advertisement panels with repeated circles of bilious light.

The scene the following morning, in which Helen wanly confronts her alcoholic sister Imogen—"A disturbance of springs and squeaking castors began; then the bedclothes were pushed aside and Imogen's head appeared"—recalls the opening pages of Elizabeth Bowen's *A World of Love*.

The heart of *Langrishe, Go Down*, the long section set in 1932, is an account of an affair between Imogen Langrishe and the German scholar Otto Beck, who lives rent-free in a cottage on the Springfield estate. Beck is a wonderful creation, feckless, arrogant, demanding, the classic opportunist and sponger. "Beck of Bavaria. He has no visible means of support. He was arrested by the Guards of Enniskerry and Dada got him out on bail. He is writing a thesis, supposed to be." For Imogen, the youngest of the sisters but no longer young, he is her last chance of finding love. Although we know from the first encounter between the two that Beck will "take advantage" of Imogen—"Ah you're wicked, you'd get round me if

I gave you half a chance," she says—and although the inevitable affair will follow an inevitable course, Higgins portrays it all with enchanting delicacy and freshness, and with the lightest touches of ironic humor. Consider this exquisitely gauged moment when Imogen first invites Beck into the main house:

> He heard her delay before the hall mirror. And as she entered the room he was rising to his feet from the sofa. The music started again upstairs. She had removed her coat and brushed her hair for him. She wore a pretty dress, walking there before him where the air was so still, in the dim light and shade of a past which he had no part in. Now that he could see her more clearly he saw that she had a pale powdered face, the skin stretched tight across the bones. Her dress made a caressing sound, *riss-riss*, as she passed, and her scent, her displacement, followed; so many cubic feet of scented Miss Imogen Langrishe going *riss-riss*.

The affair is recounted in a series of set pieces so cunningly and fluidly executed that there is nothing about them that seems set. There is a grimly comic late-night drinking session in a seedy studio flat in Dublin, where Beck introduces Imogen to the egregious Barry Shannon and the one-eyed actress Maureen Layde, "a hot-faced sprite with a wet avaricious little mouth." The night ends with Imogen insulted by the actress and helplessly drunk on Guinness: "The room swung round. Something was approaching, a kind of milky translucence. It came closer and closer. Her eyes filled with unshed tears."

Throughout his work Higgins has a magical way with louche characters and situations, never, or hardly ever, falling into the buffoonery of the "hard man" school of Irish writing. Strong drink is a constant in his fictional as well as his autobiographical worlds—on his own evidence, he begins most of his mornings with a glass of stout and a whiskey chaser—but he eschews the sodden braggadocio that so often mars the work of Flann O'Brien or Brendan Behan or J. P. Donleavy.

The affair between Imogen and Beck ends, as such affairs tend to do, in tears and small tragedy. Beck, impatient for new vistas, flees Springfield, pursued by a blast of buckshot that Imogen in her fury and despair fires off at his departing head. After the gunplay comes the regret. "Two springs, two summers, three autumns and two winters. That was all; and now all over." Imogen has turned forty, she is alone, and unexpectedly, disgracefully, disastrously, pregnant. The child when it comes is stillborn. All this may seem trite rather than tragic, but Higgins arranges his scant material with such force of feeling and beauty of style—he can veer from classical purity to demotic knockabout and back again in the space of a paragraph, or a sentence, even—that his tale takes on the lineaments of a timeless legend. As in all true art, the effects that he achieves are at once simple, profound, and entirely mysterious.

The last, brief, section of the book is set in 1938, after the death of Helen and the death, too, of Imogen's last hopes of happiness. On a cheerless day at the end of winter she revisits the cottage for the first time in years, and memories of Otto and her love for him come flooding back: "He had come when she was miserable and lost, telling his tall tales, putting his invincible mailed fist on woman's weakness." The closing paragraphs of the book are resolutely unemphatic, despite the beating repetitions of "w" words—wind, window, winter—and yet, or therefore, heartbreaking, especially in the sudden switch from general bleakness to mention of the "mild March day" with its hint of the spring to come:

When she heard a sound behind her she turned quickly. No, nothing. Grey light. The wind on the door. Nothing at all. She went to the window facing the avenue and stood there with her back to the windowsill. Tenuous air, bare fields, the beginning of a typical winter's day.

She turned her face to the window again, to a soft diffusion of winter light. The beginning of a mild March day. On the shadowed windowsill a few dead flies remained, leftovers. Hide away here, let the days pass and hope that things will change. Clouds were slowly passing across the window. Yes, that—or nothing at all. How the wind blows today!

One of the things that give *Langrishe, Go Down* its feeling of timelessness is Higgins's acute sense of history and the historical moment. For him the past is not the past but a kind of continuous, fixed present. The book is rife with quotations from such sources as the fabulist Barnaby Rich's *A New Description of Ireland*—Shakespeare took Rich's *Apollonius and Silla* as the source for *Twelfth Night*—and the Elizabethan general Sir John Perrott's thoroughly disenchanted and disenchanting *Chronicle of Ireland*. In the three books that make up *A Bestiary* there is also much recourse to old and dusty documents, especially those pertaining to the history of Springfield House, records of which, Higgins tells us, with an audible sniff of pride, can be traced back to 1734.

Donkey's Years, published in London in 1995 and now the first book of the trilogy, opens with a preface reprinting some pages devoted to Springfield House in an account of Celbridge and environs by a historian, Lena Boylan, while toward the close of the third volume, *The Whole Hog*, first published in 2000, Higgins prints four or five pages of legends culled from the headstones in the two cemeteries, one Protestant and one Catholic, in the town of Kinsale where he now lives, that same Kinsale on the coast of County Cork where the last and decisive battle was fought, on the afternoon of Christmas Eve 1601, in a violent thunderstorm, between the doomed Irish aristocracy and the English Crown. Higgins's account of the "Great Battle," tossed into the closing pages of *A Bestiary*, is as violent as the *Iliad* and as vivid as tomorrow's headlines.

A Bestiary is at once a bildungsroman, a portrait of the artist young and aging, and an old-fashioned account of a rackety literary life lived as much to the full as any full-time writer could manage. The three books of which it is comprised, *Donkey's Years*, *Dog Days*, and *The Whole Hog*, are garrulous, opinionated, frequently incoherent, packed with gnomic scraps of useless information—"Henry David Thoreau had a brother who died of lockjaw"—and repetitive to a degree which the sorely tried reader will consider infuriating or endearing, depending on mood and the quality of what is being repeated. Friends, relatives, lovers, enemies pop up in these pages like the irrepressible figures of the commedia dell'arte, always in new disguises and always instantly recognizable.

Higgins has a swaggeringly cavalier attitude to his family portrait gallery, constantly painting over old canvases to make space for new studies of the same handful of subjects. His brothers appear and reappear in all the stages of life from infancy to old age. In particular, the numerous fondly mocking caricatures of the eldest of the four Higginses, the richly eccentric Desmond, known as Dodo, are funny and affecting in equal measure; the book is worth having for Dodo alone. Meanwhile the two major portraits, of Dado and Mumu, stand on their easels at the back of the studio, obsessively worked on and never to be finished. Baffling, beloved, mourned, these people are themselves, unforgettably so, and yet they are characters too, like all the other players in Higgins's little theater. "Rory," Higgins's alter ego throughout *A Bestiary,*

> found that he could bring dead people back to life. Even when treated in a fictional manner, they came back to life. He could bring them closer. Rory could bring my mother back, as long as I called her 'Mumu' and not Lil; and my father, as long as I called him 'Dado' and not Da. I had to turn my back on the real parents in order to evoke this other pseudo-anonymous couple who were more real than my real parents, Bart and Lil. I thought, not quite believing it, that one day I would write a book about them. Well, this trilogy is it.

Auld Lang Rish and After

BERNARD SHARE

On Thursday 20 December 1956 Aidan Higgins disembarked from *Die Waterman,* out of Amsterdam, in Capetown: "Table mountain looms over us, balancing on its summit a single cloud. It's a hot day in high summer here." It was an equally hot day in the same hemisphere in the White Horse Hotel, Apia, Western Samoa, where I was spending my second Thursday 20th in succession, courtesy of the International Date Line, waiting for the Tasman Empire Airways flying boat which would carry me on to Tahiti. The previous day, also Thursday and of even date, had been spent in Suva, Fiji, partially in the company of two ship's acquaintances (I had sailed with them on the *Oronsay* out of Sydney) the Rev. Figgis and his wife, "Presbyterians but reasonably human," I had noted condescendingly. I had been relishing the travel experience: "So far it has been wonderful" I concluded on the second Thursday. Not so Aidan: "I've grown tired of the narrow regimen of shipboard life . . . the repetitive meals, the same dull decks and the same dull company . . . it's a kind of prison."

If Aidan was not then publishing his impressions (*Images of Africa* did not appear until 1971) he was observing the non-significant detail, to be represented in what was to evolve into his practised deployment of a structured banality: "These are figures cut loose from a frieze; what you see of them—the little you can see of them—it's only a very small part of their existence; their existence in my eyes. It's nothing." But it was to be both nothing and everything: the verbal equivalent, perhaps, of Cartier-Bresson's "defining moment." And that Christmas Day, as he travelled in an upper berth in the train from Capetown to East London I was battering out a piece for *The Irish Times* on my old Hermes portable before heading out to Les Tropiques in Papeete for a swim.

Though it was to be another nine years before we met, the odd concordance of our respective plunges over the Equator, to borrow Aidan's phrase, and our very different attempts to verbalise what we found continued to intrigue me. When I visited him in Nerja in the middle of his seemingly endless struggle with *Balcony of Europe* I was critical of (as I was to put it in a 1977 piece in *Hibernia*) "forays up to the plaza [which] would yield a few more shards, to be embedded in a further series of discrete paragraphs." But when, about that time, I found myself travel-writing for a living I would attempt the same technique, trying to crystallise Kathmandhu or Leeds-Bradford in a series of short takes. Later, Aidan was writing what was in essence a travel-piece for me in my then capacity as editor of *Cara* for Aer Lingus—a piece on the Kildare town of Athy to accompany a series of photographs by John Minihan, photographer of Beckett, whose home place it was. "It all hangs together in an odd sort of a way," he wrote to me on 28 April 1986, "references holding hands under the table, and smiling at you over it, in spite of everything." By then I knew what he meant: "dense particulars," as Gerry Dukes put it in a review of *Lions of the Grunewald* (*Irish Times,* 13 Nov. 1983): "the specifics of lived lives. . . ." "Nous avons oublié le poids des mots," lamented Claude Duneton in *Le Figaro* (31 Jan. 2008). Higgins, however, has always known how both to weigh and weight his words, even if the obsessive juggling was to come to oppress him: "Wrong way to write; one should slap it down. Hollow laughs" (letter, 20 Nov. 1967).

But to go back to somewhere near the beginning. In 1966, when I was a regular fiction reviewer for *The Irish Times*, one of the fortnightly bundles I was handed contained a copy of *Langrishe*. I had heard neither of the book nor its author, but it so moved me that I gave it, in the common phrase, a rave review and, I believe, its first. Some months later I found myself addressing an academic audience in the University of Newcastle, New South Wales, of which I was formerly a staff member, and had the pleasure of introducing a somewhat uncomprehending audience to a book which I had described in print as "clearly the best novel by an Irish writer since *At Swim-Two-Birds* and the novels of Beckett"—certainly *Langrishe*'s first excursion into the then remote Antipodes. In the interim I had met the author, who had sought me out in Dublin courteously to thank me for my review, and by 1967 with myself back in Ireland and Aidan at Carabeo 40, Nerja, he initiated a correspondence which was to stutter intermittently for the next three decades or so as we moved each in our very variable trajectories, paths occasionally crossing, both physically and collaboratively.

"It occurred to me that you might be able to help me in some Irish research," he began, not inappropriately, on Bloomsday 1967, "background of present labours." There followed four substantial queries, of which the last in line read: "Do you recall the case a few summers back in Dublin: an Italian couple used to lure Irish virgins (non-virgins) to their flat and the brother assault them, photograph them nude and then blackmail them? How were they caught and what was the sentence and what were their names? What you can remember of it yourself—or any friends who might recall details. Not to bother going to newspaper files, unless you have a handy office boy." *Answer all the questions. Write on at least one side of the paper.* I had no office boy.

"Am hoping to finish present, er, novel by Frankfurt Book Fair," he told me in that first letter. But in his second of 20 July, following some perceptive comments on my own first novel (*Inish*) which I had sent him, he indicated trouble: "3 ½ years more or less constant labour off and on with BOE, 1,000 pp. discarded crafts, sorry, drafts, search for le mot-juste, very exhausting, 1,000 typed settings in folders, 900 pp. MSS in 7 large notebooks, and all for what? I had 70 pp. ready this time last year; shrunk to 50 pp. (different ones) this year, deadline hurrying near, September Frankfurt Book Fair . . . I want it to be a longish novel (300 pp.) free of clichés and high-sounding effects, but is it. Cliché-ridden subject. Costa del Sol. Extranjeros. Love in the afternoon. Boozing at cafés. Guff. Adultery. All that shit. I have a narrator who bores the living daylights out of me. Rara Avis. The quinsy. I tried to omit the Irish background but it didn't work, so I have to make one, Sligo and environs."

"My younger brother says, Be simple. My older brother says, Dardanneles (spell) after Great War? (We used to call it the Great War). My middle brother says, When are you going to give up this writing lark?"

By 10 August *BOE* was "flinching away from me, the centre of a void, do you know that sensation? . . . I am working all day and should be working half night as well and may be by then. Must get this bloody thing finished. Trying to afford a typist, pesetaless Americana woman. My wife detests the stuff and won't touch it, have anything to do with it, no wonder . . . Eugene O'Neill I believe (now on US stamps) used to give a great roar when he finished one of his marathon plays and jump into the sea. I wish I could do all that. Profound mistrust (growing rather than diminishing) of all forms of communication, particularly fiction, particularly my own. Did you ever feel that way, Sir?"

My visit to Nerja in the summer of that year confirmed the continuing struggle, but following my return the detailed questioning continued. Aidan thanked me for coming up with something
which must have been of use concerning the Felloni case (the Italian couple accused of luring the Dublin virgins/non-virgins—see
above). But the questions were getting harder:

1. Meteorological. Winter of 1962–63. Worst since 1740? What
do records say. For Europe, Ireland. Spain? What was happening
around 1740 anyway?

2. Nautical. What liner sunk off Galway in first day of war 1939,
could you get data from Irish Times (they call all those local rags
the Times)? (An allusion to a repetitive phrase in *Inish*.) Remember being shown Irish Press (they call some of those local rags the
Press) with pictures en route to Aran three years back. What ton-
nage, what loss of life. Sunk how? Some details. Whereabouts.

3. Religious/topography. Name of RC church off Johnson's (spell)
Court off Grafton Street, facing the fumes of Bewley's best ground
coffee. What order of priests? (b) Do you recall old harpist who
played there. Hazard guess. I Dreamt I dwelt in Marble Halls? Harp
tune? Patriotic? Mangan to music?

4. Beltaine. Solstice? June 22. Is it Beltane? Winter solstice Dec.
Irish pagan background, couples jumping through fires. When is St
John's day? June? Fires lit on Clare coast, bonfires on Aran. Why?
Would it be St. John's? All Souls? All Saints? Here they have candles
floating on water and the passing bell all night. Old custom I think
finished. Difficult queries. *And how.*

"I didn't go to Frankfurt," Aidan confessed in the letter of "Oc-
tubre 6 (San Bruno y San Emilio)": ". . . They say I am uncoopera-
tive in interviews. Just as pleased not to go; was working well. Trying to finish part III this month, IV in November, V (last) by year
end. Sold MSS, notebooks, files, on drafts, re-drafts, 52nd and 53rd

thoughts to well-heeled university for £1,000. Buy your wastepaper basket." He had published 20 pages of *Balcony* in the current issue of the *London Magazine* "with spelling errors (the bane of Share) in 3 languages." He sent a copy to Sam Beckett, who "said he read it with what little feeling he had left for that kind of *decent* writing, liked the strange words beginning 'A death-blow is a life-blow to some,' which is from Emily Dickinson. He has cataracts in both eyes and goes to a specialist in Berne, in steps of the Master."

BOE was still inching along (20 Nov.): "A little greying here, a lot of rain, and this cell leaks. Going forward very slowly. 160 pages Xerox copies. Hope to Christ I can finish it this year. Little overlap. Say February. All distaste. Always the way until I see galleys, and then it looks okay for the first time . . . . Read: Querelle of Brest/Genet. Writing degree Zero/Barthes. Miserable Miracle/Michaud (mescaline). Very dull (me), memory in shreds. Drink and mope, eyes scorched; work and more work the only panacea."

More questions. "Name of evergreen (laurel?) bush in Stephen's Green along the railings. Types of trees (saplings) planted in Green where the rough lads play football, near Leeson St. gate, but back a bit, there towards the urinal midday (*sic*) to Merrion Row. . . . What trees planted along pathways of Green as you enter from Grafton St. gate and walk by pond to the bridge, overhanging in summer. Beech?" As I put it in my 1977 *Hibernia* piece marking the awarding to Aidan of the American Irish Foundation prize, "A hopeless botanist, I did my best. Whatever about the accuracy of the information he used it in a manner very different from that in which he handled his Nerja source material."

That piece, entitled "Down From the Balcony," was accompanied by a Higgins self-portrait, as was his 1983 interview in *The Irish Times* marking the publication of *Bornholm Night-Ferry*. Aidan's first paid job, as he was to tell the *Leinster Leader* on 6 March 2008, was with Domas, a Dublin advertising agency in Grafton Street, much at the same time as I was doing a stint in the rival O'Kennedy-Brindley in O'Connell Street. William Trevor, Salman Rushdie, Dorothy Sayers, Fay Weldon, all cutting their teeth as admen or women; there is a thesis hiding there somewhere. In Aidan's case the visual had from early on represented an alternative calling, as Trevor with sculpture, and it was to continue to weigh upon his words. Question 7. "Dropping Well pub on Dodder. Tables in lounge. Covered in? glass? Veneer with high shine? (cloud reflecting material)." "But I'm a failed painter," he confessed to Anne Haverty (*Irish Times* interview, 1983): "I wanted clean pure stuff like Klee and Kandinsky but I couldn't. I always wrote."

1967 gave way to a leap year. On 29 February he wrote "Today C&B [Calder & Boyars] bring out paperback *Auld Lang Rish* . . . I should be ending BOE but amn't, not quite yet." There was a mild reproach: "I seem to ask a lot of questions of you and receive a lot of silences from you, but no matter. Small nuts and bolts . . . If you are ever in the vicinity of our old flat, have the goodness to pass through Belgrave Square, and tell me the number of the first house on the right after the traffic lights at end of Charleston Rd (our old track) and what way is that side of the square pointed—East? Is the door still painted red. I saw a girl in furs and a Negro hand lifting aside a half curtain one rainy morning." *BOE* was continuing on its erratic course: "160 pp. Balcony Xeroxed in Dublin November reached here last week, by long sea after I'd given package up as lost. I am being charged a very reasonable £8.10.0. by Arthur Power's broth of a son Roddy, of Xerox in Dawson Street. Could you pay this by cheque and I can pay you via Hibernia cheques (he was now reviewing fairly regularly for John Mulcahy's journal)."

By the next letter, 30 May, things were looking up. "Offloaded 144 pages of Balcony to C&B, and now in throes of beginning to finish it. Marion Boyers comes here for August, takes it back, whatever remains." Encouragement came from that fact that he had, he said, been awarded a "Berlin scholarship worth I think $10,000 and will stay there for a year, try to produce another book." *BOE*, however, was not to be disposed of without a struggle. "Forget all other questions," he instructed me on 12 July, "and answer these as soon as you can. 1. Dry-cleaning shop near DBC on Stephen's Green near Huguenot cemetery—called? Bells? Swastika? Is there a Swastika laundry or dry cleaning place on Baggot Street?" My marginal scribbles suggest that I made some reasonable attempt at these. After that it was back to the trees in Stephen's Green, the statues in College Green "facing what way, with which arms upraised . . . Were they all there in '22? Were things normal in Dublin that year?" *Probably, give or take the odd Civil War.* "I have a woman realizing she is pregnant looking at the statues, their hands upraised (some of them). Check. In 1922."

By this time Aidan was clearly getting as impatient with the novel as I was, but relief was at hand. I saw him when he came back to Dublin on his way to Berlin, which city was to act like a shot in the arm: "We are going to like it here. A new way of . . . life for us." From 51 Beskidenstrasse, Schlachtensee, 2 July 1969, he wrote: "We have a most loverly modern huis at Schlachtensee with garden of currents (*sic*), goose gobs, wines, cherries, and pines mit squirrels, and jets banging through the sound bar. Nacht und day . . . Kids swam in pooey underpants at Wansee last eve among swans and resolutely wading blubbery Fraus und Frauleins, wading towards woody Heckeshorn shore, as a male voice intones something of other over a loudspeaker. Very queer kind of sight to see at the end of the Weg; the doors, the roses and then der milchy lake full of der frantic life. Yokes like paddle steamers with 2–3 tiers of gawking passengers (faint blobs in der distance). Rowing boats nil, but speedboats lepping out of der wasser, and Oxford und Cambridge skulling like der mad. . . . Stout Greek f. colleague lent me Vintage Giacomo Joyce. The words were coming back, and inside the wrappings of the words there would be thoughts lying there." New directions. About this time both he and I contributed to John Ryan's collection of essays on Joyce, *A Bash in the Tunnel,* but "Calder & Boyars were here after Frankfurt Book Fair," he wrote on 25 October, "trying to straighten out Balcony . . . I begin to grind to a close." He had dinner with Sam Beckett, "here rehearsing Krapp, which we see Saturday night. SB very thin and brown gone to Tangiers . . . says the word is finished, but still praises Pinget ("a shamefully neglected writer"), who is very wordy . . . Pinter is after all doing screenplay of *Auld Lang Rish* and comes here next month to discuss first draft, ready by then. I had prepared a treatment that I thought would do. Bang goes £7,500. I get instead £200 consultant's fee. How's that for low?"

The seventies. Aidan moving from Berlin to London, from London to Spain again to Dublin to Galway and back to London with a few other refuges in between, while half way through the decade I found myself, by a curious concatenation of circumstances, living in the wing of Springfield (not, please, Springfield House, a relegation of *Langrishe* to the corporate headquarters of a minor multinational). Celbridge was, then, much as Aidan had left it: the 20 minute walk into the village was through largely open fields, the single-decker Edenderry bus (known locally as "Peter's bus") pottered past the entrances to Springfield once or twice a day at unpredictable hours, there was no supermarket, and when the Big Snow came in 1982 the small shops quickly emptied and, with the bridge frozen, the village was cut off from the outside world for the best part of a week. If Alistair Campbell, an Aer Lingus pilot who worked to a timetable, had not managed to commandeer a passing tractor to clear the front avenue, Springfield would have remained equally inaccessible. As for the house itself, Alistair and his wife Rachel had added a kitchen at the rear but otherwise, as Aidan was to confirm when he came to stay, had made few other changes. We helped Alistair and family save the hay in the front field and every so often the water was cut off, as a result, it was said, of farmers tapping into the supply further up the line.

By this time, 1976, I was editing the nascent *Books Ireland* as well as *Cara* (Patrick Rafroidi, co-editor of *Etudes Irlandaises*, referred to me as 'un veritable homme-orchestre,' which I am not sure implied a compliment). But it meant that I could offer Aidan reviewing, for a very modest fee, in *BI*, and something a bit more substantial, both creatively and financially, in *Cara*. To the latter he contributed on three occasions; on Berlin (March–April 1978), Spain (Jan.–Feb. 1982) and the impression of Athy (Sept.–Oct. 1986) which almost got me fired and made that town an immediate no-go area. "A mood piece I hope or trust not too leery," he commented when he sent it to me, "because the place itself was and is DESPERATE. Had quite forgot what a miserable place Kildare can be . . ."

Berlin's time was up. On 12 March 1976 he wrote to me from 252 Muswell Hill Broadway, London: "A mighty mixed spring comes in here, with snow and bombs. Spent 10 months in hill hideout between Nerja and Málaga and began another novel, now accepted by Viking Press on very theoretical synopsis and 30 actual pages. Novel about Berlin under another name. Trying to complete a thing for Calder." (This was to emerge as *Scenes From a Receding Past*). "It resists being writ. Trying to compose something less convoluted than previous works, shorter too, in a gliding effect without too much morose delectation."

"From the only excerpt I have seen," I wrote in the August 1977 *Hibernia* piece, "it is clear that the forming motivation of the new book is again autobiographical. This causes no surprise. Higgins claims that he cannot create a fiction, by which he means that he cannot draw upon sources outside his own immediate experience and dislikes the hurdy-gurdy mechanism of the conventional plot. Though he admired both Joyce and Beckett and other innovators, he is not himself an experimental novelist in the accepted sense: the narrator/observer is too firmly installed for that. Certainly, in common with many other serious novelists, he mistrusts the form, perhaps that is, in the last resort, the only way to squeeze anything original out of it. What he is trying to do, I think, is to create a stasis embodying movement and colour but denying progression, again the analogy of a painting is difficult to reject. From this there stems his intense preoccupation with detail, the sentences and paragraphs so larded and compressed that they seem in danger of exploding in one's face, the frequent recourse to the present tense." If I have presumed to quote myself *in extenso* it is because, after the passage of some thirty-odd years, I see little cause to revise that opinion.

In that same year of 1977 the French academic and critic Serge Doubrovsky, well-known as an authority on Corneille (and with whom I had once played violin and piano duets during his time as a *lecteur* in Trinity), published his second novel, *Fils*, and devised the term "autofiction" to define its fictionalisation of autobiographical material. The term, in common with the earlier "faction" promulgated by Ginsberg, acquired a certain resonance in critical circles, with a particular focus on its coiner, whose subsequent novel, *Un Amour de Soi* (1982), served further to authenticate it. The blurb on the back cover of that edition, the work of the author himself, suggested that "Seule, en effet, une 'autofiction' assume réellement, dans le vif, le fardeau des vérités pénibles, que l'on support uniquement dans l'abstrait, ou sur le dos des autres." Old wine in new bottles? As Gerry Dukes put it (*The Irish Times*, 13 Nov. 1993), with reference to *Helsingør Station & Other Departures* (subtitled 'Fictions and Autobiographies 1956–1989'): "'Fictions and Autobiographies'? Which is which? Higgins promiscuously heaps them together, blurring the supposed lines of demarcation. For in our autobiographical or self-narrative mode our past history is a plastic material shaped by present exigencies. We invent ourselves as we go along and finally, as we go."

The previous year (1976), Aidan had hinted at his new project (*Muswell Hill, 4 May*): "Viking novel about Westberlin, I think. Writing for who? Old belief (vanity?) wavering, going. Maybe gone." And on 8 July 1977, accompanying his Berlin piece for *Cara*: "These are exploratory sorties in epistolary form for new novel, SCHOENBERG'S LAST PUPIL, letters a sort of cover to convey indiscretions that seem embarrassing in any other form." And later (*letter*, 1 Mar. 1982): "Fiction as I done her seems now impossible, for no readers can take it, nor me neither." The following year, in his interview with Anne Haverty on the occasion of the publication of *Bornholm*, he was, according to the interviewer, "in a mood of skittish pessimism": "I'm baling out of fiction. It's a mug's game. Fiction has shot its bolt. People live in such calamitous times it's superfluous. And it makes me feel I've been digging a hole and I'm getting in deeper." And much later, from 2 Higher Street, Kinsale, 14 April 1994: "I wrote Lions in about three months, rising at 5.00 am and worked like Crusoe building his stockade. Your quibble about veracity of narrator seems to me just a quibble. Dedalus is Joyce and Gavin Stevens in Faulkner and Father Zossima's opinions are also Tolstoy's and no matter how you may crank up the invention the author is the I that writes, so it hardly matters what you say he does, is supposed to be doing, in the fiction. Is this not so?"

During the late '70s and the 1980s, with Aidan making fairly regular visits to Ireland from Muswell Hill and for various periods living in both Bealadangan, Co. Galway and Ballyhara, Co. Wicklow, our correspondence understandably became less frequent and largely resolved itself into the unappetising mechanics of the writer's trade: review copies, fees (paid or unpaid), commissions, publication and promise of publication (frequently broken), the jetsam of the creative process. He returned to Spain for the summer of 1981, where, he told me, he "did a lot of work." On 10 June he wrote from Calle Rivera, Competá: "Very odd to write to your country address; all the miserable years I wrote it from Clongowes, Killashee, asking for jam, always jam, always starving, longing for home. And now?"

Now, after twelve years, we too were to leave Springfield. Alistair Campbell had been talking for some time about selling, fearing that in the harsh economic climate then prevailing Aer Lingus would make him redundant. Ironically, a few weeks after he resigned they called him back to relieve a temporary pilot deficit. It was a sad parting: the 200-year old beech outside the window, the black rabbits on the back avenue, the abiding sense of place and the drawing down of a fortuitous connection which had fructified in so many ways. But, in the event, I was not yet finished with Springfield, nor it with me. A commodious vicus of recirculation, Aidan's interrogations were to return, ghosts of subverted Langrishes. On 14 April 1994 he wrote from his now secure haven in Kinsale:

> Am putting finishing touches on a sort of memoir, a mixture of *L'Opopanax* (Wittig), *Speak, Memory* (Nab), *A Writer's Beginnings* (Welty) but not like any of them, going over Langrishe terrain and proving that everything in it (253 pp) was and is a lie, the Langrishes never existed. Anyway I have 37 out of 38 chapters finished, going on for 300 pp, a very smoky bonfire that may yet catch fire. I

wrote it even faster than Lions and in between (punching with both hands) a Secker text for Minihan Beckett photomontage: a scream. In the sense that men (and indeed women) of Kildare might say "Share's a scream," meaning: we don't understand him.

I am trying to understand the nature of Kildare history in this latest effusion, dreaming back, and could do with some help if you are up to it.

Possible (phone?) to find cost of land per acre in Kildare in 1900, 1960, 1970. What did land go for in 1750?

Would it be possible to find what Springfield and lands changed hands for since my Da's day? I think he sold it for £16,000 around 1943. Now going for a million . . .

More or less where we came in.

A Chance Meeting Outside
the Irish Tourist Board

DERMOT HEALY

"Asylum" has travelled with me since I first read it in the seventies in London. I might have read it three or four times then, and delved into it on many journeys and praised it in workshops as one of the finest stories I'd read; but now that I have read it in its entirety again—for the first time in a few years—I realise again the truth at its core. There are always a host of small details I will have imagined happened in the story that did not; I have invented changes in place since the last time I read it; and now I'm again suddenly aware that I had forgotten the actual tough, physical and religious terrain his writing has set down on the page.

Then I realised that was his ploy—he was leaving the door of the imagination open to the reader. You will always want to return to see what really happened. Then you set off again to make it up all over. For years I have been adding to the story in my own imagination, and now I recognise again the debt we all owe him in the writing world.

What Aidan has done has left us a vast map of London with the small roads that lead there from Kildare, and elsewhere; via a host of historical backgrounds and demeanours and aromas and cemeteries. Smell is one of his literary tools. Undergrounds reek. And sound is his echo. Rain falls off sagging trolley bus lines overhead while London wakes. Brazill, with a puce tie outside his green knitted cardigan, has left home for good after saying goodbye to his father, and taken up residence in a world of panel-beaters somewhere off the long drag of Uxbridge Road. There are bad times, so rich in detail, that the sorrows are well hidden.

I had forgotten the poverty Brazill underwent because Higgins has allowed his personality such a great deal of wealth and perspective.

The cliché meets the unexpected at the corner.

As five o'clock strikes from some windy steeple Brazill is off to work again those long hours we all did at times but now reading the pages we have to relive the doldrums, the clocking in and the clocking off; the shredding of memories; the mystery of working out a four minute cycle on the semi-automatic press; the lipstick going up in smoke; the long marches through side streets with the spleen jolting; and then to encounter fits brought on by the roars of laughter, and hunger; while coming in another direction is Mr. Boucher, fresh from the sixteenth century, a close neighbour of his from back home, an old golfing friend who comes from another class, a bigger house and an even more tormented mind.

I always thought that sanity met insanity when they both happened to look into the one window of Piccadilly Circus at the same time, and recognised each others' reflection; but no they just meet, with no dramatics, outside The Irish Tourist agency in Regent Street, and head off to eat a hamburger seated among gentlemen in check trousers and bowler hats and tweeds. We have entered the other world. I can hear the laugh of unreality in the distance, because the encounter rings so true. The cliché is afoot breaking new ground.

Brazill is employed as a caddy, companion and listener to a deaf man trying for one last grip on sobriety. "Questions, questions," says Boucher, "what are they but our memory of what we have forgotten." To seek out Boucher's cure we enter the world of the jester and the clown and the single girl on stage singing her heart out. Love enters through the back door with all its attendant mistakes.

With the flourish of an orchestra the writing enters the theatre of pantomime. Enter Elizabeth. When she sings the hair on my head stood. Then home. At night the lives of the great women of history are given in a rant that lilts as Boucher rages through the past while Brazill nods. The rant is growing. There is terror afoot. The clowns are turning into demons. The jester is growing skeletal. With a nail brush last thing at night Brazill the companion cleans the golf clubs, next morning Boucher's spine curves as he goes up on his toes at the first tee.

He is turning round. And round.

Right to the end Aidan Higgins never lets go of the brute physicality of being. The cheap shirt has as much importance as a hatpin stuck in a doll. The characters are dressed with solid quaking adjectives. The colour of each vestment howls. Fumes rise from the brewery and the armpits. Veins stand out like repressed shouts on the necks of two men carrying a drowned child. As Brazill walks he can feel his lights and kidneys on the go. Out comes an inarticulate noise from the throat. Air holes are drilled into the penitent's box in the church to let out the blasts of sin.

When a character looks into despair, the melodrama is in the shape his shoulders take. Out comes the rattle of the human tongue. Then, just fondly at the back of his mind, the presentiment switches off a light.

The death cart, with its hollow rumble, travels on through the names of London thoroughfares. The pantomime is the everyday, and in the background, the gallant piano plays on.

"Asylum" is a masterpiece.

Now after reading it I know that down the line, I will imagine things in the tale that did not take place. The author has scored a story into the brain that grows and grows in the imagination afterwards. In "The Dead" you forget that you have been at an extended dinner party. Joyce has slipped the host of characters so well into the text that when we enter the Gresham to cross the bogs of Allen we only remember the acute loneliness at the end. In the same way

Higgins in "Asylum" has entered the physical and the musical so thoroughly that the reader is left standing on the first tee, club in hand, about to swing.

He is handing on a text that lets the perspective and characterisation veer so much out into the world of reality that you come up against the sneer, and the fib and jolly, and are left scraping your boots on the mat at the door. The poor in heart are impervious to another's suffering. Because he fell for a girl the servant did not take care of his master who began to count to himself in French. Austerity takes a swing at ignorance. "Spit on me," says Boucher. "Spit on me!" then he collected his deaf-aid, and they go to bed. There are a few stiff whiskeys. The poor lights a candle for the mad.

It is a narrative where Dickens leads Camus to Church, not by the hand—but by the ear, and all because of a chance encounter between two paddies outside The Irish Tourist Board on Regent Street.

When the girl on stage sings her doleful lines she *looks as if she were trying to remember something else.* Higgins's prose has the same effect. He is letting the reader take the story away to tell to some other poor soul afterwards, but when you look back at the original the debt grows and grows. "Asylum" questions the inevitable with a rare joy that bring on remorse, "and remorse—in a word—is continuing with the farce," as Boucher says in one of his speeches.

Then a few pages later, he puts away his hearing aid, reads a few passages from Brazill's missal, and steps out of the story.

The puppeteer, that Aidan Higgins once was, knows that someone is working the strings that make him, and the rest of us, act like we do, in the afflicted city and in the deplorable house.

He has added fiction to the groves of memory. Long after you have finished the story you will be making it up again.

It's a gift he always had.

The Blithely Subversive Aidan Higgins

Derek Mahon

The remains of Miss Emily Norton Kervick were committed to the grave one cold day in March of 1927. On that morning—the third—a Mass for the Dead had been offered for the repose of her soul, and she was buried without delay in Griffenwrath cemetery. Thus did Aidan Higgins, in 1960, make his ceremonious debut with a fine short story entitled "Killachter Meadow," about the decline of, yes, a Big House near Celbridge, County Kildare, a theme taken up at greater length and to memorable effect in his first novel *Langrishe, Go Down* (1966), an outstanding work of the time and a modern classic. It won the James Tait Black Memorial Prize, quite a thing then, and established its author as Ireland's finest contemporary prose stylist (it has now been reissued by New Island). Traditionally, as with Elizabeth Bowen and J. G. Farrell, the Big House novel concerns an "Anglo-Irish" family, urgent political events bearing on the immediate situation, and preferably a good old blaze in the final pages. *Langrishe, Go Down* is at an angle to this. The family, once Protestant and now Catholic, has grand but distant connections, political events (the rise of fascism in Europe) seem far away, and instead of incendiarism there is entropy.

Set in the 1930s, in De Valera's Ireland, the novel traces the last days of the once prosperous Langrishes of Springfield House, now reduced to a trio of shabby-genteel sisters. Helen, the eldest and least irresponsible, has consulted their Dublin solicitor about the financial situation and been advised that they will have to sell the house. The others, silly Lily and lazy Imogen, take the news glumly, without knowing what to do about it: Lily being preoccupied with the hens and Imogen, the youngest, with thoughts of a past fling. Bitter and desolate, Helen dies soon after and the book comes to an end; but, in a long flashback that forms its main substance, we hear the six-year-old story of Imogen and Otto Beck, a visiting German research student: "She had a little touch of colour on her cheeks. An old love had put it there. The memory of past obscenities gave her that rose glow on sallow cheeks when she was old."

The lovers are beautifully realized. Imogen is a good-natured, ironical, sensual woman not in her first youth, imaginative and discontented. Otto, the same age, is a hard, cold, pedantic, domineering character, impressive, annoying and dangerous: "He runs his tongue over his dry lips like a fox licking its chops." An outlandish, "legendary" figure ("that face among the leaves") with green eyes and red hair, he wears corduroy and dirty tennis shoes without socks: "Vengeful manner, cruel lover; I wouldn't mind being his trollop." He lives rent-free in the back lodge, made available to him by Major Langrishe, the women's father, since deceased. Perched in a tree-top, he observes Imogen at her flighty "air baths" in the woods. Together they spend "gin days" and summer nights till the rows begin. His manners are brusque, his views peremptory and severe; he speaks of "culturally inferior" nations: "Oh, he was hard on people."

An important feature of the novel, and one largely responsible for the stately pace at which the narrative moves, is the leisurely and minute contemplation of the Kildare countryside where it takes place. Helen and Imogen, from snobbery and indolence, are not greatly interested in their surroundings, but "foxy" Otto, naturalist and opportunist, has made himself familiar with the fauna;

he takes trout and rabbits and keeps a weather eye on the clouds. The sexton in the local graveyard discourses to morbid Helen on mortality and the swift passage of the centuries, recalling the grand folk thereabouts as far back as Bartholomew Vanhomrigh, "the Dutchman, Vanessy's da." The Celbridge of Higgins's youth is vividly recalled in all its practical detail.

A graduate of Freiburg, Otto is writing a thesis on the eighteenth-century "Ossianic problem" in relation to Goethe. He can tell you about the night sky and the Munich whores with equal detachment; to his foxy eye, life is a hen-run. But for all his brisk information and quickness to learn, he is temperamentally incapable of sharing the organic character, lovingly described by Higgins, of the Springfield demesne and its surroundings. Were the sisters more closely identified with the landscape we might read Langrishe as a parable of sexual politics in the larger, ecological sense; but they too are parasites. The family money came not from the land but from the stock market (American mining shares); their father was no good at running the estate, and now the place is going to rack and ruin. "Such filth and disorder in the old rooms, a smell of poverty, disuse, rotting wainscoting and dirty beds. Wind echoing in the deserted cottage . . . It looked as if someone had been living there."

"Killachter Meadow" first appeared in book form in *Felo de Se* (1960) and reappears in *Flotsam & Jetsam*, a collection of shorter fiction, travel notes and miscellaneous pieces, as "North Salt Holdings" (the Barony of Salt is in Co. Kildare). Another five of the original *Felo de Se* stories reappear there too, together with reworked material from *Balcony of Europe* (1972), *Helsingør Station* (1989) and *Ronda Gorge* (1989). "Lengthening Shadows," a grim view of the present state of England, is adapted from a series of "Texts for the Air," a BBC radio commission. *Donkey's Years* (1995), *Dog Days*

(1998) and *The Whole Hog* (2000), remarkable memoirs now available in one volume as *A Bestiary* (published, with *Flotsam & Jetsam*, by Dalkey Archive, distributed in the UK by W. W. Norton), received less attention than they deserved first time round, and in those reviews that did appear a hostile note was sometimes audible; for Higgins, who is eighty this year, is an austere and often difficult writer, more than a touch old-fashioned, with an astringency that can stir the bile of whippersnappers. He is known for an elaborate and exigent style derived from, among other sources, Elizabethan and Jacobean prose, Swift, Joyce, Djuna Barnes and Beckett. He can be expressionist and baroque, lyrical and grotesque, fastidious and colloquial by turns, and presumes a like-minded "browser" of comparable erudition and unsentimentality. His whole practice and attitude are about as far as one could get from current aesthetics, though it would be wrong to think of him as conservative. Not at all: he is, paradoxically, the most blithely subversive of writers, though grandly aphoristic on occasion: "Absence makes the heart less fond, au fond"; "Notions of vulgarity vary from vulgarian to vulgarian"—not that we bother much about such things now.

Two instances of his picturesque and comically vehement technique. "Asylum" is rife with startling similes: "She sat upright with knees drawn together, her spine curved back like a bow; from the waist up she was as unadorned as the town of Trim, not a stitch anywhere to spare her blushes." (That Trim, Co. Meath, is actually quite decorative need not detain us here.) "Berlin after Dark" has this:

> As certain burrowing creatures, in order to gain their ends or to exist at all, are resolved down to one anxious or bitter form of themselves, so his features seemed to narrow down to one place and one gesture; his face was a falling

back to function. As winds in their persistence stretch and sharpen boulders, and as these in turn indicate free access to territory beyond, so his features spoke of only one preoccupation, and that preoccupation, venery.

The mock-heroic simile, Homeric in origin, is associated with Pope and Fielding, and it is good to find it alive and kicking in modern Ireland. But what's it all about?

"We shift about, all that great glory spent" (Yeats, "Coole Park and Ballylee," 1931). Higgins's principal theme is the decay of old decency, the atomization of life, personal and social; our decline is figured in sexual chaos, wickedness in these matters being a traditional sign of the end of civilizations. His settings, when not Irish, are typically peripheral London and rural Spain; seaside resorts out of season; winter golf-links, rentier havens and expatriate watering holes—wherever there is a last ditch for the singular, the marginal and the disregarded: for alternative lives. While business proceeds in the financial centres, somewhere an eccentric "spinster" slips Ophelia-like, for the last time, into a river, or a disconsolate exile studies cloud formations, adrift in gin and Unamuno's "ether of pure speculative contemplation." Wise to expatriate decadence, like Durrell, Bowles and the rest, Higgins is attentive too to the newer and even more pernicious decadence of universal package tourism: "We shift about." There is an apocalyptic undertone in everything he writes, however circumstantial or debonair; ominous epiphanies are everywhere. He returns constantly to the same material; it's all autobiography, "a life as story told." *A Bestiary* is the summation of this project, a getting closer to the bone, the persona now that of a curmudgeonly if witty recluse. Despite a good start his reputation, until recently, was a fugitive one, a thing of hearsay among initiates, for he is unfashionably "literary" (his friend Samuel Beckett, alas, thought *Langrishe* "literary shit") and detached from the more obvious contemporary fixations, which he views with horror—as he views the "loudly pictorial" future being prepared for us, when the writer's trade will be "extinct as falconry."

The Whole Hog is good on Kinsale, where Mountjoy scattered Hugh O'Neill's Hispano-Gaelic confederacy on Christmas Eve, 1601, and where Higgins now lives. He reports the famous battle as an international rugby match. But the best of *A Bestiary* is in *Donkey's Years* (the account of his mother's death) and in *Dog Days*, where the author, in search of peace and quiet after a difficult divorce, returns to Greystones, Co. Wicklow, where he spent part of his youth—a locale he re-creates here in the fine opening section, "First Love." This thirty-four-page overture is a virtuoso short novel in itself, remarkable chiefly for its portrait of the severe though sensual Philippa. Some years her junior, randy "Rory," as he calls himself, drags her off to sheds and dunes, "the pair of us naked as salmon on the sea-shore, panting, our unchained bikes propped up against the broken fence, one lying on top of the other as if engaged in rapt and silent copulation, the heavy Raleigh on top, the dainty female model underneath."

Now he spends two years in a borrowed bungalow, his field-watching solitude oddly reminiscent of Otto Beck. He quotes Henry James: "Next to great joy, no state of mind is so frolicsome as great distress"; and there is much here that is frolicsome. Rory has an ear for pub talk; like Beckett he is good on the seasons ("the fields in frantic stir at lambing time, placentas blowing about like refuse . . . saw bullfinch in bush") and times of day and night. He hears blackbirds, "music that would have delighted Messiaen; it delights me"; and there is life yet in the old art simile: "Combine harvesters working in the dark with powerful headlights; glow of stubble burning in the fields, smoke swirling up: a nocturnal Turner." He is mostly alone, except when his teenage son comes to visit, or his friend Anastasia from Austin, Texas, where he once taught Creative Writing ("Don't make me laugh"). Radio, not television, relieves the rural silence. Time for reappraisal, for close attention: "A wren on a fence in the rain; inky clouds at sunset; a white breast feather falls from the sky. Boom of rising wind in the chimney . . . saw sickle moon." This is the higher vagrancy, in tune with an older reality. "Homeless," he suggests, is one of the saddest words in the language; yet this is not a sad book but a waiting book, a book of "mysteries, revealed truths we cannot comprehend."

Aidan Higgins in Berlin: The Great Walker—A Personal Omnium Gatherum

MARTIN KLUGER

> "Je te tiens, tu me tiens par la
> Barbichette. Le premier de nous
> deux qui rira, aura une tapette."
> French Children

In 1971, the walled city of Berlin provided a home and a none too safe shelter for an estimated twenty-thousand of the species mus muscúlus, or common house mouse who, when some sort of spring eventually came after a pang of snow in May, fled the houses in a frenzy as all genuine Berliners did and do, to frolic in the bushes lining the local lakes. One specimen, not forgotten, must have crossed our path as we were walking round Schlachtensee in the *green lungs* district of Zehlendorf. Did you see that? Higgins asked me, obviously baffled by this sudden hint of wild life in the city of the ceaselessly digesting pet dogs. No, I had not, would not, still very awkward in his presence, blind to the visible world, lost in the contemplations of the young about what to say next on this planet. Then open your eyes, the fastidious taciturn Irishman remarked. Was he serious, this scribe from the end of the world?

Apart from a novel-manufacturing uncle turned diplomat whose daughter Imogen had married an Irish sculptor, and full-time-fatherer of carefree girls, the famed author of *Langrishe, Go Down* was the first writer I met in person. For a young aspiring member of the utterly extinct tribe of *Denker* and sometimes also

Dichter, to become acquainted with a living practitioner of that invitingly doomed trade was, as it still might be, a matter of honour and great expectations and furtive thoughts about what to say next. Higgins's admonitory advice to open my veiled or altogether sealed eyes haunted my wishful dreams, and later my writing days, for many years. Perhaps it still does and will go on doing so. Not that I would mind. Walking with the writer in the Berlin of 1971, I began to investigate my native grounds which before I had only vaguely sensed, like a blind-born animal, in unspoken affairs of the heart. Walking with him was excellent exercise for the eyes or "beepers" as I think Cole Porter called them, obviously referring to some ethological threshold change in adolescence. Nothing escaped Higgins's weather-proof eyes. I had learnt the alphabet at the age of six and thus did not trust a "creative writing course" so generously offered and executed in the busy hives of North America. But I placed high value on the mouse that Higgins saw. It had disappeared for all time.

Der große Spaziergänger (the great walker) was a name my mother found for Higgins. She admired his hands, his work, his ways. Both guarding their distance, unable to understand each other's language, they had the most serious exchanges on Grass (a mutual favourite) and Thomas Mann (a controversy). They agreed on Céline and the great McNab. When staying over at our place after prolonged intakes of *Apfelklarer* at the Dahlem "Annapam"-pub (notable then for its rapid and stylish decline: a sort of guilt-ridden self-service while the proprietor was sound asleep in a dim corner, clutching an empty bottle of *Perversiko*) Higgins rose late, wanted raw bread for breakfast, "with some spreading," commented acidly on my constant "abuse" of radio or record-player. My mother stood on the balcony, facing the green tunnel of trees into which our friend vanished, and said: *Da geht der große Spaziergänger.* There he went, into the unknown. Where did he live in Berlin? There were friends in Wannsee, a tall brown beauty on Güntzelstraße, driving her Karman Ghia to the limits. He never stayed in the tiny monk-cells offered by the Berlin Academy of Arts to the very shy (Beckett) and the very poor (Herbert) and the very dangerous (Burroughs). He did not take part whatsoever in Berlin's literary life, a full-time tour de force for walking self-advertisements with livers of steel, nor did he fall for the professional lickers of names from both the Free and the Technical University. He walked, he worried, he wrote. He was going from strength to strength, to weakness, to strength again. He had his own life to *denken* and *ditchen* about, seldom talked about it. "My life is a mess, but I think that's what I want it to be," I noted him saying. Passers-by did not stop for his autograph. A Higgins in full stride, all out for Berlin's wild life, mice and bigger mammals, could do without that. Young girls were not amused and not impressed. My own friend Fatima, dentist's daughter from the poor plains of Afghanistan (a blank spot on the map then) did not for the life of her want to meet him (although her raven-black helmet of hair could be seen spying round the corner now and then), she sensed trouble, the man was too *intensiv* (intense). Too odd. Too old. Moreover, one had to listen to him and listening to him was, just then, not very popular with us young people. Women in their early thirties were attracted to him and attracted him, tall hardheaded beauties named Lore or Hanne (pre-war names), makers of misery, "with them," Higgins said, "I see how Europe goes."

I was disappointed by his total lack of self-dramatisation. To me, in those days of my indecision between drumming and writing, *Dichter* and even writers were big beasts, monsters, tragic figures, Lowry with an open fly, Grabbe howling, Kafka coughing last love to Dora Diamant in the Botanical Gardens. Higgins's friend from early DAAD-days in Berlin, the poet Zbigniew "Zbignaw" Herbert sinking fast at the beginning of this European entertainment. In love with zoology, biology, biography, more painting than music, lacking anything known as "story-telling" but telling a story from what used to be called the soul (a certain wholeness in the course of bioparanoia, a certain *pierre de touché* in history): *Balcony of Europe* is the work of eight years which almost killed him, as Aidan wrote in a letter, ". . . of boredom and something else I cannot describe, something electric on the far side of that mountain Inertia." But all the big circulation glossies, *Time* and *Newsweek* illiterates, hated it, panting for a plot, unhappy with anything "less." Even the more benevolent Brits missed their good old patent leather "character-development," i.e. Forster's Flat or Fat. Many mistook the book for fiction (a novel) when it is quite something else: a sort of old testament for the lusty, droppings into the dictionary of despair, a Who's Who in Ghosts, cyclopaedical poetry in the meteorological tradition of *The Anatomy of Melancholy*, a map of the Garden turned bad, a love-story untold, a horrible and haunting procession of lost souls, a remembrance longer than a sleepless night, if I may paraphrase Karl Kraus. No soul-utions, nor solutions, nor tricks. Dialogue and help drowning in the sea, the Atlantic Ocean. To be re-read in the grave, the dark school.

Fidgeting through Lelouch's film *Vivre pour Vivre* in old Capitol Dahlem, not impressed by Yves Montand, Higgins decided in 1971, rightly, that I had bad taste. Which I still have, especially in films. Both mistrusting the medium, we founded our "Morningstar Productions," dedicated to the pursuit of Kitsch in a sober world. That is, I had to go through a maze of Kitsch while he, over all the years, did the fine writing. I guess that's what used to be called a modal action pattern in ancient behavourism. It was strange, that time in Berlin in 1971. I learnt a lot but was officially forbidden to learn. You Germans need your masters, Aidan told me, but I am not willing to be one. We sat in the "Theaterstuben" at Ernst-Reuter-Platz, drinking Dortmunder Union Beer, and I tested his nerve, talking away. He scratched his goatee, scratched it again, remained silent. I was not sure what to say next. I loved the situation, its awkwardness, Higgins not. Later, through many meetings, more letters, I saw his point. He introduced me to: Yves Berger, Djuna Barnes, Tanja Blixen, Eudora Welty ("her use of light"), Richard Brautigan, Brian O'Nolan, George Steiner, Tacitus. He introduced me to Berlin. I played Coltrane for him, Miles, Sweet Paul Desmond, Glenn Gould electrically "writing" himself through the Goldberg Variations. We spoke English alone. Much later my wife asked: Has he ever read one of your stories? No?

Yet, in those days, I always wrote thinking what he might say. Higgins as a customs-officer, multilingual as Peter Ustinov, searching my luggage. Any Kitsch to declare? I learnt the art of smuggling, romanticism in disguise, syrup declared as Vodka. My customs-officer became more ambitious to find pure sticky Kitsch as the years went by. Translating his *Scenes from a Receding Past*, another novel from ghostland, I discovered, late in our friendship, just what I owe him in the craft of putting words together. Most of all courage, feeble as it may appear to be. Courage to switch a point of view against the point of time, gently. Who wrote that Higgins is a lonely figure tiptoeing through disaster? Perhaps I learnt that, too. Not that I would mind.

We walked Schlachtensee. I was twenty-three. Had never been to Ireland. Waited in Berlin, this great station, for the arrivals and departures of friends who travelled as far as Africa. I scribbled down most of Higgins's remarks, kind or unkind, imperative or incidental. Mostly later, alone at night, or break of dawn, sometimes while he was talking. I tried to behave like an adult, smoking big cigars with him, drinking Mosel wine at the "Kurgarten" in the summer under a strange foreign tree. But I was no adult and might never be, I was an admirer, fascinated by his sad sentences, the world he had known, the faces he had seen, the mice he saw. Later I enjoyed answering his eccentric queries about Berlin, the details that should be many or none. Then, one day, he had walked enough here, did not show up anymore for a long stretch of "time," gone to Spain again or his troubled Ireland. It was my turn now. I began to investigate my haunts. I began to take a closer look, I began to walk alone. The past had begun. The only element we are fit for.

A lot of suicides later, still in the European capital of suicides, I walk the *green lungs* alone, and I still stop and stare and listen to an occasional faint rustle in the bushes of Berlin from where the ghost of a mouse might appear any moment. Are you asleep, little mouse? Answer me.

More I cannot and will not write about the Great Walker. Hard to say anything about a long-time friend, hard to avoid the Kitsch and cant he hates so much. He came back to Berlin, recently, we walked again, but nothing can replace those first walks through landscape and literature. His own walks are there, recorded in his books. Books one can read and re-read and re-re-read in times of disorientation, when one gets lost in the woods, when one needs the clear voice of insomnia only great poets and a few great prose-writers can supply, when the *aurora borealis* of the silver screen and the flickering handkerchief of TV or video just won't do.

It is much too early to write about Higgins's contribution to the literature we live. He will go on writing his unique stuff. He will remain, like some of the animals the World Wild Life Fund is trying to preserve, in his own biotop. Remain when people will not read anymore (which could happen, even might happen sooner than we know), nor see, nor feel. He knew and knows that art is for the birds, in a world defying the word, blinding the ancient mirror we

Balcony of Europe is set in Andalusia, Spain, in 1962–63 and the novel shares much with Antonioni in its abandonment of conventional narrative, little forward momentum, unexplained characters and relationships, dead time, architectural design, chunks of history, sick Eros, and relationships in limbo. There are of course sections of the novel set in Ireland but these were added at the suggestion of editors to help "explain" it. For our purposes here we are looking only at the Spanish material. The Author claims the overall writing took eight years but he also states that much of it was written while the *events* he is describing were actually taking place. This seems true in respect of the Dan/Charlotte affair which appears to be taking place in an uncertain present as if the narrator has just got his wind back after another semi-successful tryst with the seemingly available yet strangely elusive Charlotte. He is thus recording events before they vanish; also we suspect, to prove to himself they actually happened in the first place. In the novel Dan and the others in Andalusia are trapped, either by location or simply copper fastened through marriage, duty, children. The endless time-serving and the reluctance to throw off the shackles, remind us of the protagonists in Paul Bowles's *The Sheltering Sky*. Dan Ruttle is in Spain following the death of the first great love of his life: his mother. He spends his days avoiding his wife Olivia, he is furtive, scuttling from bar to café, chatting, making notes, observing, needy for Charlotte his lover and tormentor. Dan Ruttle should be thriving but he is not. What has happened to him? And why is a young married woman risking her marriage with a needy much older man? It is interesting to compare Dan and Fitz from *Bornholm Night-Ferry*. Dan needs Charlotte to brighten him up, lift him out of the gloom. She never really wants him, to her their affair is fun, almost an irrelevance, she can replace him quite easily. In *Bornholm* Elin really does want Fitz but ultimately Fitz shies away.

Dan "loves" Charlotte because of the excitement she brings. She is an elixir. An escape from the drudgery of life with Olivia and sons. Olivia remains a silhouette, not a fully fledged "character." Indeed Charlotte is also finally a silhouette. Imogen in *Langrishe* is possibly the one true female fictional creation. In *Langrishe* the central relationship is riveting; here the central relationship is almost peripheral. It is more about the effect of not having her.

"The Plaza was damp; it had been hosed down like a ship's deck. And I was engaged in a shipboard romance with a young married woman from another class, from another continent. I walked there with a void in my stomach, as on the mornings after breakfast on the Cunarder Sylvania ploughing back from Canada. Mind not poor lovers who walk above the decks of the world in storms of love."

It's about Dan, not about Charlotte. We know what Dan feels, his loneliness, his romanticism, his self-pity, but we never learn what Charlotte feels. Is Charlotte, and all she represents, a mere image of escape and not a real alternative to Olivia? Charlotte's daughter is called Daisy and this seems to add further weight to the notion of an image attempting to convey what is missing. *Jay Gatsby* on the edge of the dock looking across the bay to the green light where his lost love lives. Dan is a *painter* though he might have greater credibility as a blocked writer, projecting onto Charlotte his hope to escape from writerly limbo. If Dan were truly a painter he would have painted Charlotte nude many times and thus would have had a perfect cover in which to meet.

For the Theatre the material would have to be chopped to the essential characters: Dan, Charlotte, her husband, Olivia. But what is at stake? Does the adultery really matter? No. Very little dramatic value there. Limbo or inertia? How do we dramatise that? Chekhov's "The Cherry Orchard" is closer to the model, where hardly anywhere does anyone take hold decisively of his or her own destiny. On stage Dan's desire for Charlotte might appear comic and not the intended soul searching torture of the novel. Although Harold Pinter's dramatisation of *Langrishe* created two great acting roles for Judi Dench and Jeremy Irons the film had a chilliness, much to do with Pinter's style, which negated the warmth of the book. But then again it is difficult to transfer such rich prose from page to screen or stage.

Aidan Higgins, a non-driver, has always explored what the passenger sees. It's not the High Street but all the little side streets that interest him. His narratives are flawed just like that other great modernist Antonioni. In 1995 Antonioni received an Honorary Oscar ("in recognition of his place as one of Cinema's master visual stylists"). If the equivalent existed for writers Higgins might receive a similar citation. But also might be added: master prose stylist, creator of extraordinary sentences combining great charm, colour, feeling, complexity and comedy. How is it possible to dramatise that? It can't be done. Can it?

Aidan Higgins in Conversation
with Neil Donnelly

Aidan Higgins in conversation with Neil Donnelly on 28 April 2008, reflecting on *Balcony of Europe*, first published in 1972 and due to be re-issued in 2010.

DONNELLY: Some contemporary critics have drawn parallels between you and W. G. Sebald.

HIGGINS: What parallels?

DONNELLY: His use of history, autobiography, travel, photographs, breaking the conventions of the novel.

HIGGINS: Sebald is too grim. I'm not like him. I used to be accused of being grim and difficult but I'm not, I'm much more a joker.

DONNELLY: Joker Higgins!

HIGGINS: Joker Higgins, yes.

DONNELLY: *Balcony of Europe*, first published in 1972 is about to be re-issued. The original manuscript was over a thousand pages later reduced to 463. It has at its centre a love affair between Dan, an Irish painter and Charlotte, a Jewish American free spirit. Both are married to other people. The story is set mainly in Southern Spain in the early 1960s. Apart from the love quartet the manuscript is peopled with an array of quixotic characters. "Purity of race does not exist. Europe is a continent of energetic mongrels" is one of the rejected epigraphs. So, a big oak with many branches. You kept sculpting away at it.

HIGGINS: *Balcony of Europe* took me eight years. I suffered for it. I thought I'd write a book that I wouldn't have to invent at all. Whatever happened to me I'd write down. I'd make notes of, I'd invent nothing. I'd just have to follow my notes on what was going on. I could leave things out but I couldn't put things in, except of course I would elaborate. For example, the character Finch, who goes to Russia, stories he told me, I didn't invent anything there. All I invented was his name. He was a tall guy but I gave him the name of a small bird.

DONNELLY: Why so strict a discipline?

HIGGINS: When you are finished with one book you are in a void until you begin another. The gap between the first and second book, and in the case of *Balcony*, the third book, gets wider and wider. I was wondering how to begin. I began in the family story in Ireland. I wanted to write books that were as un-Irish as possible. In *Langrishe, Go Down* I got up to about page 100, let us say, before I realised, *It's Irish, for Christ's sake! It's all Irish!* I had to do something about it and then I had the luck to end up in South Africa and to make a buddy of a German who was in fact writing the Big German Book and I got a great deal of Otto out of watching him and listening to him, in fact he gave me Otto. In truth Otto was really a copy of a chap called Adam Czewski who has since died. So he wasn't quite as invented as at first seems. He came into *Langrishe* of necessity in order to bring Europe into the book. To associate what I was writing with greater Europe. That Ireland wouldn't be as isolated as it seemed to me most Irish writing was at that time. It was all about Ireland, in a very narrow way. Writers like Frank O'Connor and Liam O'Flaherty, that my mother read to me that I liked very much as a young lad, but when my critical faculties became more critical, I couldn't stand. It was a great relief when I discovered *At Swim-Two-Birds* which is very Irish and not *very*

Irish at all in a curious way. It jumps over the parochialism of much Irish writing of that time. Irish writing seemed to me reductive in its themes. It didn't seem to move at all, except backwards into our glorious past. It couldn't touch me in the way foreign writers could, English writing didn't help much but American did. Reading somebody like Faulkner, using jargon in a non-patronising fashion—the poor blacks are poor blacks, the poor whites are poor whites—

DONNELLY: *Balcony* also begins in Ireland then moves to Southern Spain.

HIGGINS: Yes.

DONNELLY: Where you are inventing nothing.

HIGGINS: Almost nothing.

DONNELLY: I want to read this brief coda to Chapter 58:

> She's never in her life before had such attention, such love, Bob Bayless told Olivia. She doesn't know what to do with it. Olivia repeated this to me: that never before in her life had Charlotte Bayless received such attention, such love, and that she didn't know what to do with it.
>
> From Whom? I asked. From him?
>
> No, Olivia said, from you.

Dan is the narrator and Olivia is his wife. Are Bob Bayless and his wife Charlotte based on real people?

HIGGINS: Yes.

DONNELLY: Did Bob Bayless know that Charlotte was having an affair with Dan?

HIGGINS: Yes.

DONNELLY: Did he know at the time?

HIGGINS: Yes. I couldn't hide it.

DONNELLY: Did he object?

HIGGINS: He did. But he didn't do anything about it. Except one day he said to me when we were in a bar, *I'll stop pimping for you*, and I said I didn't realise he was pimping for me. And he said, *You wouldn't have got very far with her if she hadn't strewn a few roses in your path.*

DONNELLY: What was his reaction when the book was first published?

HIGGINS: I don't know. I imagine he didn't like it, but I don't know.

DONNELLY: And what was her reaction?

HIGGINS: She didn't say anything.

DONNELLY: There is a lyrical poetry in *Langrishe* but there is no attempt at this in *Balcony*. In it there seems a tendency to deliberately puncture moments of lyricism.

HIGGINS: Banville is looking for a beautiful sentence which I think is a mistake. I look for a simplicity which I found in Robbe-Grillet, Cheever and early Hemingway.

DONNELLY: *Balcony* does not have a conventional plot.

HIGGINS: I was writing a true book as events developed, so I didn't have to worry about plot.

DONNELLY: You are never interested in plot?

HIGGINS: No. In *Balcony* the plot was what happened to me daily. I didn't put in *everything*. I put in only what I thought was relevant to keep the thing moving.

DONNELLY: It's almost a documentary?

HIGGINS: I sum it up this way. It has an acerbic bitter sweetness. You can read a page of it and it can only be *Higgins*. And that is the hard work on sentences and out of the hard work on sentences came this characteristic tone.

DONNELLY: In *Balcony* you appear to reveal everything, yet it is full of unsolved Mysteries.

HIGGINS: What you read and what I read is a different book. The author is really the worst judge of their own book. Borges said a very true thing about the reader and a book—a book is read by ten people say, each time the book is read it's a new book, a new person reading it makes it a new book, naturally because he is a different person with different abilities, different interests and some of the stuff is very interesting and that bores the hell out of another reader. So, there are good patches and bad patches and they occur for different readers in different places. So there are ten different books.

DONNELLY: Are there any new Higgins books on the way?

HIGGINS: As a matter of fact there are. Two.

DONNELLY: Two new books?

HIGGINS: The first is *March Hare*. It's 300 pages and is hard to categorise. In the past I tried to suppress the humour in my writing but no longer. The second book is *Darkling Plain*. A book of conceptions and misconceptions. Two free flowing books.

DONNELLY: When are they due for publication?

HIGGINS: Next year.

DONNELLY: Three books altogether next year, *March Hare, Darkling Plain* and the re-issue of *Balcony*.

HIGGINS: I'm very excited about the new books. I haven't re-read *Balcony* for a very long time. Of course reading for me now is very difficult as I am technically registered blind.

DONNELLY: You are looking very well.

HIGGINS: So they keep saying.

Prose Familiars

AIDAN HIGGINS

Most Irishmen, I think, must have accepted on hearsay that "in Drumcliff churchyard Yeats is laid," that there is an inscription on his headstone with some instructions to a Dark Horseman, and that, on another grave above Zurich, a further inscription says simply: *James Joyce, 1882–1941*—because few Irishmen have ever read either. Any time they might have visited them (a somewhat remote possibility in the latter case, in every sense of the word) in order to pay belated obeisance to what poor remains of the immortals might there adjacent lie, their visit has been in vain, and they are deprived of even a sight of the grave, so thickly are the abstracted crowds of prose familiars gathered already there before them—small, vague, monkey-sized forms sitting in the haze, rather like Shelley's old atomies, and so unsightly that their own shadows have disowned them. Most of them crouching on the famous headstone in a sort of coma; tapping away on minute typewriters; squatting on the bramstokerish glass covers over the frozen flowers ("and others sate chattering like helpless apes on vulgar hands . . ."), or digging reverently into the topsoil of the grave with tiny trowels, meticulously depositing the earth in envelopes which they seal and tidy away in breast-pockets before transplanting clay from another grave into their own shallow one; and this in spite of the fact that they are *all* doing it, so prose familiars must *always* have been doing it; and, consequently, the clay in their envelopes is just earth from a grave, any old unknown grave. No, that does not stop them; it never has stopped a familiar, and it probably never will . . . So, in the face of all this rather unsettling ritual and hubbub, the deferential Irishman is compelled to beat as unobtrusive a retreat as possible, hat in hand; as it is a well-known fact that familiars will not be shifted.

You may say now, "Yes, yes! We can see all this, and it's undoubtedly very terrible, if you say so. But what harm are these prose familiars—as you call them—doing? What *do* they do? What do they look like? Do they live in graveyards *all* their lives?"

Well, I'll tell you the harm they do.

What do they look like? Nobody knows that; as nobody has actually seen a prose familiar face-to-face. I am inclined to imagine myself that they are indescribable-looking elementals from the great common psyche, like the things one finds in the Kafka short stories. But then again of course, your guess is as good as mine. First of all, they hang about, invisible, in the air, like conscienceless guardian angels, refusing to materialize until a dead and forgotten author is ripe enough to be exploited by them in print, or until a promising new author has made a big enough impression for them to swoop down, adopt him as their own, insinuate themselves into his vulnerable confidences little by little, and generally learn all they can about him.

They *may* write books about him while he is still extant, but usually the exploitation does not start in the earnest until he is safely out of the way. Then they write a great deal about him; biographies and safe tautology that can be spun out at length. Inevitably they make a great deal of money out of him. It's as simple as that. Prose familiars are the accepted pirates of print; the seas they sail in are the old discarded documents—diaries, letters, drafts, possibilities for biographies, etc.—of (preferably) dead authors. Not all of them are ghouls and intellectual blood-suckers: some of them, the best of them, attached themselves to their masters and patrons even before the latter had "made their name." No, not all of them are ruthless; but a lot of them are, whether they admit it or not.

To qualify as prose familiars at all, all they have to do is to answer a few questions correctly (theirs is the easiest trade union in the world). "Did they actually know the author—*their* author?" "Had they anything further to add about him?" and, "Was it worth adding?"—as Joyce would have said: "Were they trying to express something they *understood*?" Should they answer "Yes" to all these questions, nothing further is allowed stand in the way of their ambitions, least of all the solemn, gathering of familiars already there before them, in all probability staring into their master's face in a sycophantic manner. A prose familiar worthy of the name must trample ruthlessly over the crowd in possession, pointedly ignoring their indignant futile squeals. Such a familiar must never walk in step, never be content just to gall other wretched servile kibes. A true familiar must always be prepared to act on the insolent assumption that he himself, furtive egomaniac that he nearly always is, knows more about his master than the latter does himself. And only in this way can he justify the meaning of his existence at all.

Broadly speaking, prose familiars come in two categories. Firstly, the household kind: whose self-imposed duty it is to prey into the most private details of their master's life, keep his bed warm for him if necessary, and, provided he is still alive, a cagey eye on his work. If he is dead they keep it on his copyright, which they somehow always manage to corner, depriving the avaricious publisher of this lucrative possession for a few years at least. He is referred to as the Definitive Biographer. The very least we ought to expect from him is that he exchanged a few words, however banal, with his master on some unspecified occasion. (Proust and Joyce sat through a protracted dinner-party seated next to each other in a silence unbroken but for one question—*who* asked it is beside the point—*Was he fond of truffle?*)

And, secondly (the title is almost self-explanatory) the Critical Appreciator; a more scholarly and intellectual brand of familiar altogether, whose interest is centred more on the master as an artist than as a man. This one, we should expect, has an, avowedly, comprehensive knowledge of the master's text, with a special insight into its more clouded aspects, figuratively speaking, of course; which implies a duty in honour to reveal all to the less fortunate at the very first opportunity in print—not that the published interpretations need necessarily be correct, indeed they seldom are, but they must sound convinced that they are. An urge which is not, needless to remark, allowed to lie in abeyance very long. Thus, in theory, at least, pipping other more or less irresponsible prose familiars from profiteering overmuch in their questionable old practice of attempting to pin *a priori* deductions on texts they are probably more ignorant of than otherwise, or opinions on a subject who is posthumously thrashing about in his grave in a vain effort to evade such unwelcome castigation.

But, of course, one is really as bad as the other. Honour, with unnecessarily self-righteous people, is always fighting at the last ditch; its own truculence is in itself an indication of how little it feels it has to lose. So, like lots of excellent theories, this one does not always work out in practice as we might have hoped (though in this context Joyce has little to complain of); and we need not be surprised to find that the familiars who were the trusted friends and confidants of their masters made them suffer most for that very friendship in the end; while those who had prose familiars thrust upon them, profited accordingly.

These groups of Definitive Biographers and Critical Apprecia-tors coalesce and even expand sometimes, as every now and again a more than usually determined prose familiar defies analysis within a single category. Such a one was Boswell. So big was Dr. Johnson's familiar that he acted as surrogate for his non-existent twin; indeed, so big was he that he probably had a few familiars of his own, sucking away enthusiastically at his unprotected supernumerary while his attention was otherwise engaged. The converse, peculiarly enough, does sometimes happen as well. Joyce, for instance, was at one time in Ibsen's small army of familiars. Though later he appears to have gone out of service: *Exiles* going on from where *The Wild Duck* left off—though as a dramatist of course Joyce was not in the same class as Ibsen—surely implying that the greatest "saving lie" of them all was the implication that, once Werle senior and Berta Sörby "knew each other as they were," all their troubles would be over. In that stage in *Exiles* their troubles would have only begun. But these transitions are to be welcomed in accordance with the amount of vanity, greed, presumption, certitude, or dedication, predominating in the familiar in question. Before leaving the point I would like to remark in passing that the contemporary Boswell is a scholar called Henn; his Dr. Johnson is W. B. Yeats.

It is impossible, I imagine, to know either Joyce or Kafka without, some time or other, bumping into their respective familiars. Both of them, as you can see in any of the better bookshops, have one particularly faithful—or, if you wish, particularly insidious—one apiece. Proud and remunerative positions which the indefatigable little things have won for themselves by sheer weight of print. The pair of them, you know them as well I do, derive a comfortable livelihood from farming-out their undeniable firsthand knowledge of their respective masters. Who are both, fortunately for themselves, now dead.

So now you know about the noxious Prose Familiar, and in future you can watch him weaving in print, and remain immune to his dangerous appeals. For prose familiars, not satisfied with undermining the reputations of immortals—of some, only of some—have, by their very existence, falsified hard true things that were said regarding those immortals. They falsified that wonderful cynicism of Cocteau's: *A hundred years after my death I shall retire, having made my fortune.* Now, this is no longer true. It should, perhaps, read: "Rather than sink my credit in a remoter posterity, my familiar is willing—as frequently as he thinks necessary—to commit the most pious of self-deceptions; namely, ever so often, to dig me up again, and always pretend to be astonished to find a stranger buried in my place." This is the kind of sensation the public never tires of, because seasonally, and almost in spite of itself, the baleful public eye turns to the idols it feels it ought to kneel before, but is loath to all the same; possibly because the same idols are human enough, once they find their old tormentors in that position, to kick them shrewdly in their undefended parts. In these seasons of public heat you will always find the prose familiars somewhere around, attempting, with varying degrees of success—depending on their own plausibility—to convince a doubting public that such treatment ought really to be welcomed—it was either good for them or, in any case, was done out of sheer kindness.

No, as far as I can see—certainly as far as the mortals are concerned—Chamford was wrong—*Prose Familiars* are contemporary posterity. Because they judged them with a lack of severity usually reserved almost exclusively for the dead; and that they should do so sometimes while they, the immortals, were still alive, seemed to them the highest compliment they could be paid; and they never forgot it, because they, like ourselves, were human once. But it should be pointed out that they had no right to be human—after

Section II: Critical Responses

For the Record:
Aidan Higgins's Autobiographies

PETER VAN DE KAMP

In *The Whole Hog*, young hormonal Rory of the Hills (Aidan Higgins's autobiographical self) sneaks inside the former lamp room now transformed hyperbolically into the "reference library" of his peculiar older brother the Dodo:

> Tidy mounds of magazines and newspapers were arranged in alphabetical order along the shelves, a morgue of out-of-date newsprint yellowing and smelly that still retained some things of interest for the Dodo, the ruby and cricket records. (*The Whole Hog* 81)

Rory's quest is for one of the issues of *Lilliput*, a magazine with black and white photos (by Douglas Glass, we learn) of naked English girls—"to take [a] model for an outing [in the wheat field] with an Irish boy after months of being cooped up in the stuffy study." It is the boy, we presume, and not the model, who has been cooped up for months—his sexual ardor must be acute. But the narrative is not informed by any urgency, and calmly and comprehensively catalogues the Dodo's periodicals:

> And here were the London *Daily Mail*, the *Dispatches*, the *Wisdens*, the *Illustrated London News* and *Tatler & Sketch*, the *Irish Times*, *The Field*, *Good Housekeeping*, *Home & Beauty*, *Lilliput*. (ibid.)

The booty is on a lower shelf. Off runs our frisky handyman with his spoils. He is indeed bursting to undress "in a trice" (undressing in Higgins is mostly done "in a trice") and "soon ejaculating for dear life into a pocket handkerchief spread out." That comes later; as the boy hastens out of Springfield House, we're given six paragraphs of background information about the erotic quality of Mr. Glass's "studies" ("as good as a private viewing of blue movies"), about censorship during the War Years ("what Dev and his Dáil were calling 'the Emergency,' an elusive Irish euphemism if ever there was one"), about The Hayes Office and the Daughters of the American Revolution, about Betty Grable, whose emblem decorated the fuselage of a Boeing 707 ("part of the war effort, like selling war bonds, when Irish bread was getting darker"), about Rita Hayworth, Jane Russell, Jennifer Jones, Margaret Lockwood, James Mason, Phyllis Calvert, Celia Johnson, Trevor Howard, Michael Wilding, Anna Neagle, The Irish Episcopal See and even John McEnroe.

At last the randy pup reaches his destination, but still he has to wait:

> The young wheat stood a good three or four feet high in a field of five or six acres protected by some scarecrow leaning sideways at drunken angles, with faces of straw swaying in the breeze as if it was the wind blowing over a body of water. . . ." (*The Whole Hog* 83)

Poor lad!

Critics have compared Higgins's work to that of Joyce, a fellow Clongownian and lapsed Catholic. *A Portrait of the Artist*, which he read at the age of twenty-two, made Higgins realise that "a novel could be more than a story" (Introduction 8).

But his "more" is very different from Joyce's: not for him the hall-mark Joycean collocation of experience and expression—the lusty lad above is held firmly in check by his autobiographer, who has more important matter to convey about the spirit of the age than mere intimations of his younger self in it. Higgins genuinely loathes vanity; not only does he look askance at writers who are concerned with their own greatness, and fulminate regularly against vain artists (foremost among whom is Norman Mailer), he also indicates his lack of self-importance, and does so with commendable modesty, through juxtaposition:

> On 3 March 1960 I was thirty-three years old and beginning to think of myself as a writer, for Calder and Grove Press had contracted to bring out the first stories, *Felo de Se*. In sixteen recently made independent African territories eighty-five million new black citizens had also begun to think differently about themselves. (*The Whole Hog* 136) [1]

Higgins continually pits the world against the self out of a sense of genuine engagement which is unique in Irish literature: "It is not enough to live," he contends, "you need to know as well" (*The Whole Hog* 104). This engagement does not stem from any political ideology; for him literature and politics don't mix.[2] Writing his life necessitates chronicling men's atrocities; they inform the spirit of the places which Higgins or his alter ego, the wandering Rory of the Hills, or those closest to him, inhabit or inhabited; "the land itself, never a spent force, is in its turn an instrument of the remote past" (*Dog Days* 179)—from the battle of Kinsale, evoked with unparagoned vividness, in terms of a rugby match, in "The Great Battle," the "sadists . . . having their day," to the

Provos "scatter[ing] about the bodies of their victims as heartlessly as cannibals would discard human bones" (*Dog Days* 376). Munich elicits the Palestinian hostage drama, and the slaughter of the Jewish Olympians. The atrocities unleashed by the Nazis are often on his mind (and he muses now and then on Rudolf Hess and Albert Speer in Spandau); the Siege of Stalingrad is documented, as is the erroneous bombing of Dublin by the Germans. Everywhere "predators [have] pattered after victims like stoats in search of blood" (*Dog Days* 398).

But Higgins's narrative control is about more than just "no moaning, no boasting" (*Windy Arbours* 106), or about bearing witness to men's atrocities. It attests to a fastidiousness, not unlike that of his highly neurotic (if not psychotic) older brother. Higgins is an archivist who makes every effort to get the record straight. He authenticates. He has an archivist's fascination with statistics:

> EEC Eurobarometer reveals that the Irish are a little less gloomy about the future than a year ago, while the majority remain pessimistic all the same. Forty-five per cent believe the world situation will disimprove this year. They are not as down-hearted as the Belgians, of whom only 12 per cent believe that the matters will improve, while 51 per cent believe the contrary. . . . Women are slightly more constipated than men and the young in the 15–25 age bracket more so than those older than them. Eighteen per cent of the Irish fear world war, as do 25 per cent of the Dutch. (*Dog Days* 62)

> Thirty thousand condoms have been imported into the country since 1980. . . . Fourteen thousand Irish emigrated

to Britain during the 1940s and 1950s. The official figure in 1985 was down to 6,000; today it would be more like 30,000. (*Dog Days* 95)

"The imprecise" is one of the faults he attributes to John McGahern's fiction, with its "fetid reeks of old socks" (*Dog Days* 146; *Windy Arbours* 229). "It is better to be precise than to be imprecise," he avers in *Dog Days*, "for you can be imprecise in many ways but only precise in one way, the correct and only way. . . . Only in such discipline can we hope to find freedom, if it exists" (*Dog Days* 104). A similar fastidiousness manifests itself in his use of catalogues. They include the device of old family documents which the young John Cheever had exhumed and deployed as part of the fictional progress of *Wapshot Chronicle* (*Windy Arbours* 88). The ones that jump off the page are: the comprehensive list of items with which he and his younger brother the Dote are fitted out for boarding at Killashee prep (run by a French order of nuns); the list of names in his class there; a list of the inhabitants of Castletown from the time of William III; a list of his Aunts and Uncles; a list of the price of rent for profitable local land from *c*.1660; a six-page list of the dates and venues in South Africa visited in 1957 by John Wright's Marionettes National Theatre Organisation with whom Higgins went on tour; a list of places visited by same in Rhodesia in '58—all in *Donkey's Years*. *Dog Days* is fairly "list-less" (though certainly not listless) but *The Whole Hog*, once well under way, presents a list (mercifully truncated) of illnesses (in Afrikaans) cured by natural healer Dr. Rex Ferris; a list of Danish place-names; and then, in one orgasmic chapter close to its end, and hence the finale of *A Bestiary*, a list of headstones at St. Multose Protestant Cemetery (beside the present dwelling in Kinsale of Aidan and Alannah); of the anglicized names of Irish villages and townlands; of the fish that swam "under the arches of the Archdeacon Duggan bridge opposite Folly House" ("whilom home" of his friends the Simpsons); of the birds that wintered in the Commogue Marsh; and, as a final elegy, a list of the remembered dead.

In the Prophetic Books of Blake, for whom exuberance is beauty, such lists have been interpreted as ontological devices, as in Joyce's *A Portrait* and *Ulysses*; in Higgins, they have come in for criticism, to which the man himself retorts:

> Carping reviewers, those journeymen ever hasty in their judgements and not too prone to split hairs, have objected to the prevalence of lists in the Higgins *oeuvre*, still emerging and changing, which they took at best to be an indulgence and at worst a poor imitation of James Joyce's worst excesses. . . . But hold your hearses, carpers.
>
> Lists or catalogues of proper names can be ambiguous—and sinister—as processions, be they military, religious, funeral or Klu Klux Klansmen [sic] burning effigies by night, preparatory to hanging some unfortunate next day. . . . I took the notion of lists from Rabelais, via Urquhart two centuries before James Joyce. Crusoe was obliged to keep lists in his head, ink being in short supply on the island. (*Donkey's Years*, in *A Bestiary* 244)[3]

Neither ambiguity nor sinisterity can fully account for Higgins's fascination with lists. They are part of a wider scheme of things, which includes snippets of poems and songs, proverbs and sayings, newspaper cuttings, an auction sign, and a copy of the score card of A. C. Higgins, 3 handicap—a course record of 66 (net 63) at the Grand Hotel Cup (nothing sinister or ambiguous about that), as well as diary entries and letters. In Sterne's *Tristram Shandy* such matter is a nominalist exercise in the expression of sensational experience, testing epistemological boundaries (as Neil Murphy has argued persuasively in *Irish Fiction and Postmodern Doubt*, there is much of that in Higgins); in early Joyce, whose very first story produces two signs on the door of the sisters Flynn's drapery, and whose "The Dead" flouts the economy principle by offering all the surplus words of the world's most familiar birthday song, it instances ultra-realism, the writer paring his fingernails, while at the same time commenting silently on the vacuity of verbal communion (and there is much of that in Higgins too). But perhaps most of all in Higgins, these extra-narrative devices exemplify the authenticator's troubled relationship with memory. "Are the memories of things better than the things themselves," he wonders time and again throughout his oeuvre—from *Langrishe, Go Down* through *Lions of the Grunewald* to *Dog Days*.[4]

Memory cannot approximate reality, but the subjectivity of personal memory can be fortified with the—semblance of—the objectivity of facts. They extend referentiality beyond the restrictive plot of a life-story. At the same time, the reporting of memory is in itself a distortion, which requires its restoration—"What aches a man is go back [sic] to what he remembers, wrote Faulkner. As you taste it you destroy it, say the wine buffs" (*Dog Days* 34). Yet time "attenuates memories," Byron writes (and Higgins quotes in an epigraph); to retain them requires continual recall (*Dog Days* 37). As such, Higgins's autobiographies are *recordations*—not just in the contemporary meaning of the word ("the action or process of recording or committing to writing"), but also in its obsolete sense of "an act of commemorating or making mention; a commemorative account."

Higgins's autobiographies, his memoirs, his "Memories of Life as Story Told" (the subtitle of *Donkey's Years*) are a *record* of his memory; they bear out the original meaning of the verb "to record," *viz.* "to get by heart, to commit to memory, to go over in one's mind." They are not just the product of his remembrance, but also an act of cognition proper—the mind at work. "I am consumed by memories," he writes at the very start of *Donkey's Years*, "and they form the life of me; stories that make up my life and lend it whatever veracity and purpose it may have" (*A Bestiary* 11).

Small wonder that Higgins champions Robinson Crusoe, that role model of Cartesian cognition. Just as Crusoe keeps lists in his head, Higgins goes over the same matter time and again in his memoirs. But where Crusoe survives and is restored to civilization, Higgins's recording is a life-long activity which is doomed to Beckettian failure. Like Beckett he cannot but keep on recycling the same memories, even the same phrases, in ever-changing contexts. Neil Murphy posits this quandary perspicaciously apropos *Balcony of Europe*:

> Any account of past events which raises the problematic issue of memory invariably challenges the validity of its own writing. Higgins's particular response to memory, and therefore to life, directly conditions the nature of his fictions. If the universe is in a state of flux, if life is ephemeral and refuses to be imprisoned by man's power of communication, then the act of writing must respond accordingly. Not only do events alter in one's memory, but so too does the mind that remembers. . . . Thus, if both the present and the past are in flux then how is it possible to transcribe events or states of feeling? Higgins's fiction insists that it is not possible to transcribe life: "To seek to paint that which cannot be painted—the Deity's human form— was considered by the wise ancients to be human imbecility" . . . Upon this artistic principle, the text is built. . . . flux is a constituent part of memory. (Murphy 62)

Soît. Let us return to that "reference library" and our adolescent Rory; here is the same episode but then in *Donkey's Years*:

> Among the books in the study I had come upon *Paris Salons, Cafés and Cabarets* by Sisley Huddleston and spent much time poring over a monochrome nude posing in a shadowy studio. On the orderly shelves of the Dodo's reference library I found neat piles of *Lilliput* and in them stark-naked English ingénues photographed by Douglas Glass in a field of English wheat. "With yourself or with others?" questions the priest from behind the wire. . . .
> (*Donkey's Years*, in *A Bestiary* 65)

The pernickety detail which we got in *The Whole Hog* has been replaced by a modest but telling white lie. Gone are Rita Hayworth and Betty Grable; they are offered ample space elsewhere, and given a whole chapter to themselves, "The Shapely Flanks of Rita Hayworth (*The Lady from Shanghai*)," later on in *The Whole Hog*, while *Lilliput* features once, and the Dodo's reference library twice, more in *Dog Days, en passant*.

Any biographer, like any composer, is engaged in a struggle against the tyranny of time. Lives simply aren't chronological; events and experiences do not follow a linear progression. Happenstance (or "happenchance," as Higgins calls it) reigns supreme. Things happen all at once, or don't happen, or happen differently than we thought or felt—and their effects aren't instantaneous: pennies, or the "agenbite of inwit" (Higgins calls it "aginbite"), can drop years later, or drop into different slots, or never drop at all. Language, however, *is* linearly ordered in time, and thus can never capture all those complexities, the blood and mire of human veins. A composer at least can use counterpoint.

What Higgins exposes through his recordation, masterfully, is the biographer's incontrovertible dilemma: pursue a theme in a biography and the time-line gets lost; stick to a time-line and important themes will dwindle into insignificance. Of course, no biography is written from beginning to end but is constructed like a puzzle, on the basis of trickling evidence and haphazard inspiration. Higgins says as much in his own work: "People sometimes ask me what kind of writing you do," he confesses in *Dog Days*. "I tell them 'Writing without a beginning, middle or end.' It still has no beginning, middle or end" (*Dog Days* 273). After all, "there are no pure substances in nature. Each is contained in each" (*Scenes from a Receding Past* 200). Indeed, in *Dog Days* the beginning of Rory's life is relegated to Chapter 21, "My First Arrival"; "My Second Arrival" follows six chapters later, the intervening chapters being set in 1980s Wicklow.

Begin at the end was the advice that Peter Costello gave me when in 1986 I wrote my first biography, on Flann O'Brien, with him, and wriggle your way back to the start. Even then, the biographer yearns for a second dimension, and a third. And this multi-dimensionality is what Higgins tries to achieve by recording the same episodes of his life in varying contexts or co-texts. For example, the start of *The Whole Hog* revisits the ending of *Donkey's Years*. He writes like a three-dimensional chess player. *Donkey's Years*, which ends on the death of his mother, *Dog Days*, concluding with his departure from Wicklow after that strange year of moving statues, murders and the *Big Wind* (1986), and *The Whole Hog*, finishing on the now-aged Higgins in his house in Kinsale beside the Protestant graveyard, should not be read consecutively but all at once. Ideally, the pages of *A Bestiary* ought to be transparent, and time put in its insignificant little place—on the back-seat.

You could call Higgins a meta-biographer (or "self-reflexive," if you prefer that pleonasm). His use of extra-narrative material fits the bill—like any biographer at work he queries how much circumstantial evidence his book will sustain: "How many facts does a life story require?" he asks in *Dog Days*, "what is fact and what life story?" (*Dog Days* 104). Reviewing *Donkey's Years*, Dermot Healy claimed, I suspect jokingly, that Higgins has "for years been fighting fiction by inventing fact," but now, with his autobiography, managed to write a "straight narrative."[5]

For Higgins there is no such thing as a "straight narrative." What he hopes to convey is "movements from the past (movements of the hidden heart), clear as sand in running water" (*Dog Days* 47). He quotes Huizinga (whom he calls "Huizenga"), the author who sees man as *homo ludens* in *The Waning of the Middle Ages*; "There is not a more dangerous tendency in history than that of representing the past as if it were a rational whole, dictated by clearly defined interests" (*Dog Days* 39). Time and again in his critical writings, as in his Preface to John Minihan's photo-book of Beckett, he cites Pascal, "Nature is an infinite sphere whose centre is everywhere, whose circumference is nowhere"; with considerable glee he explicates Beckett giving his anthropoid Miss Counihan a bust which is "all centre and no circumference," and he tells of Borges hunting down this metaphor all the way to Xenophanes, who "offered to the Greeks a single god," six centuries before Christ (Introduction 11). His main objection to realism is precisely its straight narrative. Its snug, regimented order of events, its glum coherence and causal cohesion leave no space to "record." Hence his reservations about Henry James, whose fiction "was always too highly organised, too concerned to prove its point, to move us or work well as fiction" (*Windy Arbours* 261). He dismisses James, "the Londoner by proxy, with overtones of camphor balls and port," as "an interminable parenthesis with little you—'the ultimate male destiny backed by means and position'—in short, the hard unreality of things deliberately arranged" (*Windy Arbours* 125).

"Reality stands in no need to be true to life," writes Anna Olsen/Reiner to Rory in *The Whole Hog*.[6] Realism belies the limited control that cognition can exert over nature's infinite sphere. And realistic fiction for Higgins, as for his favorite authors, Conrad and Borges, is just a fantastic story, because "the world is fantastic and unfathomable and mysterious" (*Windy Arbours* 235). To seek out reality and leave things that seem, is for the singer-born to lack a theme. Themes, defying the comfortable experience of reality, stem from what Stephen Dedalus towards the end of *A Portrait* so aptly phrases as the "reality of experience," which is fed by a fardel of stories, newspaper reports, movies—in short, the stuff that myths are made of. Higgins cites Thomas Mann writing of the genesis of the novel: "My own growing conviction, which I discovered was not mine alone, was to look upon all life as a cultural product taking the form of mythic cliché, and to prefer quotation to independent invention" (*Windy Arbours* 237).

"Reality of experience" allows us to feel that we're not just living Theroux's lives of quiet desperation but that we are the heroes in our own novels, like Eveline in Joyce's *Dubliners*, whose "reality" is constituted by Cinderella and three-penny romances. Lives imitate art—Higgins instances Goethe's *Leiden des jungen Werthers* resulting in the suicide of hosts of young men at the pinnacle of *Sturm und Drang*, just as Céline, another favorite of his, has pointed out that the gallantry of officers in rollicking turn-of-the-century novels enticed the reading men to sacrifice themselves in the field of Flanders before their unlettered soldiers.

It follows that for Higgins there is no real distinction between a life and a lie. "All biography is ultimately fiction," he writes apropos a book of interviews with his favored Djuna Barnes, "and fiction, a form of autobiography" (*Windy Arbours* 15). Indeed, all his books are a blend of autobiography and fiction, even his successful take on the Big House novel, *Langrishe, Go Down*—which his friend Beckett called "literary shit." The four sisters in that book, he explains in *Donkey's Years* and *The Whole Hog*, are his brothers and himself "in drag"; its protagonist, the venial Otto Beck, who acts as catalyst and mediator, is based on Bernhardt Adamczewski, the German-Polish second husband of Fiona, his first wife's best friend.[7] "Most of my books," he admits, "follow my life, like slug trails. . . . I don't invent anything—all the fiction happened."[8] And so he lifts, shamefacedly, from his fiction *and* criticism, and inserts it in *A Bestiary*. Higgins, a chess player, is nothing if not methodical—his recycling conjures up the image for me of an orderly archivist in front of his filing cabinet (something which one would not associate with Mr. H.). *The Whole Hog*, for instance, contains chapters from *Lions of the Grunewald* and *Bornholm Night-Ferry* (from Elin's side of the correspondence). He admits to this process of recycling in the Appendix to *Donkey's Years*:

> The sullen art of fiction-writing can be a harrowing procedure; an inspired form of pillaging. The writer has never scrupled to beg, borrow or steal from other sources, languages and times when occasion seemed to demand it. . . .
>
> "Borrow" may be a misnomer; say rather, put to better use, refined and improved out of all recognition. Both *Balcony of Europe* (1972) and *Scenes from a Receding Past* (1977) are out of print, and will remain so in my lifetime. I have freely pillaged from both for sections of this present work—bold Robinson Crusoe ferrying booty from the two wrecks.

The transported elements of these "liftings" now serve different purposes—as Crusoe had to cut down a great hardwood tree to make a plank—so too the castaway's necessities when conveyed with the stockade contrived a cave-dwelling from the side of a hill.

They have become my own stories again. (*Donkey's Years*, in *A Bestiary* 243)

Stories have their source in dreams; "as to dream," writes Higgins's fictional alter ego in *Bornholm Night-Ferry*, "(perhaps the only word we cannot put quotation marks around) and 'reality,' whatever that may be, well they are for me one and the same" (*Bornholm Night-Ferry* 93). His autobiographies are "all dreamy stuff, all dreams" (*The Whole Hog* 386). And dreams feature prominently, full of auguries, in *A Bestiary*, from his mother's nightmare about the suicide of his Uncle Josef Moorkens in *Donkey's Years* ("the corpse of a naked man laid out on a cold slab in a windowless room") to Higgins's dream of his mother transformed into a slosh ball for Russian pool at the end of *The Whole Hog*. The latter absurdity tames any urge in the reader to go hunt for symbols in Higgins's unconscious. For Higgins disavows the mythic method of Yeats and Joyce.

Higgins keeps it cool. This, together with the confessional nature of his autobiographies, and the inclusion of so many facts, make us want to believe that his biographical revelations *are* as real as the places he visits, the people he meets, and the historical events he depicts—and that his frame of reference is fairly fixed in this sublunary world. This belief he does his best to dispel, or at least to qualify, like any good artificer. He blatantly doctors the spelling of Elin/Anna's letters in *The Whole Hog*. In the Appendix to *Donkey's Years* he calls his life-story "this bogus autobiography, bogus as all honest autobiographies must be," and towards the end of the trilogy he acknowledges: "I had to turn my back on the real parents in order to evoke this other pseudo-anonymous couple who were more real than my real parents, Bart and Lil."[9] Both confessions of course harbor the paradox of artifice: bogus autobiographies are honest, or honest ones bogus; made-up parents have become real, their real counterparts having dissolved into "the seminal substance of the universe that is always becoming and never is" (*The Whole Hog* 233). And Higgins the artificer is not beyond Nabokovian game-play: in *Dog Days* his Brother Bun is seven years his senior and the Dodo five; in *The Whole Hog* ten and eight years separate them. This disparity is noted in a letter by that old Danish flame twenty-five years on:

> Why do you call yourself Rory? And how can you be seventy-one in the year 2000 when you were born in 1927? Or more interestingly where did you spend the last two years? (*The Whole Hog* 400)

So much for explication. It might not prove all that relevant for an assessment of Higgins's *Bestiary*. And assess we must, for fear of being asses, counted one among that set whom Higgins frowns upon: "Settle back in your armchairs, gentle browser, we are in the presence of bores, *arch* bores, academics trimming their fingernails" (*Windy Arbours* 220).[10] After all, epistemology does not interest him; it gives him the creeps: "It is not good for man to keep reminding himself that he is man. Lukacs, Adorno, Benjamin, Goldmann, Karl Kraus, Chomsky, what good did they ever do us?" (*Windy Arbours* 256).[11]

Please, dear reader, do not demand a paraphrase of Higgins's life from me—his growing up in affluence in Celbridge, with a mother who gave him notions, a dad who was that rare thing: an absentee landlord *in residence*, his childhood timidity, two older brothers (Brother Bun, a virgin for life, set in his anglophile ways, and that queer fish the Dodo) who treated him like shit, the immensely likable Dote, that constant companion of his youth, two years his junior whose super-ego never knew any bounds, the rough treatment he received from French nuns and from the National School, where he suffered but a day or two before being sent to the Jesuits who gave him (and me) a healthy dose of cynicism, his parents literally running headlong into debt, the odd first job for a golfing boss whom he saved from the scourges of alcoholic despair without ever getting paid for being a Samaritan, his meeting the South-African first wife in a pretentious London entourage ("had coffee with Joyce last night"), their touring South Africa and the then-two Rhodesias with that puppet theatre, the gradual dissolution of their marriage as Higgins, like his son James, yearns for love's replies, from Hannelore Schmidt in Berlin, where he does a stint for DAAD (DILDO, the Deutsche-Internationale Literatur-Dienst Organisation, in *Grunewald*), from Mrs. Harriet Deck of San Francisco ("OK, I'll let both you guys do it into my behind!"), from Anna Reiner of Copenhagen ("Uuuh you make me lude! I always seem to have your preek in my mouth when we are in the mountains"), *et al.*, time and again experiencing that the tragedy of sexual intercourse lies in the perpetual virginity of the soul, right down to his settling in Upper O'Connell Street, Kinsale, with his second wife and true love, Alannah Buxton-Hopkin, who was born in Singapore of an English father (Dr. Denis Buxton-Hopkin, a voluntary POW staying with his patients after the fall of Singapore) and an Irish mother, one of the Foleys of Summercove.

For that life I refer you to *A Bestiary*.

My empathy with Higgins? Well, at least partly his showing up "the hoax that joke bilked" (the phrase from *Finnegans Wake* which he quotes frequently), that exploitation of Ireland by its men of letters, and by *Bord Faoilte*, for what it is worth. "The smaller the island the bigger the neurosis," he intones time and again. He has no time for any of Ireland's small-mindedness, and scalpels its faults. He does acknowledge that the country bears the scars of "fixed subjugation," but that is no excuse for its "farsoonerite" mentality of interminable prevarication, or its "parochial miasma," or its begrudgery, or its exultation of violence ("the old Irish cruelty directed against itself"), or its mindlessness (of his friend the un-philosophical philosopher Arland Ussher he writes, "all his long life he was engaged in that most un-Irish of occupations: thinking").[12] I also warm to his splendid sense of humor, his epigrammatic wit (he can come across like a father full of good advice about women), his eye for the ridiculous, and his ability to pun, which recalls Beckett, Joyce, and Flann O'Brien, but also Mangan and Swift. As for his taciturn modesty, it is absolute requirement in any writer who really dives beneath the surface, or for that matter in any man worth his salt.

But empathy clouds judgment.

Higgins's is not the Modernist mythic method. For that he is too much an authenticator. He does require his reader to distill and instill meaning from his structural, contextual ventriloquism. Under all the apparent spontaneity of form lies an architectural dorm. The title of *The Whole Hog*, for instance, is announced in the first chapter of *Dog Days*. Like the best modernists he demands a lot from his interpreters, and pays them back piecemeal. One example, full of unspoken pathos, must suffice—the dentures; in *Dog Days*, Higgins cites a letter from his younger brother about their father's final days in hospital:

> The doctor gives him a week or two. He just about holds on, mind almost gone. Now they call it cancer . . . The operation caused the symptoms to spread all over, and to

the mind. Person & events have become confused & inter-changeable for him. He says you were fitted with false teeth when you were here but lost them, & himself and Jimmy Martin looked for them but didn't find them. (*Dog Days* 37)

A couple of dental appointments are mentioned in passing later in *A Bestiary*—they only seem to signal Rory's inevitable decay.[13] But then, towards the end of *The Whole Hog*, old and hoary Rory writes to Mary Alice Simpson:

> . . . Something wakes me at 3.30 and I get up to work on this book I'm finishing, but I suspect my mother is writing it. She always felt that she had a book in her. Now it's coming out.
>
> I took a break at 11 A.M. and searched high and low for my teeth (mi teef), the frontal bridge that produces such a winning smile (if I care to use it), compliments of P.J. Power, dental genius of Kinsale, without which (and whom) I am a sorry sight. The search proved fruitless, as lesser writers would put it. Guess where I found the teeth?
>
> In my mouth. (*The Whole Hog* 392)

The trilogy bears out Yeats's "Myself I must remake / Till I am Timon, Lear, or William Blake / Who beat upon the wall till truth obeyed his call"—that quality in Yeats which Eliot most admired. *Donkey's Years* is the fairly serious Higgins, full of elegiac pathos—the pages of his mother hanging on, impishly, and dying are among the most moving in Irish literature. *Dog Days* explicates his oeuvre with self-mockery, as men do *nel mezzo del camin*. Why should not old men be mad, he could have asked in *The Whole Hog*. It is Higgins at his most picaresque, not unlike the footloose and fancy-free Dutch author Jan Cremer (who he calls Jan Cramer), and when Higgins adopts that picaresque personality of a sybarite (and a sodomite) seeking salvation through love, itchy for response, as he does in *Grunewald*, he is very, very sexy. But where *Grunewald* is written in a healthy dose of self-mockery, like Donleavy, its re-visitation in *The Whole Hog* becomes more moralistic, T. S. Eliot-like. There is a touch of *O tempora, o mores* in his description of German rock cellars, and of mindless materialism:

> Shoppers, passive as fish, stunned by pumped Muzak, ascend and descend by escalators. Overpriced commodities were sold by ingenious advertising campaigns in an all-out psychological war not on want but on plenty. Everything was oversold, overstated, overheated; fraternity too had gone to Hell. The cities were splitting up from within, supermarts and car parks replacing cathedrals and concert halls. On fine summer evenings the long cinema queues waited silently in the north. To flee the world and dream the past was their intent; a sourceless craving now externalised, brought close. For them it would always be *Spermüll-Tag*: throwing-Out Day. Say rather, Throwing-Up Day. (*The Whole Hog* 204–05)

As he bemoans the Americanization of Ireland, first signaled by those disgusting baseball caps, and its accompanying opulence and greed, his prose becomes infused with a touch of *O quam cito transit gloria mundi*, a nostalgia for the pre-TV authentic Ireland (as if it ever existed!). Contemporary Ireland has no past to evoke, and that past is precisely what Higgins has evoked in his trilogy.

I would not be the first to say that Higgins is a superb stylist. Style being personality deliberately adopted (Yeats), he can surprise us with a sudden personality shift. For instance, the author, elegiac, visits the corpse of his mother in the mortuary and is moved to plaintive epigrams about the soul, but then, as he walks into a pub with his father, he suddenly dons the cap of Joyce's Arranger, straight out of *Cyclops*: "We were hardly into the steaming pub when whom did we run into but one of Dado's cronies . . ." (*Donkey's Years*, in *A Bestiary* 243). Like any good Irish man it seems that Higgins does not want to run the risk of appearing sentimental. The arranger, that Thersites-like narrator, makes some appearances in *Dog Days*:

> One fine May morning I was walking west along Waterloo Road when whom should I see approaching on the same pavement but a small-sized, brown-faced man in a pale serge suit and tan brogues, hatless, a miniature lariat serving for a tie, that gave him a look of Hopalong Cassidy. He glances at me as he passed by. It was Frank O'Connor.
> (*Dog Days* 31)

The arranger's cynical appearances increase as Higgins gets older, and funnier. He is very present in *Grunewald*, that book about the author as adulterer (or willy-nilly beast), squirming for romance and pained by the existential void. And he may well be behind the mock formality of such descriptions as the one of the patrons in the bar of the Shelbourne on a day in 1980:

> Meanwhile up in Dublin, in the Horseshoe Bar of the Shelbourne Hotel on Stephen's Green, in amiable juxtaposition sat Randal, Count MacDonald of the Glens, the

honourable Garech de Brun, heir to Guinness millions, and Lord Henry Mountcharles whose forebears had stood shoulder to shoulder with or near enough to William of Orange, King Billy at the Battle of the Boyne, the upshot of which upsets and disturbs the body politic to this very day. (*Dog Days* 91)

When Higgins addresses the reader directly he projects a colloquial affability that is reminiscent of the same technique in Mangan's prose (which I doubt he has ever read). What is typically Higginsian is his masterful modulation—the rhythm of his prose, the way he controls the reader's pace, the ease of his periodic sentences, the synesthesia of his style, as in "semen and seaweed smell of nocturnal sea" (he has a sensitive nose and a lot of people, from Elizabeth I to his father, fart in *A Bestiary*), and his informed allusions to all of the arts, "all five senses engaged" (*Windy Arbours* 125). He captures dialects and accents in their most distinctive features so that we know where the characters hail from in Ireland, and sometimes also in England or the States; here is an unmistakable Dublin bus driver: "Anywan with half a fukken brain wouldn't drive today. Fukken ice—*hard!*" (*Dog Days* 60–61). And here a working class urban English:

> Yew git outah bed inna mawnen an luke aught d'windah an ooow d'yasee? (Pregnant pause, rolls eye, gulps lager.) 'Nuffen. Nabaddy! . . . It ain't flash, see. Wot's the point? (*Dog Days* 102)

Higgins does not even need direct reportage to signal the dialect of his characters. Listen to the Californian computer nerd, captured in indirect reporting:

> We're in a loop in history, man. The world is being recreated and we're right in the middle of it. People have a lot of power right now. Right? That's why it's important for us to spread the possibilities on the higher side of force. Trippy spiritualism. Right? (*Dog Days* 68)

Higgins is at his best when he expresses his reality of experience with immediacy, without the archivist's intervention—in dialogue, or in the epistolary form of *Bornholm Night-Ferry*, and in the passages from that book in *The Whole Hog*. At his worst he repeats himself annoyingly within a couple of pages, endeavoring, I suppose, to approximate musical *motivs*, as in Bach's *Art of the Fugue*, but really just sounding like an old man who has lost the run of his thoughts. His foreign tongue, which Annie Proulx prides him on, is nearly always wrong: "*Ni* [sic] *me frego*," he defies, with a wink at Italian fascism, after admitting to practicing golf shots at night in the nip with a hard-on. For all his fastidiousness he can be sloppy, forever hyper-correcting objective pronouns as if there is no such thing as an English dative ("to him and I"). And then there are those typos—basically, Higgins has never had the luxury of a good copy-editor.

"All dreams turn into pointless stories as soon as we tell them to someone" (Introduction 20). Our life is such a pointless story told, its dream never really shared. Higgins looks with wonderment at the stories constructed by his *dramatis personae*, at their impenetrable dreams. For a second he flirts with postmodernist solipsism towards the end of *The Whole Hog* when the man met on the street protests he ain't he. The incurable loneliness of the soul informs Elin/Anna's wistful observations:

> So many stories are about "the lust of the flesh and the irreparable loneliness of the souls." . . . So many stories are

songs about men's loneliness, men's search for that picture of love which is only given by glimpses. (*Bornholm Night-Ferry* 66)

But no, Higgins is not a solipsist. The core of the story may never be quite found, but the dreams themselves are by their very nature extraordinary—the true nature of the human condition—as is his human urge to commune—to love.[14] Now that his circus animals are all on show, Higgins must lie down where all the ladders start—"*Za vaschyezdarovyie!*"

WORKS CITED

Higgins, Aidan. *A Bestiary*. Champaign, IL: Dalkey Archive Press, 2004.

—. *Bornholm Night-Ferry*. London: Allison & Busby, 1983.

—. *Dog Days*. London: Secker & Warburg, 1998.

—. Introduction. *Samuel Beckett: Photographs by John Minihan*. 1995. New York: George Braziller, 1996.

—. *Langrishe, Go Down*. New York: Riverrun Press, 1980.

—. *Lions of the Grunewald*. London: Secker & Warburg, 1993.

—. *Scenes from a Receding Past*. London: John Calder, 1977.

—. *Windy Arbours*. Champaign, IL: Dalkey Archive Press, 2006.

—. *The Whole Hog*. London: Secker & Warburg, 2000.

—. "Writer in Profile: Aidan Higgins." Interview with Aidan Higgins. *RTE Guide* 5 February 1971: 13.

Murphy, Neil. *Irish Fiction and Postmodern Doubt: An Analysis of the Epistemological Crisis in Modern Irish Fiction*. Lewiston, NY: Edwin Mellen Press, 2004.

NOTES

1. Those dear to Higgins are similarly put in their place—take for instance the momentous day of his son coming to age: "It was Bloomsday and my eldest son's eighteenth birthday, the thirty-third anniversary of the destruction of Hiroshima. It was a lovely blue morning in 1945 when the cylindrical bomb with its packed canister of unholy death came drifting down out of the sky on its little parachute like a child's toy, to explode over a city fragile as if made on papier mâché and some 200,000 Japanese civilians with a great cry gave up the ghost" (*Dog Days* 48).

2. "I encountered him [Günter Grass:] once at a Book Ball in Amsterdam. . . . I was asked to participate, discuss the equation Literature and Politics. I said there was no connection. Ah, but that's a political comment, they said. Not my cup of tea, I said, thanks all the same" (*Windy Arbours* 303).

3. This rare explication occurs in an Appendix to *Donkey's Years*, the title of which alludes to Rabelais as much as to *Finnegans Wake*—"Farsoonerite Fears, Preverbal Chaos, Undertow of Time, the Mulligrubs."

4. *Langrishe, Go Down*, p. 71; *Lions of the Grunewald*, p. 274; *Dog Days*, p. 177.

5. Quoted in Murphy, p. 96.

6. *The Whole Hog*, p. 263; the letter is also included in *Bornholm Night-Ferry*, where Anna is called Elin Marstrander and Rory, Finn Fitzgerald.

7. "In Johannesburg I became friendly with Bernhardt Adamczewski. He was the German-Polish second husband of Fiona, Coppera's best friend from King, her home town in the Eastern Cape. Adam gave me the idea for extending and widening out the novel I was working on sporadically. I called him Otto Beck and included

him as the catalyst and mediator between the Langrishe (Hill: Higgins) 'sisters,' who in reality were my three brothers and myself in drag; wedged between an Irish past and the European present" (*The Whole Hog* 385).

8. "Writer in Profile: Aidan Higgins," p. 13; also quoted in Murphy, p. 37.

9. *Donkey's Years*, in *A Bestiary*, p. 244; *The Whole Hog*, p. 386.

10. In his review of Kathleen Worth (ed.), *Beckett the Shape Changer: A Symposium.*

11. How Higgins includes that deluded grammarian Chomsky in this list is beyond me.

12. *Donkey's Years*, p. 188, 245; *Windy Arbours*, p. 140, 202, 216.

13. By the bye, the answer to his question, "Are there dental surgeries in Westland Row" (*Dog Days* 164) is aye, or at least nearby: Trinity's erstwhile dental hospital.

14. ". . . dreams are by their very nature extraordinary; the true nature of the dignity of man is that all is extraordinary, at least potentially. The core of the story is never quite found, the centre never quite arrived at but gestured to, from a safe distance" (Introduction 20).

Aidan Higgins's Ear Plays: Narrative as the Sport of History[1]

Daniel Jernigan

Aidan Higgins's literary reputation is largely founded on his fiction, travel books, and autobiographical narratives. What is less known is that beginning with *Assassin* in 1973, Higgins had nine radio plays (Higgins prefers the term "ear plays") produced for the BBC and RTE. Four of these ear plays either broadly intersect with—or are repeated wholesale—within the larger canon of Higgins's own work, a practice which, as Neil Murphy explains, is much in keeping with the Higgins's aesthetic generally:

> Higgins has reissued, relocated, and revised much of his writing in several ways, something that poses significant difficulties to serious readers of his work. . . . Some of the material from *Felo de Se* is included in *Helsingør Station & Other Departures* (most notably the stories "Killachter Meadow" and "Lebensraum") and in the collected fiction and prose, *Flotsam & Jetsam*. *Ronda Gorge & Other Precipices* contains many autobiographical echoes of *Bornholm Night-Ferry* and also includes a reprint of *Images of Africa*, the early travel book. Many of the short fictions and prose pieces of *Helsingør* and *Ronda Gorge* are reprinted in *Flotsam & Jetsam*, and the stories of *Felo de Se* again reappear, though they are renamed and revised. (Murphy 51)

Fleshing out this self-referential mode of intertextuality to include the ear plays, we find that the play *The Tomb of Dreams* (1984) eventually finds its way into Part IV of *Dog Days* (1998), *Texts for the Air* (1983) is reproduced in *Flotsam & Jetsam*, and *Zoo Station* (1985) is transformed into *Lions of the Grunewald* (1993). In explaining Higgins's tendency to reproduce and relocate, Murphy quotes Higgins:

> All of this is not to suggest that Higgins simply recycles his work. He has continually revised, added new material, and even renamed some of the shorter fictions and has, as he says in the Apologia to *Lions of the Grunewald*, tended to transplant "fugitive Ur-fiction" into its "proper context, relocated from embryonic themes" (vi). (Murphy 51)

Zoo Station is itself perhaps the most notable example of such relocation in the plays, as it finds its "proper context" in the opening sections of *Lions of the Grunewald* by means of near wholesale relocation. Finally, *Boomtown, Texas, USA* (1990) is reproduced in its totality as *As I was Riding Down Duval Boulevard with Pete La Salle*; however, in this instance it is more as if the radio play has simply been published in book form, as Higgins doesn't provide any significant revision to the published version except that it has the appearance of a personal narrative, not a play.

Winter Is Coming (1983) has a different publication history, as it comes after the novel which is its apparent source. Like *Balcony of Europe* (1972) it is set in Andalucía (and is subtitled *A Rhapsody for Andalucía*) and includes both characters (Antonio Cerezo, for one) and locations from the novel (the Plaza Balcon de Europe—the very bar which is the namesake of the novel). And so, while *Winter is Coming* doesn't explicitly rehash material found in the novel, it is a reasonable assumption given Higgins's methods that the material might have come from the original draft of *Balcony of Europe*, as, according to Higgins, the original manuscript was over a thousand (Share 57).

Given the degree of intersection between these five plays and Higgins's novels and autobiographical works—which to date have received the bulk of the critical attention—I will focus on two of the plays which have not been represented elsewhere: *Assassin* (1973)[2] and *Vanishing Heroes* (1983). As for the remaining two ear plays, *Imperfect Sympathies* (1977) and *Discords of Good Humour* (1982), they are each tied so explicitly to historical literary figures (Flann O'Brien and Charles Lamb, respectively), that they deserve separate, literary historical analysis that goes beyond the focus of this essay.

What these two plays share is an investment in engaging significant episodes in history, the assassination of Franz Ferdinand (*Assassin*) and the exploration of the stratosphere and of the ocean depths (*Vanishing Heroes*). Moreover, what we find in these plays is that Higgins is no more respectful of this history as an objective and static discourse than he is of his own prior works, as what we see in the plays might itself be described as "fugitive *Ur-history*" transplanted into its "proper context."

HISTORY AS HUMILIATION

Of all Higgins's radio plays, *Assassin*, which focuses on the assassination of Archduke Franz Ferdinand by Gavrilo Princip, is the most notable, both for the continuing relevance of the topic as well as for its literary innovations. Indeed, despite the fact that there are clear signs of a traditional linear objective narrative just beneath the surface (a consequence, perhaps, of its importance within those numerous historical narratives purporting to describe the origins of WWI), the play explicitly appropriates a non-traditional chronology, with much of it narrated by the central figures in the past tense as if from some sort of trans-historical afterlife. Moreover, because the early draft (*Assassin*) is much more innovative than the produced version—and is innovative in ways which resonate with Higgins's larger aesthetic agenda—it is *Assassin* which receives the bulk of my attention.

One of the more surprising characteristics of this early draft is how it explicitly employs various metanarrative techniques and, moreover, that its object of self-reference has nothing to do with the medium of the play itself, radio, but instead pretends as if it is a teleplay for a live studio audience:

> Narrator: (*Brisk*) "Assassin," a television tragicomedy in two acts for a revolving stage. The End of the Hapsburg Empire, or History as Humiliation.
>
> POLITE APPLAUSE AS FOR SMALL CHAMBER ORCHESTRA.
>
> WOODWINDS TWEETING UP. TWEETING, piccolo. Coughing.
>
> Narrator: Act 1. Vienna, May 1914, a month before the assassination at Sarajevo. In the Hapsburg Palace Archduke Franz Ferdinand stands alone, looking out over Vienna. (5)[3]

Given that the opening narration reads like stage directions for a teleplay (with the narrator suggesting that a revolving stage be employed) it is almost as if the subject of the radio play itself is not the assassination of Franz Ferdinand but, rather, a "television tragicomedy" about the death of Franz Ferdinand; the performance, moreover, apparently has its own live audience providing "polite applause." Only a few lines later the Narrator announces that "A curtain is opening on a play. . . ."

It is worth considering what aesthetic mileage Higgins might hope to get out of such a formulation, odd as it is with its mixed-metanarrative levels. In his seminal book, *Metatheatre* (1963), Lionel Abel theorizes the impact of metatheatre as follows:

> . . . for metatheatre, order is something continually improvised by men [which] gives by far the stronger sense that the world is a projection of human consciousness . . . glorifies the unwillingness of the imagination to regard any image of the world as ultimate . . . assumes there is no world except that created by human striving, human imagination. (113)

This turns out to be a very reasonable perspective from which to consider Higgins's metanarrative approach, in addition to its metatheatrical framing there is much about the play which continues to remind us that even as the facts of Franz Ferdinand's death are being reconstructed for us in the play itself, they have been similarly reconstructed time and again within various histories of the period.

This constructivist attitude is best recognized as part and parcel of how ill-defined the difference is between fiction and non-fiction for Higgins, which Murphy explains as follows:

> In Higgins's writing human experience is already a fiction in the living (and remembering) of it. He does not, finally,

differentiate between life and fiction, because life, once
apprehended, is already a fiction. (81)

In this instance Murphy is specifically discussing how Higgins's autobiographical work blends with his fictional work. However, this
attitude that "life, once apprehended, is already a fiction" is equally
true in Higgins when it comes to rehashing the lives of others; in
fact, it follows quite naturally that if the lives of Franz Ferdinand
and Gavrilo Princip are something akin to fiction for themselves,
they must also be for any given third person author, such as Higgins. Indeed, Higgins's own reliance on third person historical narrative would not have been lost on him and, likely, explains some
of the more self-consciously metanarrative announcements from
the narrators.

   That Higgins is once again engaged in blurring fact and fiction
is only further reinforced by the fact that even the most traditional
historians such as L. C. F. Turner have argued that the importance
of Franz Ferdinand's assassination in instigating WWI is notori-
ously hard to pin down (a fact which might explain Higgins's attraction to it):

> The full story of the Sarajevo assassination has yet to
> be told and, in spite of much learned research, many vi-
> tal points remain obscure. Whether the details of the as-
> sassination merit the torrents of ink expended on them by
> historians may well be doubted. Sarajevo provided the
> spark which started the Great War but, in view of the in-
> flammable shape of Europe in 1914, a major international
> crisis could hardly have been postponed for very much
> longer. (78)

It would seem, then, that despite all of the best efforts by historians, the fundamental motives for the assassination remain as obscure today as they did in 1914, with some regarding the event "merely as a violent expression of South Slav patriotism," and others interpreting it as "a deliberate provocation intended to lure Austria into the course of action which she actually pursued" (79). The clear implication is that historians themselves have difficulty differentiating fact from fiction, and that Higgins is onto them.

Perhaps the key to this early draft lies in the subtitle provided by the narrator: "The End of the Hapsburg Empire, or History as Humiliation" (5). What, then, is the project of history as it concerns the origins of WWI except for a continual revisiting of the humiliation which finally saw the end of the Hapsburg Empire, especially considering that a fairly standard take of those events leading up to war is that they didn't warrant the eventual outcome, wherein the Entente Powers of France, the United Kingdom, Russia, the US and Italy defeat the Central Powers of Germany, Austria-Hungary, the Ottoman Empire and Bulgaria, ultimately remaking the map of Europe in the process? History as humiliation, indeed.

But what then of Higgins's own play? Is it an attempt at further humiliation, perhaps? Or, rather, a sympathetic representation of those (such as the Hapsburg Empire) who, for whatever reason, continue to be humiliated by historians? Or, rather, is it a direct response to the historian's humiliating methods that instead we finally get this turn to self-conscious historical pastiche and its explicit rejection of the veracity of historical narratives generally? This last possibility is the most compelling, especially given that making such claims about Higgins's motives returns us to familiar territory given his aesthetic objectives more generally.

There are, moreover, occasional and very specific pronouncements in the text supporting this particular reading. In one telling instance, the Narrator offers a direct response to Gavrilo's brother's

(Jovo) description of how poor Gavrilo's health had been as a child: "Narrator: (*Urbane*) No doubt, no doubt. We know that history at all times draws the strangest conclusions from the remotest causes." The implication is that the Narrator thinks that Jovo is searching for an excuse for Princip's actions, and that the Narrator is dismissing the argument for proffering only "remote causes." The irony of the passage, however, cannot be overstated, as its very dismissiveness speaks to the truth of the matter, which is that those in the position of narrating events are the ones who so often "draw the strangest conclusions from the remotest causes." Moreover, this perspective is not inconsistent with the idea that Higgins is espousing a bit of sympathy for the way in which the history of the end of the Hapsburg Empire has become a history of humiliation. The implication of this passage is that if the Hapsburg Empire (and its allies) had only won the war, the "remote causes" of the war might be read much differently (i.e., even more strangely) than they are today. Perhaps, even, the very importance of the assassination of Ferdinand would resonate very differently as well.

In the play's concluding sequence the metanarrative playfulness goes one step beyond simply espousing historical constructivism:

> Narrator: (*Benign*) Two actors, got up as Bishops, but now behaving as stage-hands, quickly assemble the three sections of a First Class Smoker. And sit facing each other by a window. (55)

Only now do we find that even the play within the play is meant to be recognized as *explicitly* metatheatrical, as the audience is first allowed to see through the costumes of the two Bishops and to recognize them as actors (and at this point the metatheatre is akin to what we saw in the beginning) but then it is also told that the actors themselves behave "as stagehands," suggesting that even for the fictional audience, which itself only sees the actors as Bishops, the play has explicit metatheatrical features. It should be noted, moreover, that the multi-metanarrative layering is, in some sense, explicitly critical even of constructivist perspectives, as it suggests that the constructivist attitude of metanarratives are themselves "improvised by men." Constructivism is itself a construction. Something carried on stage by "men behaving as stagehands."

The final draft of the play is, however, a radically different and less interesting product. Instead of a diverse cast of characters each pitching in from some ambiguous future and describing the event in the past tense, Higgins allows his narrator and the occasional "historian" to do much of the work, such that the result is a much safer product, where none of the gaps between history as reality and history as construct are investigated (needless to say, all of the metanarrative elements are purged as well). As this is Higgins's first ear play, perhaps we should be little surprised that he ultimately chose to play it a bit too safe (if, in fact, the choice was even his own). And while there is nothing explicit in the final text to suggest disgruntlement on Higgins's part, reading in tandem with the early draft it is hard not to feel that it is a more cynical treatment of the same material, especially when you read that as sources Higgins mentions "James Joyce (Letters), John Berryman, T. S. Eliot . . . John Hawkes (The Cannibal)" alongside other more typical historical sources. A more traditional work would quite simply require such references, whether they are relevant or not. As such, Higgins provides them. But he does so with a wink and a nudge of his elbow, as they remain outside the actual narrative, never to make their way into the radio performance itself.

The Sport of Science

Except for the fact that both plays are at least nominally historical, *Vanishing Heroes* is a very different play than *Assassin*. The
"heroes" of the play are a father and son, Auguste Antoine Piccard and Jacques Piccard. In 1932 Auguste set the altitude record
at 15,785 m (51,775 ft), a height to which he ascended in order to
study cosmic rays. Some twenty-nine years later his son, Jacques,
would descend with Don Walsh into the Challenger Deep in the
Mariana Trench, the very deepest part of the ocean. While *Assassin*
is grand in the scale of its human dimensions (so much so that the
numerous characters carry with them a keen sense of the historical
importance of the event), the characters of *Vanishing Heroes* ultimately come across as much more local in their import.

Dermot Healy's essay on *Texts for the Air* and the novel *Bornholm Night-Ferry* provides the sum total critical reaction to Higgins's ear plays, aside from a few brief radio reviews in *The Listener*
(in fact, there is very nearly as much about *Vanishing Heroes* in
Healy's essay as there is about *Texts for the Air*). Healy's thoughts
on *Vanishing Heroes* provide a nice complement to what we have
already seen in *Assassin*:

> *Vanishing Heroes* mapped out the journey, a radio play
> concerning a flight into the hemisphere in an air balloon,
> and a voyage under the sea in a prototype of the subma-
> rine where the adventurer/narrator's experience of the
> world is brought to its extreme. Higgins respects the travel
> writer above all, one who brings back a story from a hith-
> erto unknown place, in the mind or on the earth. And to
> bring back the story without disturbing its essence by sub-
> mitting it to the laws of easy consumption. Common
> sense from letting the senses have their say. (Healy 181)

Aside from the fact that the bathyscaphe that the Piccards used to explore the ocean depths is not a "prototype of the submarine" (which has its own history which greatly predated that of the bathyscaphe), I find this to be a particularly prescient understanding of *Vanishing Heroes*, suggestive as it is that the play refuses to treat history as "an objective and immediately consumable object." For not only does Higgins bring "back a story from a hitherto unknown" geological location, but he also further defamiliarizes for a late twentieth century audience what has of late become the rarest of world travelers (a "Vanishing hero," so to speak), the scientific explorer, whose "expeditions are the sport of science" (40).[4]

Given that *Vanishing Heroes* doesn't just question the reliability of historical narratives but, also, the reliability of scientific narratives in particular, it is hard not to see a kinship to what Jean-François Lyotard has had to say about the increasing incredulity towards grand narratives (call them the "Vanishing" heroic narratives) of the postmodern era. In this sense, Healy's description resonates with the very attitude that the play takes towards science; that is, in how the play is invested in the debate between those who privilege science as pure of essence (i.e., as pursued for its own sake) and those who value how easily its products submit themselves to "the easy laws of consumption" (i.e., how easily it becomes a means to an end). From this perspective Lyotard's importance as the theoretical touchstone for this discussion comes into clearer focus, given that in his explanation of the two methods by which the sciences have traditionally legitimized themselves we find a compelling explanation of the play's various and divergent attitudes towards the sciences:

> We shall examine two major versions of the narrative of legitimation. One is more political, the other more philosophical; both are of great importance in modern his-

tory, in particular in the history of knowledge and its institutions. (Lyotard 31)

The first "political" version finds knowledge legitimated according to how beneficial it is in helping to liberate humanity: "According to this version, knowledge finds its validity not within itself, not in a subject that develops by actualizing its learning possibilities, but in a practical subject—humanity" (35). (Call this the "emancipation narrative" and note that in this version science is valued as a means to an end.) The second "philosophical" version holds that knowledge is legitimated according to how it assists in the realization of a unified whole: "In this perspective, knowledge first finds legitimacy within itself" (34). (Call this the "unity of knowledge narrative" and note that in this version science is valued for its purity of essence.) *Vanishing Heroes* queries the fecundity of each of these narratives in turn before, finally, adopting an attitude which is equally incredulous of both.

While focusing on science is new territory for Higgins, focusing specifically on the scientific expedition allows him to play to his strength as a travel writer. This is a wise choice, as the remoteness of the new worlds he explores in *Vanishing Heroes* ultimately has as much to do with the fact that his travel companions are scientists as it does with the unfamiliarity of the locations that these scientists take him to. And so while Higgins did not travel ten miles up into the stratosphere—or ten miles down into the Mariana Trench—in venturing into a narrative concerned with science he was forced to contend with a world that is perhaps even less familiar than either of these other environments, and one that is maybe only a little less hostile to a visitor of artistic temperament and occupation. In *The Two Cultures*, C. P. Snow famously describes the divide that exists between the two "Cultures" as follows:

For constantly I felt I was moving among two groups—comparable in intelligence, identical in race, not grossly different in social origin, earning about the same incomes, who had almost ceased to communicate at all, who in intellectual, moral, and psychological climate had so little in common that instead of going from Burlington House or South Kensington to Chelsea, one might have crossed an ocean. (Snow 2)

If we are to believe Snow, an endeavor such as Higgins's is not something to be taken lightly, a fact which makes it worth considering how Higgins—given his own aesthetic commitment to conflating the literary and the biographical—responds to the precise factual narratives that scientists tell themselves about the work that they perform.

That Higgins replaces what more typically might be the role of the narrator in such a historically grounded narrative as this with a "Chorus of Censors" (1)[5] immediately suggests a rather glib attitude towards his task, especially given the fact that the narrator so often plays the role of arbiter of truth and objectivity in scientific documentaries such as this one. Moreover, that The Censors seem particularly slow about getting to the task at hand—and evade not with prudishness but, instead, with an irrelevant risqué narrative about "a lovely Thai girl . . . giving herself to a bearded student in the commodious toilet on the second floor of the Grande Hotel del la Loire" (3)—might be seen as reluctance to get to the subject at hand, if not (once again) for the excessively glib nature of the approach.

That there is more than mere reluctance at work here—and instead, perhaps, epistemological doubt on Higgins's part that narratives such as the one he is about to undertake are essentially futile—is made especially apparent when The Censor is itself, censored:

> Censor: Bull-faced Lully, Keeper of the King's Musick, be-
> lieved that creation was a book in two volumes. The first
> volume of which was (blast of factory whistle drowns out
> word) . . . I forget the second. (4)

That The Censor is at first censored by seemingly random external
sources—and then by his own inability to remember his point—
indicates the seriousness with which Higgins questions the veracity of this and (by implication) all such similar narratives. We are,
moreover, also reminded of the fact that each and every historical
narrative faces numerous challenges in discovering its audience,
not the least of which is the static of competing events and the
poor memories of unreliable narrators. How is science to be pure
and pursued for its own sake when it faces such environmental
constraints?

To better understand this take on scientific narratives it is worth
remembering that Lyotard's theorization of the "unity of knowledge" narrative has a corollary aesthetic formulation, outlined in
his essay "Answering the Question: What is Postmodernism?". As
with the "unity of knowledge narrative," Lyotard's postmodern
aesthetic is also concerned with the epistemological difficulties inherent in appropriating and representing the complete idea, with
postmodern literature reacting to such futility by consciously and
explicitly rejecting it:

> The postmodern would be that which, in the modern,
> puts forward the unpresentable in presentation itself;
> that which denies itself the solace of good forms, the
> consensus of taste which would make it possible to
> share collectively the nostalgia for the unattainable; that
> which searches for new representations, not in order to

enjoy them but in order to impart a stronger sense of the unpresentable. (81)

This fit between the aesthetic and the epistemological is compellingly rendered in Higgins's hands, where the all-too-familiar narrative method so often employed for representing scientific success is finally exchanged for something which very explicitly refuses "the solace of good forms, the consensus of taste which would make it possible to share collectively the nostalgia for the unattainable."

Indeed, the particular way in which Higgins puts to use the parallel stories of father and son provides a good opportunity to understand how he disrupts natural forms to anti-epistemological ends. In the play's opening scenes Higgins at first makes much of the parallel, noting that the father had traveled ten miles into the air, while the son had traveled ten miles into the ocean depths. In his mostly favorable review of the play in *The Listener*, Neil Hepburn points out that Higgins gets this information wrong ("the son [. . .] finding bottom at 6,000 fathoms—which the programme irritatingly equated to 10 miles"). Hepburn, however, fails to consider that such a simple error might be intentional on Higgins's part; in fact, the wording suggests as much, as we are told that Jacques "descended to a depth of 36,000 feet, some forty–two fathoms, *say* ten miles" (emphasis added). The use of the word "say" in this context clearly indicates that it isn't being said for accuracy, but, rather, for some other purpose (i.e., for the sake of narrative structure we may as well "say" that the depth was ten miles). Such a change does little to disrupt the essence of the subject at hand; in fact, it quite nearly does the opposite, as essence and form (if we can call Higgins's focus on the fact that the two expeditions traveled ten miles in opposite direction a formalist invention) in this instance appear to be privileged over the "facts" of the matter.

On the other hand, the exaggerated parallel does, perhaps, lend itself a bit too quickly to "easy consumption" on the part of the reader. What, for instance, are we to make of this fact given that Higgins never considered formal techniques to be central to his own aesthetic? When, however, Higgins finally refuses to exploit the parallel to advance his narrative in any obvious or meaningful way, we find ourselves in familiar terrain. For even while we might expect such a narrative device to be employed as a transition in the narrative—with the passion for "the sport of science" being passed from father to son—we get no such easily consumable narrative devices from Higgins, even though a very real opportunity to rely on such a narrative device is available in the simple fact that father and son had themselves set diving records together in the years before Jacques and Walsh dove seven miles into the Mariana Trench.

The transition from the father's expedition to the son's instead comes in fits and starts, beginning with Piccard expressing curiosity about how closely the image he is witnessing ten miles below his balloon mirrors actual maps of Europe:

> We passed over Cadiz, Toledo, Madrid... the Bay of Biscay, Arcachon. We could see the Straits of Gibraltar and the Rock, Morocco and the Atlas Mountains and beyond, the Mediterranean. All looked exactly as on the map. And yet the map was drawn long before any human eye was able to see all these places as a group. (22)

The Censor then cuts in by drawing a parallel between the way that Piccard is navigating across Europe and the way that bees and other animals similarly track the sun across the sky for their own navigational purposes:

> Bees maintain straight courses by offsetting the sun as it passes across the sky. Plants flower and bear fruit according to the length of the day. All life responds to rhythmic time—all life, that is, excluding the denizens of the deep. Astronomical tempo does not reach below the deep-scattering layers of the Twilight Zone. (22)

Thus, even as Higgins defamiliarizes the human impulse towards mapping and exploration, identifying them as traits shared by other species, the apparent transition from the father's narrative to the son's comes into focus. Or at least it seems to, as even this carefully orchestrated transition is itself temporarily evaded as The Censor first gets distracted by how various random types of animal life measure out boundaries: "only the sperm whale ever plunges below the twilight zone [. . .] only water striders [. . .] live a purely pelagic existence [. . .] Wild trout in a stream have a home spot [. . .] Owls hoot at night to claim ownership of a specific group of trees" (22–24). In turn we also meet territorial great apes, an eel with a puzzling life-cycle, one more brief glimpse of Auguste surveying "The Sahara on a moonless night," and a species of crab which can be induced to "lead an upside down existence" with a grain of metal and a Magnet, before we finally descend "Into the Abyss" with Part Two of the play. Consequently, much more attention is given to addressing the essence of natural phenomenon than to providing an easily consumable narrative, with the added implication that perhaps the categories of science are themselves as arbitrarily random as are the conventions of literary form. And while the structure Higgins finally provides his audience with ultimately owes much to formal conceits, it is also quite clear that Higgins could have taken much more advantage of the natural structure of this particular episode in the history of science should he have wished to play party to "the solace of good forms, the consensus of taste." Indeed, Higgins proves himself quite adept, as Murphy explains it, at "rejecting sequential plotted narrative for spatial narrative [. . .] refus[ing] chronological order in an attempt to surpass the intrinsic inaccuracy of that order" (59).

The play is, finally, as suspicious of the motives of the scientists (i.e., their emancipatory commitments) as it is of the supposed organic beauty and form of their work, as the Piccards' scientific pursuits ultimately fail to come across as the selfless pursuit of scientific research that it pretends to be. Consider, for instance, that when the President of the Swiss Aero Club expresses the sentiment that Auguste Piccards's record "not be beaten for many years," Piccard is "*obliged* to disagree with him" (17; emphasis added):

> Voice of Piccard: (*Echoing in a Large Chamber*) It will be a fine day for me when other stratospheric balloons follow me and reach latitude greater than mine. My aim is not beat [sic] and above all not to maintain records, but to open a new domain of scientific research and to aerial navigation. (17)

However, even while Piccard may well have felt obliged to proclaim that his expedition into the stratosphere had all been done in the pursuit of science, he apparently felt no obligation to do any actual science during his journey, occupied as he was with recording elevations and surveying the scenery below. With Higgins, expedition does indeed become "the sport of science," except that it is finally characterized as important not so much because of how it serves the interests of humanity as for how it serves the private ambitions of individual scientists.

There is, finally, a brief episode in which Higgins even more explicitly decries the emancipation narrative, although even in this instance he does so in a way which so forcefully refuses the solace of good forms that it is a bit difficult to know what to make of it. Midway through Part II of the play (which focuses as much as Higgins is capable of on the deep sea mission), the Censors provide the following narration:

> Second Censor: It's snowing and it looks like the mad dance.
> In Tokyo the streets smell of sulphur.
> In Chicago the air is bad. A brown air, more gas than air, crosses the lake from the great steel and oil complex . . .
> In the West Forties in New York in summer carbon monoxide is thick.
>
> First Censor: In San Juan the lagoons bubble and smell like stewing tripe.
> Though carp and catfish still live in the benzene-smelling ponds. (36–37)

It is hard to know what to make of this seeming non-sequitur, until we reach the following description of the bathyscaphe's descent from Jacques Piccard (which follows immediately upon the heels of the above narration):

> While the Trieste was resting on the bottom of the Tyrrhenian Sea under a pressure of 325 atmospheres, I carefully

> examined the great joint of the cabin. I did not find a sin-
> gle drop of water on it! (37)

Apparently, prophylactics capable of keeping out 325 atmospheres of water pressure are available on demand when and if scientific expedition should require it, but are all too hard to come by when it comes to protecting The West Forties in New York from carbon monoxide, or carp and catfish from lagoons bubbling with benzene. So much for "science finding its validity . . . in a practical subject—humanity."

Lyotard's next important gesture completes the parallel to Higgins's thoughts on science and historiography, coming as it does in his realization that in the place of the metanarrative, postmodern society has come to favor the "the little narrative" (60). According to this perspective, constructivist narratives are postmodern for how they refuse the belief that biographical and historical research yields accurate accounts of those issues under investigation; instead, constructivist narratives are always and already explicitly self-conscious of the fact that what they are providing is only a "local narrative." Perhaps, then, the only real difference between postmodern fictional narratives of the type provided by Higgins and the historical narratives provided by historians is that Higgins's narratives wear their constructivism on their sleeves. The difference between *Assassin* and *Vanishing Heroes* lies primarily in how this is accomplished, with the hyper-metatheatricality of *Assassins* suggesting that metanarratives are themselves something "improvised by men" while in *Vanishing Heroes* the focus is on how even the most privileged of contemporary narratives (that of the unflinchingly objective scientist) are themselves improvised in various and sundry ways.

WORKS CITED

Abel, Lionel. *Metatheatre: A New View of Dramatic Form*. New York: Hill & Wang, 1963.

Healy, Dermot. "Towards *Bornholm Night-Ferry* and *Texts for the Air*: A Re-reading of Aidan Higgins." *Review of Contemporary Fiction* 3.1 (1983): 181–192.

Hepburn, Neil. "Traumaturgy." *The Listener* 24 June 1992: 26.

Higgins, Aidan. *Assassination*, 1973, Box 5; Lot 12.1, McPherson Library Special Collections, University of Victoria.

—. *Assassins*. Personal Library.

—. *Vanishing Heroes*. 1983, Box 7: Lot 19.2, McPherson Library Special Collections, University of Victoria.

Lyotard, Jean-François. *The Postmodern Condition*. Minneapolis, MN: University of Minnesota Press, 1984.

Share, Bernard. "Auld Lang Rish and After." *Aidan Higgins: The Fragility of Form*. Ed. Neil Murphy. Champaign, IL: Dalkey Archive Press, 2010. 54–67.

Snow, C. P. *The Two Cultures*. Cambridge: Cambridge University Press, 1993.

Murphy, Neil. "Aidan Higgins." *Review of Contemporary Fiction* 23.3 (2003): 49–83.

Turner, L. C. F. *Origins of the First World War*. New York: Norton, 1970.

NOTES

1. Special thanks are owed to the McPherson Library Special Collections at the University of Victoria. I am especially indebted to Danielle Russel, without whose prompt assistance in provid-

ing access to Higgins's radio plays this essay would not have been possible.

2. With the exception of *Boomtown, Texas, USA*, my sources have been the scripts themselves rather than the actual radio plays. However, as the scripts are unpublished, I have provided the original air date of each in place of the publication date.

3. For more information about the various versions of *Assassin*, see the Introduction to *Darkling Plain: Texts for the Air*. All subsequent references to the screenplay refer to the version known as *Assassination* (1973), housed in Box 5, Lot 12.1, McPherson Library Special Collections, University of Victoria.

4. Auguste Piccard's actual quote was "Exploration is the sport of the scientist."

5. For more information about the various versions of *Vanishing Heroes*, see the Introduction to *Darkling Plain: Texts for the Air*. All subsequent references to the screenplay refer to the version (1983) housed in Box 7, Lot 19.2, McPherson Library Special Collections, University of Victoria.

A Glimpse of Aidan Higgins through his Critical Work

Angela Frattarola

On first reading Aidan Higgins's collection of literary criticism, *Windy Arbours*, one is immediately struck by his wide range of literary knowledge, his illuminating wit, and his ability to immerse himself in another writer's work with a mind that is (as much as humanly possible) uninhibited by trends and self-promotion. Higgins presents an array of details from the literature he reviews, demonstrating a focused attention to each and every word on the page. He then looks at the piece within its particular context (American, English, Irish, among others), before he makes his way to considering how the work fits into the larger literary tradition—an invaluable critical step requiring a great erudition that few critics have. Aside from seeing these impressive critical faculties at work, however, we can also catch a glimpse of Higgins, the writer, in this collection. We become acquainted with what he values most in literature, as his short critical essays often display the very formal qualities being discussed. Hence, by looking at Higgins looking at literature, we can gather an idea of how to approach his own literary works. Yet, more importantly, these reviews offer the reader something that his fiction cannot, something that, according to Higgins, should not be discernable in a work of literature: they allow the reader to flesh out Higgins as an individual with a distinct face and a discriminating, sometimes even righteous, voice. After surveying what Higgins consistently appreciates in the works he reviews, and examining his particular style as a reviewer, this essay will argue that *Windy Arbours* ultimately warrants our attention because it reveals what Higgins refers to as the "hidden narrator" or "faceless creator"—a side of Higgins that, while informing his fiction, typically remains in the background.[1]

In almost all of his reviews, Higgins begins at the level of language. Word choice is essential to the art of writing for him, and he takes personal offense at writers who are too dense or lazy to choose their words with care. A novel must have more than an interesting story to tell, and it must tell the story in an accurate and appealing way. Higgins raises this point in his review of Deborah Tall's *The Island of the White Cow*, when he questions the "authenticity of the record," which is "marred by the manner of the telling" (45). With a characteristic eye to detail, Higgins continues:

> Fat bees are not like helicopters, and the verbs are in terrible shape; as witness, Ann mutters, Catrina burbles, Rosie croons (and "waxes"), the Postmistress gurgles (when not "crooning goodwill"); whereas Richard reiterates, while Sean intones, barks (when not "bubbling with eventfulness"), prior to suicide (understandable enough) in the cold Atlantic. (45)

By modeling such close reading, Higgins's critical observations become instructional not just for the reader of literature but for aspiring writers. Higgins always clearly justifies his complaints, and his comments have a sense of humor that simultaneously makes his analysis more pointed and pleasurable. Without sounding harsh and unreasonable, the above list of evidence clarifies his assessment and brings the ineptness of Tall's "terrible" verbs into focus. Throughout the collection, Higgins notices if a writer's "adjectives are very odd" or if "similes and metaphors are darkly jumbled" (135). He repeatedly faults John Updike for "cockeyed similes and metaphors," and proceeds to give a list of evidence, which is made more ridiculous by being taken out of context and presented in list format (77). He parodies Updike in another review, stating: "Ham-fisted metaphors and silly similes fly, for he is nothing if not inconsistent" (70). Higgins even extends these high standards to translators, who must not allow "conflicting idioms [to] intermarry awkwardly on the page" (307). When a writer or translator uses "vile" nouns and verbs or inconsistent idioms, Higgins shows no mercy in his lampooning (70). For if nothing else, the art of writing requires a finicky love and hate of words; indifference is unacceptable.

Pulling his critical lens slightly back, Higgins shows himself to be an astute critic of a writer's ability to convey speech and voice. The sound of a narrative needs to fit its subject matter, and Higgins is particularly concerned when a writer puts on airs or fails in her attempt to reflect the voice of a lower class. For instance, Higgins argues that Jillian Becker's novel, *The Union*, at times has an "irrefutably hard edge, when on line with the subject-matter and not trying to out-James Henry James himself" (258). Too often, he claims, her characters "speak in tendentious sub-Jamesian periods and sub-clauses that might have been discards from *Guy Domville*, but were never heard on either bank of the wide Limpopo" (258). Moreover, when the "white overseer [. . .] examines a class below her, her black servants" are "never quite human" (259). Tapping into the cadences and idiomatic expressions of a class or culture other than one's own is the writer's job, and if this cannot be executed with authenticity the entire work is unconvincing. Along these lines, he praises Harold Pinter's screenplay of Proust's *A la Recherche du Temps Perdu*, because "Pinter-made speech rhythms match the original" (162). Higgins has a finely tuned ear for dialect and inflection, and though he raises this issue most keenly in the section devoted to Irish writers, he rarely neglects to mention the sound of any of the pieces he reviews.

In the third section of the collection, "The Small Neurosis: The smaller the island, the bigger the neurosis," Higgins focuses on Irish writers. He continually scrutinizes how these writers represent speech because that is where one finds the pulse of a realistically drawn character. In a review of Dermot Healy's *Fighting with Shadows*, Higgins clarifies: "The energy of Irish writing is dependent largely upon the vernacular and idiomatic; street language in *Ulysses*; the frequently forked-tongued natives found they had another hidden lingo at their disposal" (192). Healy is able to present the voice of the "prototypical Irish (Fermanagh) family" as they experience the war in Northern Ireland, and Higgins is grateful for his efforts: "The forked barbs fly. Even truth itself is often bitter. And no better man to record it" (192). He similarly praises Eugene McCabe for his collection of stories about the Northern conflict. McCabe succeeds with his grim "controlled bile" because he keeps "an ear closer to the ground" than other writers (215, 216). Conversely, in *The Collected Stories of Sean O'Faolain*, Volume 2, Higgins can only find one story that "let[s] the real people, the land, through" (222). Otherwise, O'Faolain's "gabby natives perceive Ireland in Tourist Brochure prose" (222). For Higgins, such stereotyping is perhaps an even worse offense than sloppy word choice.

Reviewing a collection of short stories that he himself compiled, Higgins holds that "[s]tories have their oldest roots in folklore, the common dreams of all language: an oral tradition" (243). As he continues, he applauds Conan Doyle's work "for the energy of its verbs and the springy marksmanship of its adjectival clauses," William Trevor's "edgy diction of distress," Saul Bellow's "keen ear for argot and slang," and William Faulkner's "odd and curious" English, "replete with archaicisms [. . .] and Bible tones" (244–46). Thus, we see that Higgins's repeated stress on the importance of how a story sounds hinges on this concept that all stories are rooted in an oral tradition, which in turn is rooted in the masses. Plot is not of the greatest importance if the sound is right; and sound is often a matter of getting to what is most common and close to the land.

Higgins is able to connect with the average reader through his sense of humor, which is a key element of his style. More often than not, he uses his wit to deflate writers who fail to represent the common fabric of life. Reviewing Elizabeth Taylor's *Blaming*, he protests: "Isn't it bad enough that such pseudo-lives must be lived, call it living, paper-thin; intolerable that we must read of them too" (134). He quotes absurd descriptions of characters being "firmly snuggled down" and "most relievedly" at that, and concludes "heavens will it ever end?" (134). Using this amusing and exasperated tone, Higgins brings a serious charge against writers that waste a reader's time with superficial characters. Higgins shows that if a writer is careless with his craft, choosing words without being mindful of the actions and thoughts of actual people, a novel can become preposterous. To make this point explicit, in his review of Alexander Theroux's *An Adultery*, he asks the reader to envision Meryl Streep portraying the line: "She went visibly tense as she heard my question, glaring at me, one eye a drill, the other a slit, her lips compressed like a person tasting bitter seed" (91). He goes on playing this comical game for a couple of lines, asking the reader to imagine the actress saying the impossible and clichéd dialogue of the novel. It is through this hilarity, however, that one realizes that Higgins's constant attention to word choice is not a matter of one writer being too exacting of his peers (14). If a writer creates sentences without the common individual in mind, then her characters are doomed to be one-dimensional shells. Word choice is not just a matter of style; the construction of a character depends on the careful placement of one word next to the other. Concluding with his usual sarcasm, Higgins advises that should this film adaptation ever be made, we should "[r]un for the exits" (91).

As with the above examples, Higgins will often make the absurdity of a novel apparent by making the reader laugh. Without explicitly telling the reader that the novel is ridiculous, his jesting reveals how the work's flaws make it so. Along these lines, when Higgins is applauding a writer for skillfully using a formal technique, he will sometimes make use of that very same technique in his review. Intentionally done or not, this method makes for an interesting sort of "show and tell" in his reviews, which illustrate rhetorical devices as they are described. For instance, in his favorable review of Djuna Barnes's *Nightwood*, he remarks that the "piling on of metaphor and simile succeed, as the laying down of light artillery fire" (12). One might say the same of his own simile. Reviewing Paul Theroux's travel narrative of riding trains through the Americas, Higgins likewise takes us on a whirlwind couple of pages, briefly touching upon the many places and incidents that Theroux recounts (20–23). Just as Higgins appreciates the "free-associating account of strenuous train-rides," the reader too can experience a miniaturized version presented in his review (23). Though Faulkner is one of the few writers for whom Higgins shows deep admiration, he also mimics him in order to better demonstrate his stylistic tics. In a review of Faulkner's uncollected short stories, Higgins writes:

> Nothing was straightforward with Faulkner, least of all his syntax; fifteen and even thirty-line sentences and their attendant sub-clauses went meandering off, the long-winded parenthesis were as tracks through the Mississippian wilderness, its swamps and bayous, levee and huge river bottom; a ten-page digression (within brackets) can end abruptly on a semi-colon, to indicate where the path ends or authorial breath—or patience—gave out. (3–4)

In a sentence that outdoes Faulkner in length, Higgins shows the reader exactly what Faulkner's sentences tend to do. Moreover, as Higgins imitates Faulkner's roundabout style, the pleasure that he takes in playing with words reveals his sensibilities as a writer. As with Joyce, while writing is an art that requires rigorous work and care, there also must be an element of play—of not taking oneself too seriously.

Like Faulkner, Higgins's writing style cannot be called linear; his reviews do not present clear and logical arguments in a dry, academic voice. On the contrary, they have a particular cadence and vernacular touch. Sentences flow without a strict regard for the rules of grammar. There is an economy of language, which though at times gives the impression of a rushed story, can be appreciated for its directness and lack of pretentiousness. What may seem to be simple free association on the surface becomes a collage as one takes a step back and connects all of the fragments. "Cyril & Co.," for example, is a short unpublished piece that is not a review of any particular work but a gossipy collection of sketches about Cyril Connolly, Somerset Maugham, Joyce and Barnes, among others. Higgins presents snippets of their conversations about "large noses" and "male virility," the comprehensibility of *Waiting for Godot*, George Moore complaining that *Ulysses* is not a novel ("for there isn't a tree"), and Barnes complimenting Joyce on his waistcoat (145–48). All of these scenes are based on actual quotations from Nancy Mitford, Connolly, Richard Ellmann, and Barnes, which are cited sporadically throughout the piece. Yet, while one scene jumps haphazardly to the next and the line between fiction and nonfiction is blurred, the reader gets a behind-the-scenes snapshot of these great twentieth-century personalities with all of their idiosyncrasies intact. They are not gods to be worshipped, but writers who are great because of these very common and comical attributes.

This free-associative style is also found in one of the most interesting pieces in the collection, "The Faceless Creator," a paper read at New York University. This talk recounts a series of anecdotes, each of which presents an artist who is able to maintain a sort of invisibility or mask. The first anecdote describes how Higgins himself goes undetected, riding the buses of Dublin for free since conductors fail to notice him. When he meets Samuel Beckett, the man he encounters does not fulfill any of his expectations: for he is not exceptional in any way at all. Similarly, V. S. Naipaul "vanish[es] into thin air" when Higgins meets him (151). After telling a humorous story about being on a TV talk show with Flann O'Brien, which is cut short due to escalating drunken belligerence, Higgins explains that O'Brien had so many personas, "[n]o one knew what Flann O'Brien looked like," one man even reporting that "you had to look twice at Brian O'Nolan to make sure he was even there" (153). And lastly, though Higgins's mother held that Joyce had a "bad face," Higgins proposes that "Joyce had no face at all" (154). These fragments of narrative are deceptively simplistic. The conversational tone of the paper immediately engages the reader, and makes her feel as though Higgins is merely sharing bits of gossip and reminiscing. But of course this is not the case. Higgins shows that the artist must be invisible and faceless so that she can take on the voice of the nameless many, "the voice of the Plain People of Ireland" (155). This view of the artist is at once humble and great. It is not the artist's personality and ego that make her remarkable, but her ability to embody everyone else around her.

This concept of the artist aligns Higgins with modernist writers such as Joyce, T. S. Eliot, and Virginia Woolf. In fact, though his works were published from 1960 onward, Higgins shares many affinities with the movement. His attention to sound and language over plot, his fragmented style that so often breaks with conventional syntax and grammar, his valuing of the representation of the common and ordinary, and his belief in the impersonality of the artist, all demonstrate that above all else, Higgins is a writer building from modernism's most central tenets. The significance that Higgins places on "the collective conscious of the race of whom" the artist, "the nameless Dublin jackeen at the No. 52 bus-stop is one," echoes back to Stephen Dedalus's vision of the artist as "invisible, refined out of existence, indifferent, paring his fingernails," while forging the "uncreated conscious of [his] race" (Higgins 155; Joyce 233, 276). Woolf shares a similar view in her essay, "Anon," which was to be the first essay of the Common History Book she was planning before her death. Woolf imagines the origin of the writer in the voice of Anon, the "common voice singing out of doors [. . .] lifting a song from other people's lips and letting the audience join in the chorus" (382). Though this "nameless" artist is killed by the printing press, according to Woolf, it still is "the world beneath our consciousness; the anonymous world to which we can still return" (383, 385). The writer must remain nameless and faceless in order to connect with his audience. As the writer shows what is extraordinary in the ordinary and common, tapping into this nameless voice, any reader is able to see a reflection that is illuminating—different and yet familiar. It is because of this that Eliot, in his famous "theory of Impersonality," stresses that there is no need to look to the biography of a writer to understand a work of literature. Instead, a reader should appreciate the poet's "historical sense," which "compels a man to write not merely with his own generation in his bones, but with a feeling that the whole of the literature of Europe from Homer and within it the whole of the literature of his own country has a simultaneous existence and composes a simultaneous order" (Eliot 38). Consequently, the writer is freed from the limitations of his personal world, and is able to tap into the larger literary tradition.

In general, Higgins also adopts an impersonal stance in his reviews. He does not use the authority implicit in the form to advocate his own theories on art and writing. Nor does he treat the material he is reviewing merely as a means to justify his own artistic endeavors. Higgins floods his reviews with details from the text he is assessing, trying to give the reader an indication of the work's preoccupations. He immerses himself in the particulars of the writer, and is a "faceless" reviewer in this respect. Indeed, he faults Milan Kundera for attempting too often to explain his own writing in his collection of critical essays, *The Art of the Novel*. Higgins rightly maintains: "It is hardly fitting that authors should theorize in print about their own work, for if it's any good, the writing itself constitutes a theory" (256). Yet, although we will not catch Higgins theorizing about his own writing in his reviews, we will sometimes see the individual behind the review, unable to repress his political views.

Higgins does not see literature as the place for a writer "to discover solvents for the world's ills" (177). Writing about Anthony Burgess's *Earthly Powers*, Higgins argues that the novel is compromised by the author's "grand thoughts that were perhaps best omitted" (177). Though, worse than ruining the aesthetics of a novel by merely making it a showcase for the writer's opinions, Higgins is put off by the misogyny of the novel: "Women have rarely been seen in an unkinder light; degraded by their nature, by suffering, by female ailments, they are reduced to almost a subspecies here" (177). Though Higgins predominantly looks to the language and aesthetics of a literary work, he is unable to ignore the prejudices of this novel. Likewise, in the section devoted to British writers, Higgins draws the reader's attention to "xenophobia," sarcastically exposing writers who are intolerant of any cultural difference. Examining several works by Sapper (Lt. Col. H. C. McNeile MC),

Higgins begins by noting that in these thrillers, "[a]ll foreigners are suspect, potential bounders" (128). Higgins looks through the action-packed veneer of these "schoolboy yarns," and sees a sexism, classism and racism that is made all the worse for the seeming innocence of the genre (128). While Higgins admits that he and his brother read these thrillers "voraciously," loving their depiction of a "most exciting and exotic England," he still is able to see that they serve to reinforce "British class prejudice in all its forms," where foreigners possess an "ingrained shiftiness, [. . .] the females worse than the males" (130, 129). Whereas Burgess spoils the aesthetics of his novel by imposing his personal grievances and misogyny upon the reader, Sapper's adventure tales are perhaps more insidious in that they assume and naturalize certain biases as the status quo. As Higgins explains, the pages of these children's books are filled with "[h]aughty male voices giving orders," affirming "the effortless superiority of the English gentleman" (130). Higgins takes issue with both writers because they fail to uphold the modernist notion that a work of literature should not didactically preach a message but engender change in a reader through form and linguistic experimentation.

When reviewing nonfiction, Higgins's voice is even more distinct. He is exceptionally perceptive of the bigotry that many critics would prefer to overlook in certain famous writers. Higgins, however, does not hesitate to present a complete picture of a writer, even if it might be unflattering. In a review of Robin Maugham's recollected conversations with W. Somerset Maugham, Higgins takes note of Somerset Maugham's "Anglocentric view of the world," and how despite "massacres" and battles for the "last gasps of British colonial power," "the eating of four-course meals continues with unabated gusto" (143). Almost as an inconsequential aside, Higgins throws out that Maugham's forebears "slaughtered" the O'Neill clan to get their property in Ireland (144). He then inserts an unusually explicit comment on class: "Property is murder; the possessing classes can be ruthless, as was Somerset Maugham himself" (144). Without mincing his words, Higgins matter-of-factly presents such details without anger. He gives Evelyn Waugh the same treatment in his review of a collection of Waugh's journalism, edited by Donald Gallagher. After exhibiting several quotations that let Waugh incriminate himself, Higgins aptly sums up that Waugh was a "snob" who "did not believe in democracy" and "held a low opinion of the Irish" (169). Hence, we see another side of Higgins here: while aesthetics are his foremost preoccupation, he also cannot silently condone an ideology that he finds hateful, particularly in the nonfiction he reviews.

In a review of Günter Grass's *Headbirths, or, the Germans Are Dying Out*, which was rejected by *The New Statesman* due to its alleged "incomprehensibility," Higgins mentions his view on politics and literature, basically asserting that the two should never mix. After describing an encounter with Grass at a Book Hall in Amsterdam at some "prearranged 'happening,'" he continues: "I was invited to participate, discuss the equation Literature and Politics. I said there was no connection. Ah, but that's a political comment, they said. Not my cup of tea, I said, thanks all the same" (303). This belief, yet another aspect that ties Higgins to the modernists, makes it all the more clear why this collection of reviews is important. The reviews offer many windows where the reader can observe Higgins in a room that is interestingly both private and public; instead of the invisible "faceless" narrator of the artist, the voice of the reviews expresses Higgins's personal thoughts through the very public medium of the newspaper or magazine. Though the picture assembled through the reviews is not a comprehensive one, it certainly is different to the view we get of Higgins through his fiction, where politics almost never explicitly surface. Along these lines, in looking through the reviews, we not only see a stance against misogyny and xenophobia, but can also glean some of Higgins's views on Ireland, Irish writers, and representations of the Irish.

Higgins repeats that "playing skittles with skulls had long been an Irish game," in both his review of John Millington Synge's collected letters and a paper read at the Irish Writers' Centre titled "The Hidden Narrator" ("Fire in the Hills" 187). In the review, he examines the "death-wish" that pervades Synge's plays (187). In the paper, which in many ways echoes "The Faceless Creator" quoted above, the context is his discussion of violence in Flann O'Brien's *At Swim-Two-Birds* and *The Third Policeman* (5). Within this same discussion, Higgins states that "The Plain People of Ireland were a match for Joyce's Citizen, when it came to chauvinism and bigotry" (5). While above we have seen that the voice of the "faceless creator" must resonate with the "Plain People of Ireland," here Higgins reveals that he does not subscribe to an idealized vision of the Irish. Just as he looks with a critical eye upon British Anglocentrism, he commends Irish writers who are able to expose the shortcomings of Irish culture. Appraising McCabe's representation of the conflict between the Catholics and Protestants in Ireland, Higgins credits him for being able to portray the deeply embroiled anger and hatred that characterize the conflict without oversimplifying the issue. While historians are unable to explain logically what is at the heart of the conflict, Higgins attests that McCabe is able to get at the "tribal formulae of human existence—irrevocability, unrealisability, inevitability" (216). Rather than taking one side over the other, McCabe suggests in his fiction that violence will inevitably destroy itself from within—an indictment with which Higgins seems to agree. He bleakly ends this review with his own mixed feelings of equanimity and repulsion at the past and present: "Irish History? A servant sharpening knives: Gael versus Gall, Orange versus Green, Catholic versus Protestant; the sectarian killer, the bullet in the back, the Irish confusion, the old Irish cruelty directed against itself" (216). Yet, while Higgins appropriately condemns the violence of Irish history and the intolerance of those who resemble Joyce's caricature of the Citizen, the reader begins to notice that there is no "we" when Higgins writes about the Irish; more often than not, he discusses the Irish with an oddly distanced perspective.

Frequently, Higgins places himself outside of "Plain People of Ireland." Though he may consider the writer to be fundamentally connected to the masses, he does not seem to trust them as readers. In a harsh yet humorous review of Francis Stuart's *The High Curiosity*, Higgins laments that just as with the author's previous novels, the clichés of the "martyr complex and stained shroud" continue in this new novel (210). Following Joyce and Beckett, Higgins bemoans: "Ireland has no further use for these manifold tomfooleries; it has gone on too long already" (210). But the fact that Stuart's works remain popular with Irish readers exasperates Higgins, as he concludes that "the novel will appeal strongly to Irish readers for it is crammed with familiar lies" (211). While Higgins is conscious of these "familiar lies," the extent to which his own upper-class background sways his commentary on the "Plain People of Ireland" is sometimes unclear. For instance, Higgins praises Trevor's collection of short stories, *After the Wake*, for "dealing with the duplicity of people; an unmasker of hypocrisy, the Irish disease" (198). On the one hand, it could seem that Higgins is affirming a colonial stereotype of the Irish; on the other, however, this last line of the review could be ironic, meaning that though Trevor is specifically writing about the Irish, he is most concerned with exposing the duplicity of people in general. Higgins perhaps merely notes that some unnamed people may think of this as "the Irish disease." Of course, all writers are limited by their particular perspective and cultural background; this is as it should be. For it is this very perspective that allows the writer both to be affiliated with the "Plain People," but also to critique a society as well.

While literature is not the place for preaching politics, it does have the power to influence the "Plain People" rather than merely affirm comfortable worn-out ideas. In this sense, the writer is connected to the "Plain People," as Higgins asserts in the "The Faceless Creator," but he is also able to see and expose the entrenched biases that doom a people to repeat past mistakes. It is because the writer holds such a significant place within a culture that Higgins is attentive to the new Irish writers he reviews, keeping his ears tuned for that one writer who is able to represent the ordinary without affirming the cliché. In reviewing David Marcus's collection, *Body and Soul: Irish Short Stories of Sexual Love*, Higgins for the most part sees only the rehashing of tired plots, arguing that "the formula is as before, tried and untrue" (225). He surveys the various themes of each story, such as the "damage the Catholic Church and its well-meaning but ignorant priests have done Ireland" (224). He then inserts a one-sentence paragraph, which I assume relates to one of the stories, humorously chiding writers who romanticize love as necessary for a "normal" child: "The child conceived without love is not normal, one of eight; if that were really so, half the Irish population would be loonies" (224). After this joking, however, Higgins takes a serious turn, to ask who are the new Irish writers in this collection that will take on that slippery role of being one of the "Plain People" without conforming to a stereotype of the people. Interestingly, Higgins looks to female writers:

> Perhaps the new force in our writing will come from the women, them same women, much put-upon, in the new emergent Ireland of call-girls and massage parlours, noonday murder, a £3 million daily alcohol bill (your brain simply swirls), here hardly touched upon at all. [. . .] The female chroniclers will be tenderhearted but tougher-minded than the males—a drift of chosen females standing in their shifts itself. (225)

In addition to Trevor's short story, which Higgins praises as the "funniest," he singles out Helen Lucy Burke as a new writer who is able to offer the reader something different (224). Perhaps Higgins conjectures that female writers are the hope for the future of Irish writing because they are less dominated by a tradition of male Irish writers, hinted at by Higgins's allusion to Joyce's repeated allusion to the song "Seaside Girls" in *Ulysses*. If, as Higgins muses, female writers are simply "standing in their shifts," they are less likely to be clad in the habits of a tradition that can be burdensome. They have been down and out, making them able to be one with the common "Plain People"; but they are also outsiders, historically excluded from a patriarchal tradition. Maybe they are the ones who can hold a mirror to Irish culture that is necessarily both brutal and loving.

Higgins celebrates literature that reflects humanity with honesty and intensity, and scorns fiction that merely seeks to placate an audience. Since people are constituted through the words they speak and think, the sound of a novel—word choice, cadence, dialogue—is of the utmost importance. This is one of the qualities to keep in mind when reading Higgins's own novels, where he is particularly attentive to the language of the "Plain People." In one of the opening scenes of *Langrishe, Go Down* (1966), for example,

Helen Langrishe talks with a cemetery groundskeeper, who tells her about the history of the land, the generosity of his previous employers, the Guinness family, and other personal details such as losing his son in World War I. He informs Helen: "Oh dear God but it was a terrible waar, [. . .] Terrible murder. The mudde and the filt an the cowld. Me son Tom, God rest his sowl, seen grown min in the trinches cryin with the cowld" (41). Like Joyce before him, Higgins does away with quotation marks in this novel, for such conventions are not needed when the reader can hear the dialogue so clearly through the use of phonetic spelling and idiomatic expressions. "The life of language is in speech," Higgins writes in "The Hidden Narrator"; and his fiction is surely a testament to this (7).

But Higgins's fiction is remarkable not only for its meticulous attention to speech rhythms. He is mindful of details, both on the level of syntax and in his descriptions of characters and events. In his novel, *Scenes from a Receding Past* (1977), the early childhood and adolescent memories of the narrator, Dan Ruttle, which make up the first half of the novel, are recalled in the present tense, giving the section a sense of unreflective immediacy. Just as a child goes day to day without thinking too much about his place in life, the narrator is fixed in a stagnant syntactical form, which is only alleviated with the periodic joke:

> I write 'L.D.S.' on the top page of my lined theme book. It means *Laus Deo Semper*, praise God always. When the page is full I will write at the foot. 'A.M.D.G.,' which is Latin for the greater glory of God. So that all my work, full of errors, is in His honour. I see Knocknarae [. . .]. I miss Nullamore. I think: The place that never changes. (107)

As the narrator begins to recount his adult life, which is primarily concerned with his wife and their life together, there is a switch to the past tense, which has the effect of making the narrator seem more thoughtful. He remembers going to a party and meeting a man, who he perfectly sums up: "I heard his intestines rumbling, a blast of decay issued from his troubled interior along with unwanted confidences. His breath was foul" (181). He retells stories about his wife's childhood, remembering vivid details she told him, such as when she hid in her mother's closet, "the hems of the dresses touching the tips of [her] ears" (157). For this part of his life, he is self-conscious of his own narrative and how it fits together; it is not just a sequence of events narrated in the present, it is a story that he is constructing about himself, where he frequently repeats significant fragments that act like refrains, constants, within his life.

The last few chapters of the novel switch back to present tense, and the reader suddenly feels that after having the narrator fleshed out, she is in the present moment with him. He thinks of holding his wife in the water and her laughter, recalling: "As I sink, you rise, held up by the waist. Aloft in the air you are laughing. My head is below the surface. I can feel your laughter in my hands, as if it were the best joke in the world. The world gone from us. We are slipping away" (199). Through such simple recollections, Higgins suffuses the ordinary with a heightened signification. The assonance of "aloft in the air [. . .]" makes the words rise a little, light as laughter on air, while the last sentences of the quotation bring a weight to the scene, a sadness under the laughter. Such attention to form, his prose often breaking into poetry, further aligns Higgins with the modernists. As his own novels demonstrate, Higgins's repeated carping on word choice and the sound of a piece of literature is not for nothing—for it constitutes the aesthetics of the art.

Though *Scenes from a Receding Past* is based in Sligo, the author's note informs us that the "Sligo Town mentioned here is (or was) Celbridge, Co. Kildare," Higgins's hometown (10). The author of course takes liberties with his past, and "details given are not always true" (10); but the novel shows Higgins's way of delving into his past and reshaping moments through the form of fiction, translating memory into art. In his later writing, Higgins's work became more autobiographical. *A Bestiary* (1995, 1998, 2000), a collection of three memoirs that chart the author's life through his youth, travels, marriage and lovers, demonstrates the extent to which Higgins's personal experiences inform all of his fiction. *Bornholm Night-Ferry* (2006), consisting of actual letters written by the author, further illustrates the complicated connection between Higgins's life and writing. In his fiction and memoirs there is a formal quality, a style, which remains consistent. There is an artistic form that pervades these works, making them not terribly different in tone than the two early novels discussed above. It is only in the reviews that we can locate a more forthright and personal voice. Although the reviews are polished, they are less concerned with form and more focused on conveying information—about the art of writing, specific writers, and the writer's role in the world, which is often intertwined with politics.

When reviewing a collection of academic essays on Beckett, Higgins warns the "gentle browser" that the collection, aside from being issued by *"arch* bores" (academics, of course), would "put potential readers right *off* Beckett's work" (220, 221). As an academic, I cannot argue with Higgins here; we are often in the business of wearying our readers with fussy arguments that fail to add to the experience of reading. Unlike the "dubious bounty from the delicate hands of university lecturers and teachers," Higgins's reviews rarely can be called dull (220). In a limited space of a few pages, these critical pieces incisively spark a reader's interest in the reviewed text or assure a reader not to waste her time. Amazingly, Higgins is able to make the reader laugh while consistently pointing out why a sentence does not work, or why a particular verb is ridiculous. This alone makes them a pleasurable read. Yet, more importantly, this essay hopes to have shown that *Windy Arbours* presents a side of Higgins that is necessarily eclipsed in his fiction—over a dozen published works and counting—and even in his memoirs. What must remain "faceless" in his novels and short stories is at the very least given a profile in these reviews, and that makes them well worth the reading.

WORKS CITED

Eliot, T. S. "Tradition and the Individual Talent." *Selected Prose of T. S. Eliot.* Ed. Frank Kermode. New York: Harcourt Brace Jovanovich, 1975.

Higgins, Aidan. "The Hidden Narrator." *Asylum.* 1.1 (August 1995): 3–7.

—. *Langrishe, Go Down.* Champaign, IL: Dalkey Archive Press, 2004.

—. *Scenes from a Receding Past.* Champaign, IL: Dalkey Archive Press, 1977.

—. *Windy Arbours: Collected Criticism.* Champaign, IL: Dalkey Archive Press, 2005.

Joyce, James. *A Portrait of the Artist as a Young Man.* New York: Penguin, 1992.

Woolf, Virginia. "Anon." Ed. Brenda R. Silver. *Twentieth Century Literature, Twenty-fifth Anniversary Issue, Virginia Woolf Issue* 25 (Fall/Winter 1979) 3/4: 356–435.

Description and conclusion are inseparable in these essays and reviews. To come in Aidan Higgins's sights is to be taken, by bludgeon or by rapier thrust, and if the coup de grace is indeed graceful and the blow's trajectory lovely, as language finely turned is always lovely, we are left in no doubt that the writer of these pieces anticipates his reader's collusion in what he thinks and feels, beyond the need for persuasion.

But strata of possibility open beneath his determinations. This writer reminds us of something we might not have recognized before he set it so consistently before us: prompt judgment need not close down enquiry.

When, for instance, he writes of John Updike's *Bech: A Book*, that

> Updike employs a prose style as a Green Bay Packer's protective stuffing, as difficult to move about in as an astronaut's space-suiting with the helmet on. There hangs over the whole enterprise a stray stench of the inconclusive, the wastefully inconclusive. . . . ("A Whispering Gush" 73)

Aidan Higgins measures his subject's inside leg millimeter-perfect at the same moment as he typifies the society which provides Updike's writing with the life it has. The same may be said when his

173

sympathies are stirred. This, of Dorothy Richardson's *Pilgrimage*, is typical:

> Unspeakable family friends watch the talented daughter suffer at the piano, the Pooles and the Radners politely applaud—'poor cold English things.' No wonder she has a passion for fresh air. 'Nice,' correctly spoken, is a convulsion of the lower face, like a dog snapping at a gnat.
>
> She is in the tradition of the Brontes, compulsive chroniclers of an English disease not yet diagnosed. ("Twilight in the *Saal*" 124)

This is admirable in a way particular to him, finesse in detail and panorama in close embrace; scholarship by apercus, definitively delivered.

The confidence though, the clarity of arbitration, is so marked that it does raise a question of the center from which such conviction has issued. A question of ethos, of the custom of appreciation Aidan Higgins finds natural, arises on each occasion his judgments of literature and contemporary mores find their mark; and such occasions are frequent. This question can be summarily put: what authority does he presuppose for those positions he takes in addressing the wide range of writers, of topics, found in this collection?

I have indicated the method of presenting close work and expansiveness in a singularity as characteristic of his criticism. This applies as much to the longer pieces, the transcript of a talk given to an audience, and the several essays, as it does to the reviews. Typically, he seizes on a single perception or idea and puts it under the pressure of a language so suddenly efficient it explodes into a series of highlights which linger as they're flung from their point of origin. The allusion to Shelley's figure of the moment of poetry as a fading coal holds: such work moves the prosaic to a point where the mind may warm itself at the excellence of its own contrivance even as it watches its inevitable course to annihilation.

Sometimes, the formulation is offered as sufficient in itself. Writing of William Faulkner, for instance, Aidan Higgins locates his subject with a phrase or two, not to diminish him—Faulkner, we quickly discover, is an enthusiasm—nor to invite speculation, but simply to offer a well-made thing, like a clasp set with a semi-precious stone, to catch the light. A trinket, perhaps, but no mere bauble:

> He had a proclivity for the bracket, the enclosure, asides spoken from the corner of the mouth, not for ladies' ears. ("Below Memphis Junction" 4)

The method is sufficiently limber to apply to the august as to the relatively minor—personalities who lend color temporarily to the contemporary scene and titans such as Faulkner, or Dorothy Richardson, equally. In "hitting off" the broadcaster Alistair Cook: "His is a deceptively leisured style, like Ben Hogan's swing" ("Six Men" 35), a principle of economy is doubly enforced: Cook's presentation of self is caught by a metaphor drawn from the sport he loved best. Extension of such subtleties, a layering of them, is also available to this criticism:

> One can follow much far-fetched stuff from Mr. Faulkner, even gross improbabilities, because his novels were folk-tales made contemporary; Flannery O'Connor's vain attempts to follow him along that path end, as often as not, in Grand Guignol. But then again it's no easy matter to render convincingly the inner turmoil of imbeciles; and a

housebound invalid would have restricted contact with the Great Outside. The novels are less successful than the stories, all pervaded with the high rhetoric of Redemption, showing the same grim mendicant pride of the struggling poor. ("Hope Deferred" 66)

This is an extraordinarily compressed piece of writing, a goad to the reader's perceptions. The passage raises, for instance, the matter of the difference between a contemporary folk tale in Faulkner's, and in O'Connor's, hands. Why does one fail and the other succeed? Does failure depend on the type of folk tale attempted, or the manner of its re-telling? In what way or ways does Grand Guignol in O'Connor's fiction differ from, for example, "Little Red Riding Hood"? "Rumpelstiltskin" from "A Good Man is Hard to Find"? If Higgins is suggesting—his sentence is ambiguous—that O'Connor's novels are less successful than her stories because in the novels Redemption is pushed at us through a megaphone, are we to say that Redemption in a number of the stories generally considered successful is not similarly promoted? What of "Everything That Rises Must Converge"? If the stories are held to be more successful than the novels because in them a rhetoric comes off which fails in the longer fiction, what is the mechanism of this success? The Redemption named is Christian. To what extent might we think of the Christian account of redemption as other than a folk tale?

Other enquiries are provoked by these same few lines, not least the reasons for the trouble a housebound invalid author has in portraying imbeciles, and her effectiveness in representing the "mendicant pride of the struggling poor." What enables her imagination to extend beyond her drawing-room in one case and not in the other? Aidan Higgins compels us to test a proposition which might not have occurred to us at all before he wrote.

This style as readily encompasses the knock-out blow as it does such precisely located acclamations as the thumbnail sketch of Alistair Cook, or the ply-over-ply manner of the passage just quoted on Flannery O'Connor. Faced with something or someone he dislikes, and especially with a passage of writing which irritates him, Aidan Higgins can be exhilaratingly unforgiving:

> Biographer Atlas is no Boswell; but there again [Delmore] Schwartz was no Dr. Johnson. Prolix, free with opinions (not always his own), he stops just a fraction short of plain vulgarity. . . . ("The Henry Bear" 57)

This is a writer who clearly has his register of competency in good order. Following these plainly planted signposts, we find that those principles which stand as an undisclosed referent of the faults and accomplishments he holds near, return us to the question we began with, that of the nature of that landscape of best practice from which he writes with such acuity. What characterizes this place?

Reckoning points of detachment from behaviors he eschews help disclose the terrain.

Aidan Higgins treats unearned glamour as having all the charm of a fixed grin. Confronted by the "ornately bogus" (of John Updike, "In the Land of Glut" 77), which is felt to be as offensive as an assailant stepping across his path, or by complacent superficiality, he offers an even-handed disdain. All attempts to extend the life of a work (let alone a "career" in the arts!) beyond due term, especially if this involves a spurious realism in any of its varieties, are fair game for opprobrium. Any rhetorical gesture, including the making of fictional characters for no other reason than to pique the interest of an audience already jaded by too many of such presentations, and especially if "creativity" is invaded by a "bare-faced honesty" ("Old Porn and Corn Plasters" 230) which makes the wonder of ordinary things more dully straightforward than it is, stirs his instinct for the chase.

There is a common thread through the various tokens of this aversion to display without substance, for excellence too easily assumed, for reductive candor, for the superficial in any of its forms. Updike, again, invites a counter-attack which nails precisely the mix of over-elaboration and inaccuracy, of shallowness and a type of seeming profundity by which mere spectacle may seduce an audience schooled in self-indulgence; and with this resistance comes a sense of where Aidan Higgins takes his stand:

> Could this excessive load of verbiage be yet another form of conspicuous American wastefulness, of overload? Ham-fisted metaphors and silly similes fly, for he is nothing if not inconsistent; and this can lead to many patent absurdities. My high hopes for this novel were soon dashed. Above the 'hypothetical slice of desert' called Kush, the clouds are likened to wildebeest and giraffes compared to clouds. No desert can ever be 'hypothetical.' A girl's breasts are the shape of 'freshly started anthills' and there is an odder reference to an 'absent-minded penis' (ever encountered a rational phallus or a thinking penis?). ("Peanuts" 70)

Self-satisfied mediocrity is not in the sole keeping of mittle-America, however. Returning to a favorite theme, the dreary narrowness of English culture, Higgins writes:

In the damp kingdom of the unfunny line, presided over by Morecambe and Wise, and cuddly Coren of *Punch*, a lame English wit reigns supreme.

From whence does it derive? So cosy, so costive, so middle-class, so damned allusively complacent: *1066 and All That? Winnie the Pooh? Cold Comfort Farm?* The effortful straining for effects suggests the extended afterdinner anecdote, the purposeful drone of the club bore: Wodehouse or Beerbohm. ("How Utterly Maddening!" 136)

Underlying these refusals is a distaste for doubleness. Pretension and inauthenticity, arm in arm, swaggering stage center. Narcissus hauling his hyperbolic body over a catwalk in a coat he can't fill, effulgence of braid inviting ridicule. And what do such posturings share? A separation of versions of self from the truth at the core of these versions, whatever that might be. How to spike the guns of such hypocrisies? By binding together the aesthetic and ethic in a presentation whose immediacy requires no reasons and brooks no argument. From this imperative the compressed minimalism of Aidan Higgins's style arises, its rapid generation of multiple opportunities of perception.

In admiring the unsuperficial honesty of John McGahern, and, through McGahern, discerning Joyce ("the snowfall from 'The Dead' falls now on some peasant melodrama" ("Paradiddle & Paradigm" 226)). Higgins is saying *by* the effect in which his judgement is given—a turn of prose at least as pleasurable as Ben Hogan's golf swing—that the interweaving of a great literary predecessor with a key idea he has about a contemporary novelist can describe surfaces without dwelling there. The formulation here is "small"—a single line which grafts by bare mention a motif from a deceased novelist onto the oeuvre-in-sum of a contemporary. But it is certainly not lacking in vertical dimension, in what the New Critics, who were possibly the last to know what they really meant by the word, used to call "resonance."

It is at such points of connections concertina'd, of some scene from contemporary life mediated through a life of the mind preserved in a literary predecessor, of life and art brought together as a series of palimpsests, that Aidan Higgins's critical work excels. The presumption behind this, frail as faith, is an idea of the adequacy of language to the case in point, however complex that may be; a confidence that a representatum and its object will agglutinate; that under a sympathetic and skilled hand such immense opposites as meaning and the marks made on a page will come into transparent conjunction.

But a counter-inclination runs through these pieces, a question about the power of language, however adroitly managed, to deliver the truth of the world it puts on show. The fluency sufficiently in command of itself to resist the "relentless languidness" Higgins dislikes ("Americana" 41), stirs a certain uneasiness about the knowledge which licenses such language. Surely some foundation, or, looked at from a different perspective, some point of aim more substantial than a cultural snapshot embedded in memory by its sharpness of outline and deft shading, is required? Again we are brought back to our point of departure: what might this foundation, this point of aim, or, retrieving an earlier metaphor, this center, be? A certain stance Aidan Higgins adopts, a manner he has of addressing "whatever lies beyond the realm of words" ("Our Hero, After Babel" 239) as though he stood at such moments in the shadow of his own assurance, offers an indication.

This other manner, more hesitant than the thumbnail inscriptions of culture, to the point of reverence at times, is more often found in the fourth, or last, part of this collection, and especially in "Our Hero, After Babel," and "Dream-Zoo," the review-essay on Jorge Luis Borges. In these longer pieces, as in "The Faceless Creator" of part two, the arm thrown about a subject which characterizes the shorter reviews and other even more brief opinion pieces yields to arm's length sightings. It is as though mind may only truly know itself when its rich wanderings (Higgins, writing approvingly of Paul Theroux, p. 22) near their conclusion; only when it owns its gifts of expression that it represents itself fully.

Aidan Higgins speaks in terms of a border, of borders, in these pieces, by allusion and directly; this to the degree that we should read something of himself in the sympathy he shows for Jean Genet in the following description:

> Such a moment and such a place can only produce a unicorn. Fear, and the kind of emotion I always feel when I cross a border, conjured up at noon, beneath a leaden sun, the first faery-land. ("Our Hero, After Babel" 239)

Unlike Genet, Higgins approaches, but does not cross, this border. He stalks such moments of highest and most fanciful revelation, to lean over that "murky, depthless region of Unthought or whatever lies beyond the realm of Words" ("Our Hero, After Babel" 239), to see what might be glimpsed there. Even as he acknowledges "that reality that withdraws at the sounding of a human voice" ("Tonight in the *Saal*" 125; writing, again, of Dorothy Richardson) he will not shake sticky words from his finger ends; will not, as does Beckett, show the human voice in the process of emptying into a realm of "unthought" more spacious than anything mind may call up by its imaginings. That would be another kind of fear altogether than a trembling before the faery-worlds which keep their hold on admiration after invention is done with.

A timeless backdrop to the historical takes shape in such pieces in the final section of *Windy Arbours*. Knowing, as do Borges, and Conrad, whom Higgins quotes, that "when one wrote, even in a realistic way, one was writing a fantastic story; because the world itself is fantastic and unfathomable and mysterious" ("Dream-Zoo" 236), Higgins's gaze lifts beyond the circumscribed eclaircissements of the social dimension when he does not look through them. In one place he declares openly his capitulation—temporary, to be sure—to whatever exists beyond even the imagination which lends words their chimerical materiality, in a blank declaration reminiscent of some of Wallace Stevens's statements in *The Rock*:

> I say that that which is is. I say that that which not also is. The remote past and the future have never been so close together and the present has disappeared as the world shrinks and the imagination of man dwindles away. ("Our Hero, After Babel" 241)

And again:

> The child, who knows nothing, invents the world, and is haunted by it. A child's secret scribblings and scrawlings are a vatic spreading of the inks. ("Our Hero, After Babel" 238)

This borderland between knowing that one knows nothing and bringing back to the world of forms what one can of that nothing by "spreading [it with] inks"—the world as vatic coloring book—is Higgins's element, the place from which judgment in its variety is secured: his ethos.

It is a realm of mind, predominantly, rather than a sensuous apprehension, but not mind displaying in metaphysical meanderings as much as an instinctive going out of intelligence sufficient to render nuance concrete: a small affective universe shown in the way someone lifts a fork at dinner, it may be, or in a manner of saying the word "nice" which implicates the psychology of a nation.

When he cites Genet from *The Thief's Journal* to the effect that "I was penetrating less into a country than into an interior of an image" ("Our Hero, After Babel" 240), Aidan Higgins describes something intrinsic to his own way of working. For what may be known of the realm of unthought is represented in his critical work as it were from the inside-out—the image arriving fully realized prior to those discoveries which seem to substantiate it. So many of his implication-rich observations depend upon singular locations that, reading only a little way into him, we grow to expect his images to be instantly expansive, and are surprised when, occasionally, they are not.

Reading him in this way, we will feel no compulsion to try to separate Aidan Higgins's moral or ethical sense from the aesthetic. We will come to appreciate that it would be as much of an ethical solecism for such a writer to traduce sensibility as it would for another to talk down a political outrage. The indignation which draws him towards disparagement is, invariably, tempered—at least—by his delight in making a good sentence.

A continuous reconnaissance shadows his successes in which there is always, fundamentally, this matter of how much of truth may be brought back from the borderland, even if only as the token of something more comprehensive, instinctively grasped. We might say that it is not, as he writes of Conrad, "illusion" on the edge of darkness, but an intermittent illumination, fluorescence interruptus, which best describes this work: a flash-lighting of occasions precisely located.

Is this, then, a species of idealism? Yes and no.

It *is not*, because there is no evidence of allegiance to some universal substratum which secretly binds the world's sundry, no invisible metaphysical glue melding distinct things into a singularity whose existence is shown by a totting up of reasons, inviting lazy wonder. No god's-grandeur shining forth of things in their wholeness here, if you please.

It *is*, insofar as a formal knowledge which cannot be doubted is assumed. While there is no philosophic reaching for demonstration, "proofs" of Aidan Higgins's propositions exist in the manner of his saying them; this, naturally enough, is a creative writer's, rather than a philosopher's, *modus operandi*. Gliding by the descendents of Gorgias and stepping around metaphysic's murky pools, Higgins secures his strength to attach the strictly speaking unsayable by means of that most subtly bolshevist of ancient expedients, art. And this of course is inexplicable, especially to Platonists.

What, then, does secure demonstration, if not a reaching after axiom, censorious or sanguine?

Whether praising Paul Theroux or roasting John Updike—alas, poor Updike! thrice turned on his suburban spit—Aidan Higgins must not only expect his reader to catch nuance and social reference as they fly, but to agree with the substance of what he has to say without pausing to make crotchet points into a pattern. Recalling the passage on "nice," it is clear that in using Dorothy Richardson as a stalking horse for a notion of Englishness, Higgins expects complicity both in his association of that writer with a people's habit of speech, and the psychology this is supposed to indicate. The judgment is secured by our admiration for its execution. An ethical position (it is not nice to use "nice" in such a way; and neither is the communal mind which lies behind such a usage) is confirmed by the style in which that position is declared.

Style must register as a perception in the beholder before it can exist at all, and a writer invested in a manner as readily identifiable as Aidan Higgins's, must carry this knowledge as an enabling condition of his work, perhaps not always consciously; must be committed to the idea that communication by affect, by the language of the creatively critical, is certain. Especially for one whose style so distinctively becomes him, style is both a virtual, and a common property.

It is I think confidence that there is a decent-sized part of his audience with bankable powers of judgment, inhering as a settled part of the spectrum of reception, which grounds Aidan Higgins's critical perceptions. Writing with such assurance, he must presume that the very elect are among us in sufficient numbers, tied by a shared understanding, and listening with due attention.

In writing that "the brink, the abyss itself, is very close in a child's early feeling, experienced as a condition of convalescence" ("Our Hero, After Babel" 241), he must suppose that his reader feels much as he does. Short of consanguinity, such writing would surely be reduced to a conversation with oneself, increasingly frenzied, turning in ever tighter circles. In such circumstances, the criticism of literature would become an exercise of *He do the police in different voices*—many others indeed—but without Faber & Faber waiting in the wings to provide authenticity by imprimatur, and no expectation of accolade on the other side of publication. There is clearly a presumption of shared standards, of good taste as a type of sub-Platonic absolute which Aidan Higgins's pronouncements everywhere presume by the clarity of their address to the unknown, and their passionate distinctiveness of manner. Thus may he deal in a tangible sense of what is culturally and aesthetically valuable which readers who bring sufficient good taste to the table will instinctively affirm.

To make a sentence one cared for, as Aidan Higgins clearly cares for each sentence he writes, without the confidence that there were many waiting to take it in, could not be expected to generate sufficient voltage to carry pen over page for more than a session or two on a wet afternoon. Criticism of this high order would hardly be sustainable, across decades. The very quality of Aidan Higgins's work requires that we assume a belief in universality of expectation on his behalf. The efficacy of his art requires a commonality of understanding.

To put an example under the microscope: it must be considered, in writing the sentence just quoted from him, that the reader will understand without further explanation, at the first instant of reception, that what it is to be a child recovering from an illness (a fairly serious, or at least a trying, illness, one imagines), and what it is to encounter the *mise en abyme* of one's adult years, are somehow, in a way beyond any other words but those Higgins has given us, the same. The writer must hold that this feeling is single, coherent across both instances—that of the convalescent child and the adult in fear and trembling for his fading existence—and that this sense of the way things go can be communicated as near to instantaneously as language allows.

A more home-spun, less abstract instance underscores the point. When Higgins writes of Larry Woiwode's *Beyond the Bedroom Wall: A Family Album*: "the manner throughout is relentlessly long-winded, as if size alone could pull the matter down" ("Americana" 41), he must similarly depend on his reader being sufficient not only to appreciate the accuracy of large matters described in miniature, but to *expect* that miniatures can have it all over even your best tricked-out baggy monster.

Since the capacity of rhetoric to attach itself to reality lies at the heart of such a strategy, the matter of Aidan Higgins's relation to post-modernity arises.

A less equivocal response can be offered than in the case of his idealism. It can be said boldly that there is about Higgins the critic no tincture of the post-modern because he never comes to an admiring halt before the inadequacy of utterance, as though noting an insufficiency were in itself sufficient cause for celebration. (This measure of post-modernity is certainly challengeable, since by it Donald Bartheleme, but not Samuel Beckett, would come under that banner—or fall beneath it, as warriors caught in a conflict not of their making, as some would say.)

In the matter of the numinous which, depending on your point of view either subtends language or squeezes it relentlessly towards its point of origin until it is sucked through a black hole of reference, being neither dogmatized iconoclast nor uncritical acolyte, Aidan Higgins neither digs at the mortar of the temple wall nor slips invocations between its stones. Prepared to narrow his gaze against whatever convention he chooses to honor as a matter of course, he is also ready to incline the head if veneration is compelled from him; but not because respect washes his way from another source, and never because he feels that tearing down monuments is good for the biceps. Pride of performance goes with a humility before the immensity of what lies beyond even the best of words. An understanding of, almost a relish for, the frailty of language tempers his craft.

Behind everything Aidan Higgins writes is a wonder that things are as they are and not otherwise. Like Richard Brautigan, another of his enthusiasms, he relishes "the strangeness of natural things and the naturalness of strange things" (79), and his sharpest criticisms are called up by accounts which try to embellish such things by excessive elaboration or mannered simplicity; by any mode of description which refuses to let them be as straightforwardly strange as they are.

It is at this point that we can speak of a connection between Aidan Higgins's salon-critiques and the ethics of sensibility which superintends them. His impatience for poorly realized art, and poorly honed people, is at bottom the same irritation at the prospect of a space reserved for language which the maladroit occupy peremptorily by their interruptions.

Aidan Higgins would keep to the mark we kindred souls who overhear his conversation. Would have us cock a sharp ear always, minimally distracted by contemporary fluff and our own preoccupations, so that we may hear certain intimations which might arise where cleverness can do no more, echoes from that fine and extra-subjective place where thought itself comes in sight of its end. His most complete commentaries ride on a whelming silence. Deference to the unspoken underwrites his descriptions.

WORKS CITED

Higgins, Aidan. *Windy Arbours: Collected Criticism.* Champaign, IL: Dalkey Archive Press, 2005.

Aidan Higgins:
Forging Fictions and Memoirs

GERRY DUKES

In May 2007, in the village of Celbridge in County Kildare, a festive literary weekend was held to honor the life and work of the Irish writer Aidan Higgins who was born close by in a house called Springfield in 1927. There were lectures and seminars, a book launch, workshops, panel discussions and dramatic readings. Through most of these activities Aidan Higgins himself sat in the front row of a highly appreciative audience enjoying what he impishly called his "posthumous reputation." He was half joking and wholly serious.

Higgins has come a long way in space and time since 1960 when his first collection of short fictions, *Felo de Se*, was published in London by John Calder. That collection of six stories was almost unprecedented in the canon of Irish writing in that the stories were variously set in England, Germany and South Africa as well as in Ireland where Higgins had lived until he immigrated to Britain after the Second World War or "The Emergency" as it was called in the neutral Irish Free State. He spent some years in the London area engaged in clerical and factory shift work before joining a touring puppetry company and setting out for continental Europe and, later, Africa. Since the early sixties he has been a professional writer and has lived for considerable periods in Spain, Germany and England and has done stints as writer-in-residence at various colleges and universities in North America. He returned to live and work in Ireland in the latter part of the 1970s. In all this time he has been steadily productive—in addition to the stories there have been five novels, much travel writing, some extraordinary criticism and, in more recent years, three volumes of memoir which redefine the *genre* of autobiography.

The trajectory of Higgins's career as a writer has been odd, to say the least. Early recognition for his stories and first novel *Langrishe, Go Down* was followed by a slow sinking from public view. *Langrishe, Go Down* (1966) was reviewed ecstatically across the English-speaking world and it went on to gain for Higgins the James Tait Black Memorial Prize at a time when literary prizes still meant something more than mere publicity brouhaha. A few years later the novel was adapted for television with a screenplay by Harold Pinter and with Judi Dench in the leading role. The novel is in three parts, datelined 1937, 1932 and 1938 respectively. The main focus is on one of the Langrishe sisters, Imogen, and on her relationship with one Otto Beck, a German doctoral student in his thirties who lives rent-free in a cottage on the decaying Langrishe estate called Springfield (the Higgins' family home), near Celbridge. The novel is an extended development of the first story, "Killachter Meadow" in the collection *Felo de Se* and, as Higgins has pointed out in his memoirs, the novel is a trickily fictionalized handling of autobiographical materials, materials deployed in the first volume of those memoirs, *Donkey's Years* (Secker & Warburg, 1995). So, what began as a story became a novel and is finally revealed to be disguised autobiography. But that is not quite how the novel was received or reviewed when it was first published.

Readers and critics in 1966 and since saw clearly that the novel offered Higgins's own particular take on the traditional Irish "big house" novel except that the Langrishe family (Higgins once pointed out to me, with a pained expression, that the name rhymes with "anguish") were not members of that superannuated and hyphenated class—the so-called Anglo-Irish—but *echt* Irish and Catholics to boot, marked out by *folie de grandeur* and general fecklessness. Rising and falling, damp, decay and deterioration, dwindling resources, generalized lassitude—these are the distinguishing marks of Springfield and its resident family. The summer tennis parties are long since over and the court is destroyed by moles and weeds, the roof of the glass house has collapsed and the orchard is untended and gone wild. In the novel Higgins clearly laments the inexorable economic decline of his own family as the dividends from American mines dwindled to a trickle and then dried up entirely. To narrow the book to just that thematic is, however, to diminish its extraordinary imaginative power. What Higgins achieves in *Langrishe, Go Down*, is not just a revision of the "big house" novel but a reversion to the older Irish language lamentations of Ó Bruadair and Ó Rathaille in the seventeenth and eighteenth centuries as the Gaelic social order and culture was propelled into terminal decline. In *Langrishe, Go Down* Higgins fuses the Irish and English language literary traditions, a feat achieved before him by only Synge, Joyce and Beckett, his great precursors.

One of the consequences of the publication of *Langrishe, Go Down* was the establishment of Higgins's reputation as a fastidious and exacting writer who demanded and commanded a high level of concentration on the part of his readers. Here was a writer who wrote prose rich in cues for imaginative interpretation, a prose that opened rather than closed possibilities. It was thus hardly surprising that during the 1970s and 1980s Higgins frequently produced commissioned work for BBC radio networks. Alongside this work there is a substantial body of general criticism and reviews produced by Higgins for many of the leading literary journals and quite a few newspapers in Ireland and the United Kingdom. Many of these pieces are available in the collection *Windy Arbours* published by Dalkey Archive Press in 2005. Throughout his criticism it is evident that Higgins measured the quality of the writings he was asked to judge by what were for him the best possible models. For Higgins these were, inevitably, Joyce, Djuna Barnes and Beckett for writings in English and Borges and Kafka for writings from the wider world. It is in these provocative, sometimes brisk and unsympathetic pieces that Higgins forged a critical *persona* for himself that may have alienated some writers and readers and contributed to the diminution of his reputation.

The glimpses we catch of Higgins in the pages of his first publisher's autobiography—*Pursuit* by John Calder (Calder Publications, 2001)—suggest that Higgins may have been a difficult talent to deal with, clubbable if not particularly biddable. By the time Higgins's first novel was published he was living in London, a married man with a growing family with all that that entails. His next book, *Images of Africa* (1971), compresses a four year stay in southern Africa into a series of vignettes that yet contrives to retain a kind of residual narrative drive as public and private perspectives are opened and closed and the reader is moved forward through time, held by a prose that can register the most banal of minutiae alongside the most revealing and harrowing details. Higgins's eye is never impassive, a mere recording device; his is the satirist's eye that informs unerring judgment. The book did not sell particularly well nor was it assisted in any significant way by its publisher's idiosyncratic notions of marketing.

His second novel, *Balcony of Europe*, was published in 1972. Its 463 pages are erudite, polyglot, difficult and raunchy—the book makes few concessions to readability. At its center is a middle-aged Irish painter, Dan Ruttle, living *en famille* on the coast of Andalucía in Spain in the early 1960s. He becomes involved in an adulterous affair with Charlotte Bayless, the Jewish wife of an expatriate American scholar. Had Higgins chosen to focus more exclusively on that relationship and on its inevitable outcomes he might have achieved a more disciplined and sleeker book but his ambition was greater and he tried to annex a kind of Jamesian inclusiveness and produced what James would have called "a loose, baggy monster." Higgins himself was unhappy with the novel and he has not permitted it to be re-issued though he has allowed some parts of it (reworked) to appear in print over the years since first (and only) publication. And yet for all its manifest faults *Balcony of Europe* contains some of Higgins's most subtle and stylish prose—he is particularly good on illicit sexual desire, its pleasures and attendant guilt. He is just as good on the miserable vulgarity of anti-Semitism, on the nauseating Spain of General Franco and much else besides.

Higgins's third novel, *Scenes from a Receding Past* (1977) has similarly been disowned by him. It is in some senses a prequel to *Balcony of Europe*. Again, the central character is a younger Dan Ruttle but here featured as the central character in a *bildungsroman* somewhat in the manner of Joyce's *Portrait* but without Joyce's unremitting introspection. The Dalkey Archive Press re-issue of the novel (2005) carries an Author's Note in which Higgins advises his readers that Ruttle is a fictionalized version of himself and that the County Sligo backgrounds should be read as really those of his County Kildare childhood. It is odd that a novelist who would later become a consummate memoirist should be so forthcoming about the sources of his work and thus close off interpretive possibilities better left open to his readers. This becomes very clear when we contemplate, for example, the kind of interpretive adjustment that readers are forced to make when they view the earlier fictions of the late John McGahern through the lens he provides in his *Memoir* (2005).

Dan Ruttle is merely one of the many identities Higgins has constructed for aspects of himself. In his three volumes of memoirs (of which more below) there is a character called Rory of the Hills who also features in Higgins's correspondence. Rory of the Hills was a semi-legendary minor Gaelic "king" in the midlands of Ireland during the inconclusive Elizabethan attempts at plantation (probably more accurately called expropriation and ethnic cleansing) in Leinster and Munster. Rory was a gadfly, a thorn in the flesh, a buzzing annoyance for those with a serious sense of mission. So Higgins as Rory of the Hills is a lesser lord of misrule, a consumer of more ale than cake, a portrait of the artist as an irresponsible but irrepressible pariah. Rory of the Hills is an untrammeled free spirit, an exotic creature in the Ireland of the latter half of the twentieth century.

Higgins's fourth novel, the astonishing *Bornholm Night-Ferry*, appeared in 1983. An Irish novelist in his late forties has a brief and intense relationship with a Danish poet in her mid-thirties. They maintain their relationship through letters for nearly four years, sustained only by brief and hurried meetings. The audacity of publishing an epistolary novel in the 1980s is matched by Higgins's extraordinary skill in providing the Danish poet, whose English is pretty poor, with a serviceable and highly expressive idiolect which allows us access to her thoughts and feelings. Again Higgins was not well served by his publisher—an Anglo-Irish combine on this occasion—and the novel did not command the level of attention that it deserved.

Publication of Higgins's work passed to the London publishers Secker and Warburg in the late 1980s and in 1989 *Helsingør Station & Other Departures: Fictions and Autobiographies 1956–1989* and *Ronda Gorge & Other Precipices: Travels and Autobiographies 1956–1989* appeared, two compendia of previously collected and uncollected prose. It was with these two books that Higgins begins to blur, even to elide, the distinctions between travel, fictional and autobiographical writing—a process that he was to bring to a culmination in his memoirs. Secker and Warburg brought out his fifth novel, *Lions of the Grunewald* in 1993 and at the same time Minerva (Secker and Warburg's paperback imprint) re-issued *Langrishe, Go Down*. Minerva published yet another compendium of prose writing—*Flotsam & Jetsam*—in 1996 but by then Secker had begun publication of Higgins's three volumes of memoir. *Donkey's Years: Memories of a Life as Story Told* (1995), *Dog Days* (1998) and *The Whole Hog* (2000) constitute what Higgins has called "a trilogy." The American publisher Dalkey Archive Press published a large one volume edition under the title *A Bestiary* in 2004—further proof that Higgins has long been, like Yeats before him, an inveterate reviser and rearranger of his own work and to just as good effect.

The three-in-one volume publication of Higgins's memoirs under a new title alters the dynamics of and between the three original volumes. Their separate and punning titles are now demoted to the status of subtitles and the new title gestures towards a different reading experience, one in which the reader is led to expect encounters with strange creatures. The many photographs which were such a feature of the original *Donkey's Years* do not appear in the Dalkey Archive edition though some have been faintly reproduced in the jacket design.

Donkey's Years, the first volume, is in many ways the most traditionally pitched of the trilogy. The book is organized chronologically, beginning with Higgins's first memories—the village of Celbridge flooded by the river Liffey—and ending with the documentary details of the grave in which both his parents are buried in south County Dublin. But between those starting and end points we find all we would expect to encounter in a memoir. Memories of kindness and fear, fun and punishment, memories of the miseries of schooling, of ailments and illnesses, of the beginnings of sexual identity. Here we meet strange creatures indeed and the strangest of all are the members of the author's own family, his parents Dado and Mumu and his three brothers Dodo, Bun and the younger Dote. There are many others as well: callers to the house, teachers and school companions, relatives and strangers. The reader feels increasingly intimate with all these odd creatures Higgins parades before us and yet we never get to know them fully despite the thick impasto of detail that the author supplies. Higgins is at all points fully aware that omniscience is available only to the deity or to that pseudo-deity, the novelist. In the real world others are never fully knowable.

Higgins lays into his narrative a pattern of repetitions and repetitions with variations which disrupt the chronological flow of his book and allow us to perceive his subjects diachronically, as it were, reading character and event down through the strata of past time. In his Acknowledgements (these do not appear in the American edition) Higgins reveals that he was contemplating a sequel to *Donkey's Years* as he was bringing it to a conclusion—in the event he was to produce two—and he carries this technique over into the two succeeding volumes.

The second volume, *Dog Days*, opens around 1950 with an account of Higgins's first serious love. The loved one was a woman some sixteen years his senior who allowed him access to her in all ways but the one he most wanted and needed as a lusty youth. This hilarious adventure takes place in the County Wicklow village of Greystones where the Higgins family moved after the forced sale of Springfield and its adjoining lands. The indolence and improvidence of Higgins's father had been a prominent sub-theme in *Donkey's Years* and had been accompanied by a clear-eyed presentation of the parents' decline from bourgeois comfort in Kildare to a rented summer bungalow in Greystones and, later, to poor and damp basement accommodation in Dun Laoghaire after the four sons had struck out on their own. The fact that the second volume opens at a time which precedes the conclusion of the first is indicative of another captivating feature of Higgins's memoirs—chronological narrative can be either fast-forwarded, rewound or interrupted at will so as to accommodate the exigencies of "telling the story" in ways designed to grip the reader. Strict chronology may deliver a kind of coherence but it is not the coherence of memory or of the heart. Other modes of organization are required to record or to appease those.

Just after the mid-point of *Dog Days* there is a moment which seems to come out of the blue:

> Those were the days when Jane and I lived high up on Muswell Hill Broadway; when I couldn't extract royalties from a tight-fisted publisher; when our marriage had begun to break up; when I drank like a fish and my work went off the rails. (*A Bestiary* 358)

Such candid, personal and "confessional" moments are extremely rare in these memoirs. An account is given of the birth of the author's first son but the births of two more do not feature but are mentioned only *en passant*. The reader is made aware of a lot of drinking but at no point is its excessive nature revealed. Nor is the work gone "off the rails" much noticed, much less discussed. Higgins's memoirs are informed by the troubling consciousness that he, as author, is not in a position to tell "the whole truth," that he is at best a partial witness whose account is inevitably biased. Rarely since Joyce has there been such "scrupulous meanness" of style.

The third volume, *The Whole Hog*, brings the "story" up to the opening of the new millennium and functions as a kind of collage or midden-heap of brightly-colored scraps and fragments which Higgins feels impelled to record and display. In a lesser writer's hands these would simply distract but here each one is carefully calibrated to deliver its modicum of meaning. What the reader is left with at the end of this big, brave and bright book seems to constitute the entire stock of Higgins's incomparable imagination generously gifted to those willing to pay attention. Reading Higgins as he trawls through the past, as he sutures across the gaps in memory, as he renovates lost time is as bracing a literary experience as you are likely to get.

WORKS CITED

Higgins, Aidan. *A Bestiary.* Champaign, IL: Dalkey Archive Press, 2004.

Babel," where the mundane and the magical freely co-exist. Along-side poignantly dull wedding videos and tiresome (but strangely sinister clips) of pets doing funny tricks, there is real treasure to be found. Fans of modernist cinema, for instance, can now see Luis Buñuel's seminal *Un Chien Andalou* (1929) or Orson Welles's debut short *The Hearts of Age* (1934). Anyone interested in modernist poetry can hear T. S. Eliot reciting *The Waste Land* (1922) or listen to W. B. Yeats reading from "Coole Park and Ballylee" (1931), both accompanied by a montage of original manuscript materials. Indeed, for students of Irish modernism, YouTube is an electronic Aladdin's Cave: at the click of a button you can now see Samuel Beckett's *Film* (dir. Alan Schneider, 1965, starring the great Buster Keaton) or listen to a 1932 audio recording of James Joyce reading from *Finnegans Wake* (mimed by an eerie Joycean avatar). None of this, of course, can replace the experience of viewing these films on the big screen or reading these texts in their original form, but it does open up new ways of thinking about the multiple (and mutual) intersections between the verbal and the visual in modernist literature and film.

One of the other great pleasures of YouTube is its splendid serendipity. Recently, while searching for clips relating to "James Joyce" (736 hits and counting) and "Samuel Beckett" (428 hits at the time of writing), I came across a three-minute comedy film entitled *Pitch 'n' Putt with Joyce 'n' Beckett* (dir. Donald Clarke, 2001)—a mildly surrealist skit in which Joyce and Beckett pass the time playing pitch and putt while waiting for Yeats to arrive. The comedy depends on rather stereotypical images of Joyce and Beckett, but is no less funny for all of that. Here, Joyce is voluble and vulgar, spewing forth an unstoppable torrent of words; Beckett is solemn and silent, the mute minimalist foil to Joyce's manic logorrhea. Both longstanding clichés of course, but nonetheless the film does act out the essential difference between the two writers in a witty and entertaining manner. This contrast between the long-driving Joyce and the short-putting Beckett has been well articulated elsewhere, not least by Aidan Higgins (himself a golfing aficionado):

> A mutual mistrust of what Joyce called the 'wideawake language of cutanddry grammar and goahead plot' lead Joyce and Beckett off in different directions. The lapsed Roman Catholic believed the more the merrier and put in everything—incremental stockpiling, addenda piled upon addenda, until he went too far in *Finnegans Wake* (sans apostrophe). Whereas the sceptical ex-Anglican made it his dicta that the artistic process was a contraction, not an expansion. (Introduction, *Samuel Beckett: Photographs* 4)

Throughout his career, Higgins too has tried to find new ways of transcending the "cutanddry grammar and goahead plot" of conventional realism. However, this restless quest for more complex narrative forms has not always found favor with literary critics, some of whom seem to object to the sheer density and intensity of his language. For instance, as Roger Garfitt describes it:

> [Higgins's] heaviness of language is indicative of a persistent tendency of his style, or rather, of its particular limitation, that he is altogether too writerly, too hedged with words. [. . .] Reality is internalised, transmuted by Higgins's style into some sort of inner world, so that one could often be uncertain whether he is writing about a real or a dream world. (Garfitt 225)

Even amongst Higgins's admirers, there is often an uneasiness about the imagistic texture of his allusive (and elusive) style, which has been variously—and rather imprecisely—described as "impressionist" (Garfitt 229; Imhof and Kamm 145), "expressionist" (Garfitt 227; Mahon 12), "surrealist" (Baneham 169; Murphy 41), and even "cubist" (Skelton 215). Another related critical problem is a tendency amongst commentators to judge (or at least conceptualize) Higgins's writing almost entirely in terms of his acknowledged literary influences, Joyce and Beckett (e.g. Beja 171; Imhof and Kamm 146; Murphy 38; Skelton 220). Although I make such comparisons myself, part of what I want to argue here is that Higgins offers an alternative vision to Joyce's merry "expansions" and Beckett's skeptical "contractions." More specifically, I want to suggest that Higgins finds his inspiration not just in the bright lights of modernist literature but in the dark recesses of the cinema theater as well. In this respect, it seems to me that Buñuel and Welles are at least as important as Joyce and Beckett in the composition and development of Higgins's post-modernist poetics.

Of course, an interest in cinema is hardly exclusive to Higgins: Joyce famously opened the first dedicated cinema in Dublin in 1910 (Ellmann 300–04), while Beckett wrote a letter to Eisenstein in 1936 about the possibility of studying film in Moscow (Bair 204). However, whereas the modernist fascination with the possibilities of film is largely "epistemological" (a means of exploring the nature and limits of knowledge), in Higgins's fiction—and certainly in *Langrishe, Go Down* (1966)—it manifests itself on an "ontological" level as well (a means of exploring the nature and limits of being).

In purely formalist terms, this cinematic consciousness helps elevate Higgins's writing above the ordinary by "defamiliarizing" his language: hence the slightly off-beat visual imagery, the frequent intertextual allusions to films, the sustained use of flashbacks, and the flickering, contrapuntal viewpoints.[1] Structurally, it also allows for the development of what various critics have described as "spatial narratives" (Imhof and Kamm 158; Murphy 40), whereby linear sequence is abandoned in favor of chains of images which the reader must link together on a vertical rather than a horizontal plane. Indeed, such is the prevalence of this technique that it might be altogether more useful to consider Higgins's writing in terms of "mise-en-scène" (the aesthetic modifications of space) and "montage" (the linking together of discrete shots) rather than invoke the tired old tropes of literary criticism. As Neil Murphy notes:

> Much of Higgins's energies are directed at creating powerful images almost visual in their intensity, and these images serve to compensate for his abandonment of sequential narrative form. Dermot Healy recognises this aspect in Higgins's writing: "The key to Higgins is the 'image'—for him storytelling stopped there—if you told what was there visually, the story would inevitable follow." (Murphy 90)

To date, there is no trace of Aidan Higgins on YouTube, although a Polish user known as "mymra" has uploaded nine five-minute excerpts from the film version of *Langrishe, Go Down* (dir. David Jones, 1978), along with a number of interviews with Judi Dench (who plays the role of Imogen Langrishe in the film). This in itself says something fundamental about the scopic and erotic appeal of the cinema, where stars are always more significant than auteurs (nowhere in her accompanying notes does mymra mention the screenwriter or the director, let alone the author of the original novel). And it is this deeper, ontological awareness of the performative power of cinema that really distinguishes Higgins from his modernist predecessors (and which makes the novel of *Langrishe, Go Down* so amenable to adaptation). As Higgins noted in the third volume of his autobiography, *The Whole Hog* (2000): "The movies that came my way [. . .] seemed to reveal something of that strange threatening life, the life that other people led, the lovers who *went after* each other like carnivores after their victims" [Higgins's emphasis] (522; italics in the original).[2] For Higgins—and certainly for some of the characters in *Langrishe, Go Down*—movies don't just reflect reality, they actually help to shape and order it as well. Consequently, this present essay is not just an analysis of the adaptation of a particular novel, but an examination of how that novel itself is already adapted from the world of cinema.

"Deeply haunting": Adapting *Langrishe, Go Down*

> I rate Aidan Higgins's writing very highly. I wouldn't have written the screenplay otherwise. When I first read *Langrishe, Go Down* I found it deeply haunting—as well as being very funny. I admire the book . . . that strange vivid atmosphere. . . . (Pinter; qtd. in Emery 82)

Although Harold Pinter is primarily thought of as a playwright, over the course of a fifty-year career he has written a total of twenty-six screenplays. Of these, five are adaptations of his own plays (*Betrayal, The Birthday Party, The Caretaker, The Homecoming,* and *Landscape*), fifteen are made-for-television dramas (including *Langrishe, Go Down* and a version of Elizabeth Bowen's *The Heat of the Day*), and the remaining seventeen film scripts are cinematic adaptations of novels by other writers including, most notably, L. P. Hartley's *The Go-Between* (dir. Joseph Losey, 1970), F. Scott Fitzgerald's *The Last Tycoon* (dir. Elia Kazan, 1976), John Fowles's *The French Lieutenant's Woman* (dir. Karel Reisz, 1981), Ian McEwan's *The Comfort of Strangers* (dir. Paul Schrader, 1990), and Margaret Atwood's *The Handmaid's Tale* (dir. Volker Schlöndorff, 1990) (see Gale 5).

Pinter originally wrote the screenplay of *Langrishe, Go Down* in 1970 with the intention of directing it himself. However, he was unable to raise the money to produce it and so the project was shelved. As he later recalled: "It's on a subject which doesn't seem very appealing. It's about three middle-aged spinsters living in a house in Ireland in the 1930s. [. . .] Now [producers] don't seem to feel that this is the brightest subject" (Pinter; qtd. in Billington 268). In 1976, the director David Jones—who later filmed Pinter's screenplays of *Betrayal* (1983) and *The Trial* (1993)—became the producer for BBC2's prestigious *Play of the Month* series. As Jones noted in an interview with the *Radio Times*: "Someone mentioned that we'd got a copy of an unmade Pinter film script. [. . .] We did our sums. It wasn't too expensive. So I rang Harold, and asked if he still wanted to direct it. 'Not any more,' came the reply" (qtd. in Emery 82–83). Jones decided to direct it himself, with Pinter playing the minor role of Barry Shannon—Otto Beck's drunken and embittered friend whom Imogen and Otto (Jeremy Irons) encounter on their first disastrous date in Dublin.

As David Jones later remarked, the screenplay was in many ways "a love poem to Harold's own time in Ireland" (qtd. in Billington 268)—a reference to the two years that Pinter had spent touring Ireland as a repertory actor with the Anew McMaster troupe in the early 1950s. In his elegiac memoir of this period, "Mac" (1966), Pinter wrote that "Ireland wasn't golden always, but it was golden sometimes and in 1950 it was, all in all, a golden age for me" (32). Sentimentality aside, it was certainly a pivotal moment in Pinter's career: as Anthony Roche has suggested, "It is to this sojourn in Ireland in the early 1950s that Pinter owes the discovery of what may well be his single greatest literary influence, the writing of Samuel

Beckett" (178). Acting in *Langrishe, Go Down* was thus something of a homecoming for Pinter, who was returning to Ireland for the first time in twenty-eight years. As David Jones commented:

> Harold's immensely professional. He was very keen to know whether he was coming over authentically Irish, hitting the right degree of drunkenness, whether the comedy was working or not. He was there very much as a professional actor doing a job. Not as a writer keeping a beady eye on other people . . . (qtd. in Emery 80)

The film was shot on location in County Waterford in June 1978. Initially, there had been difficulties in finding a house that resembled Springfield in the novel, and the production designer (Roger Murray-Leach) suggested shooting it in Wiltshire instead. However, Jones insisted that "Ireland had its own values. We *had* to go to Ireland because I knew for the cast, the whole unit, [that] within a few days of arrival in Ireland the whole atmosphere, which is very much part of the story, of the film, would begin to operate" (qtd. in Emery 83). As Judi Dench recalled:

> We filmed in an old house, in Ferrybank, up river, just out of Waterford. An old Irish house, part Georgian, with a long drive and a lodge—exactly like the book. It was called Springfield—which is also the name of the house in the book. [. . .] It's very odd going to an old house, full of decay and the past, which, to make a film you decorate from decay, knowing that when you leave it's going to be destroyed. . . . Perhaps *that's* what felt so strange . . . (qtd. in Emery 83)

Langrishe, Go Down was first broadcast on BBC2 television on 20 September 1978. And that might well have been the end of it, except that it was retrospectively screened at a Pinter festival held in the Lincoln Center, New York, on 25 July 2001, where it elicited praise from a number of film critics. It subsequently received a limited US theatrical release by Castle Hill Productions on 17 July 2002, and was eventually released on DVD by Image Entertainment on 23 March 2004. In this respect, its fitful but enduring afterlife mimics the fate of its original parent text. Or as Aidan Higgins drily noted in his autobiography: "My first novel, *Langrishe, Go Down*, [. . .] sold just over 2,000 cloth copies in the first fortnight after publication in September 1966, after which sales sank to a dribble. And it has consistently sold in a dribble ever since, in five or six European languages. Beckett called it 'literary shit'" (*The Whole Hog* 459).

"Still, while absent, very much present":
The Critical Reception

[*Langrishe, Go Down*] is about three spinster sisters living in the middle of Ireland in the 30s. In a big old house. Falling apart, falling down . . . Two years of the 30s: the past, which is 1932, the present, 1938. That's the time structure. In 1932 there's a German student who rents the lodge. A student of philosophy. It's to do with his relationship [with] one of [the] sisters in 1932. And in a sense his relationship to all the sisters. In 1938 he's absent. He's long gone. But he's still, while absent, very much present . . . (Pinter; qtd. in Emery 80)

When *Langrishe, Go Down* was released in New York in 2002, most critics tended to focus on its lead actors, Judi Dench and Jeremy Irons, who in the intervening years had both become international stars.[3] Stephen Holden, writing in the *New York Times*, argued that the film was "one of those buried treasures that are unearthed for reasons that have as much to do with star power as with quality." Moreover, "unlike so many early screen performances by not-yet-stars, both Mr Irons, who affects an impeccable German accent, and Dame Judi, who is almost unrecognisable as the actress of to-day, are already in full possession of their talents" (Holden n.p.). Andrew Sarris, the influential film critic and theorist, agreed: *Langrishe, Go Down* "provides us, at the very least, with an opportunity to see what Jeremy Irons and Judi Dench looked and acted like almost a quarter of a century ago. [. . .] The fragmented storytelling is, well, vintage Pinter, but Ms Dench and Mr Irons remain mesmerizing after all this time" (n.p.).

However, the sheer presence and star power of Dench and Irons tended to dominate the critical coverage at the expense of other elements of the film. Mike D'Angelo, for instance, writing in *Time Out*, described the film as "a skillful but unexceptional chamber piece that would likely have continued to gather dust in the archives if not for its retroactive star power" (103). Manohla Dargis in the *L.A. Times* was even more scathing in her assessment:

> Pinter completists will embrace one of the writer's lesser-known works, as will enthusiasts of Jeremy Irons, in a performance that predates his *Brideshead Revisited* [1982] renown. And then there are those who have always harboured a desire to watch Judi Dench daub meringue on her breast, proving yet again—because she's also quite good even when daubing—that great actresses can and sometimes do rise above bad material. (n.p.)

In contrast to A. O. Scott in the *New York Times* who praised Irons for his "wolfish grin and elaborately precise diction" (Scott n.p.), Dargis was quite cynical in her critique: "Dench's real accomplishment here is keeping cool while Irons mouths lines in a voice straight out of Monty Python's arsenal of unspeakably silly accents. Claus von Bülow isn't the only one laughing" (n.p.).[4] Interestingly, only one critic, Ken Fox, seemed to mention any of the other actors involved: "the real revelation here is Annette Crosbie [playing the part of Helen Langrishe], who manages to express years of festering resentment and a lifetime of loneliness simply through her clipped speech and the set of her jaw." Fox also notes that "[c]ertain scenes, particularly the one in which Imogen is forced to endure a drunken night in Dublin with Otto, [. . .] feel as though they were written for the stage, but are so wonderfully played it hardly matters" (n.p.).

"A VERY CLEVER, VERY FAITHFUL EDITING": MISE-EN-SCÈNE AND MONTAGE

> There were areas of the screenplay which on the page I found enigmatic. That's not unusual for a first reading of Harold [Pinter's] work. But the screenplay is tremendously faithful to the novel. Patch after patch of dialogue which I thought was purely Harold's creation is, in fact, a very clever, very faithful editing of Aidan Higgins's writing. (Jones; qtd. in Emery 80)

Although most critics made some mention of Pinter's screenplay, very few discussed David Jones's directorial input or even analyzed the film *as* film. For instance, David Sterritt in the *Christian Science Monitor* simply noted that "Pinter's screenplay offers an exciting mixture of psychological suspense and storytelling surprise" (n.p.), and left it at that. Stephen Holden was somewhat more forthcoming: "Mr Pinter's resonant screenplay is full of veiled allusions and meaningful pauses. One intriguing device [. . .] overlaps images of characters in one place with dialogue from somewhere else." Holden also detected a mood of "doomed Chekhovian fatalism" running through the story, an atmosphere "deepened by Carl Davis's string quartet soundtrack, whose folk-flavoured classical style Mr Jones describes as a cross between Schubert and Janáček" (n.p.). However, Jessica Winter in the *Village Voice* seemed rather confused by the complex rhythms of the work: "Aidan Higgins's novel undergoes a choppy, perplexing script adaptation by Harold Pinter [. . .], further muddied by *non sequitur* editing inserts. Imogen and Otto's happenstance affair holds little intrigue or surprise, while the tawny, heavily upholstered BBC production design and languid violin score provide an inaptly somnolent context for unlikely psychosexual conflict" (n.p.).

In contrast, A. O. Scott—who confessed to being puzzled at times by "Pinter's arch, elusive writing"—seemed more alert to the subtleties of Jones's low-key direction:

> The story is a muted melodrama made strange and haunting by the manner of its telling. The pacing and chronology are, as in Mr Pinter's theatrical work, splintered. David Jones's direction, with its hushed intensity and stop-and-go rhythm, suggests the influence of Joseph Losey, for whom Mr Pinter wrote some of his earliest screenplays. A rapid collage of scenes will occasionally give way to a long, digressive passage, like the drunken boarding-house conversation in which Mr Pinter himself expounds, in a thick brogue, on the Irish theatrical tradition, and Dame Judi ends up, sensibly enough, in tears. (n.p.)

The scene which Scott refers to is a good example of just how tightly knit Pinter's screenplay actually is, and how closely it resembles both the original novel and the finished film. As Pinter wrote in a prefatory note to the screenplay, "The camera directions in this screenplay are particularly detailed as I originally wrote it with the intention of directing myself. Obviously, David Jones did not observe every direction in the shooting of the film. The structure of the film, however, remained the structure as written" (screenplay n.p.). Here is a short extract from this impressionistic scene, where Otto and Imogen get drunk with Barry Shannon and Maureen Layde (Margaret Whiting):

MAUREEN FROM IMOGEN'S P.O.V. CONSUMED IN SMOKE.

The following sequence is constructed in order to indicate a passage of time passing and, with it, the effect of drink on the characters. Each shot will concentrate on its object to such a degree that the characters will appear suspended in time, encased in themselves. Time, although dislocated, has progressed by the end of the sequence.

CLOSE-UP. SHANNON.

SHANNON: They can't hide it anymore . . . you can see it on every street corner . . . in this country. Insanity . . . that's what's under the skin. All the brave words and all the brave faces . . . are unable to keep it from bursting out . . . and that's a fact.

CLOSE-UP. OTTO.

OTTO: It was a German who discovered parthenogenesis in bees. Dzierzon, a clergyman.

CLOSE-UP. SHANNON. STARING.

CLOSE-UP. MAUREEN. (Pinter, screenplay 603)

Mike D'Angelo also discussed the rhythms of the film, praising Pinter's screenplay while simultaneously castigating the direction: "While Pinter clearly trusts the fine cast, director David Jones, sadly, does not, employing intrusive close-ups during key scenes and cutting repeatedly and pointedly to Imogen's even more uptight sister, Helen" (103). I think D'Angelo is being rather unfair to Jones here, and is also missing the point somewhat. In the first instance, the style of the film may simply be related to its origins in television, where close-ups are used more frequently than in the cinema because of the scale and ratio of the screen. Furthermore, these "intrusive close-ups during key scenes" are also the hallmark of the Ingmar Bergman's so-called "chamber dramas"—films such as *Through a Glass Darkly* (1961), *Winter Light* (1962), and *The Silence* (1963)—which is a style of filmmaking that David Jones clearly seeks to emulate in *Langrishe, Go Down*. In the second instance, all of the repeated crosscuts between Imogen and Helen are essential to understanding the interwoven narrative of the two sisters, and this aspect is very carefully delineated in Pinter's screenplay. As Steven H. Gale commented: "The close-ups are used to emphasize specific points, but it is the intercutting of images of the actions of the two women in the past and the present that is especially effective in presenting the contrast between their life of passion and a life of dry withdrawal" (Gale 373).

The best example of this particular use of mise-en-scène and montage comes towards the end of the film, when the narrative fluidly crosscuts between two telling but seemingly unrelated scenes:

firstly, a strained and lifeless birthday dinner for Helen, which is set in the present (1938); and secondly, the beginning of the end of the affair between Imogen and Otto, which is set in the past (1932). The sequence begins with the party:

INT. DINING ROOM. WIDE SHOT.

The three sitting at the dining-room table. Helen at one end, Lily and Imogen facing each other. A leg of pork, bowls of potatoes and Brussels sprouts, etc. Wine. Candlelight. They eat.

LILY: Imogen cooked the whole dinner herself.

HELEN: It's very good.

LILY: Oh, it is. (Pinter, screenplay 632–33)

Then, as the mundane conversation continues, the scene switches to the past, where we witness the gradual estrangement of the two lovers:

INT. COTTAGE. BEDROOM. NIGHT.

Imogen lies in bed, her face turned to the wall. Otto comes into shot, throws the bedclothes back, climbs onto the bed. He studies Imogen's curled body for a moment and then clasps her roughly from behind. [. . .]

IMOGEN: I want to sleep. I want my rest.

Her body tightens. Her eyes close. Otto stares down at her.
(632–33)

This scene immediately segues back to the party, until at a certain point the *tableau vivant* of the dinner table is overlaid with voiceovers from the past (the ongoing bickering between Imogen and Otto):

> *They all continue to eat, and talk, spasmodically, but the sound ceases. Imogen's voice heard over:*
>
> (*VO*): Looking for compliments from you, honest to God, it's like boring down a mine.
>
> OTTO (*VO*):   I am expected to make pretty speeches?
>
> IMOGEN (*VO*):   What is it? Have I done something wrong? Tell me what I've done wrong?
> (635)

Finally, the sequence ends in bitter voiceover recrimination between Imogen and Otto, while in the present moment life goes on, in all its poignant dullness:

> *During the preceding, Lily has brought a birthday cake from the sideboard and lit the candles. Helen blows them out. Imogen and Lily begin to sing Happy Birthday.* (636)

It is a deeply affecting moment—possibly the highlight of the film—as the viewer is invited to make the link between two seemingly discrete scenes, which are separated in time as well as in space (in this respect, the visual and acoustic style remains very true to the spirit of the novel). As Pinter noted in an interview:

> I took advantage of film time. What you can do with it. There is a great deal of voiceover. Imogen and Otto have their intensely private relationship, but you only hear their voices over shots of Helen. What I was trying to say there is that what was going on [. . .] was happening to Helen too. [. . .] Even if she never saw it, was never physically involved, it was also happening to her. (qtd in Emery 80)

Although this particular use of time is written into the screenplay, some credit must surely go to the editor of the film, Chris Wimble, as well as to the director. However, it is in the atmospheric mise-en-scène that the director's signature is most strongly evident. Throughout the birthday party/lovers' quarrel sequence we get a wide establishing shot of the three sisters sitting around the dining-room table, claustrophobically enclosed by vivid red walls that seem to expressionistically echo the repressed anger and desire that lies behind their polite, meaningless talk. This stifling *tableau vivant* is highly reminiscent of Bergman's 1973 masterpiece, *Cries and Whispers*, which is also about three sisters—one of whom is dying—coming to terms with the past in a large country manor. As Roger Ebert wrote of this film (although he could equally be describing *Langrishe, Go Down*): "*Cries and Whispers* is about dying, love, sexual passion, hatred and death—in that order. [. . .] The movie is drenched in red. Bergman has written in his screenplay that he thinks of the inside of the human soul as a membranous red" (Ebert n.p.).[5] To evoke direct comparisons with Bergman is a brave and bold gesture on David Jones's part, but one which is in keeping with the spirit and cinematic textures of the original novel.

"EMANATIONS STRAIGHT OUT OF TSARIST RUSSIA": INTERTEXTUALITY

> Otto Beck [was] the catalyst and mediator between the Langrishe "sisters," who in reality were my three brothers and myself in drag; wedged between an Irish past and the European present. Jeremy Irons played [Otto] in the television production directed by David Jones, where Springfield garden and the father and daughters resembled emanations straight out of tsarist Russia, life in a dacha there, in that time and place. (Higgins, *The Whole Hog* 733)

Throughout their reviews of the film, critics constantly made reference to the European theatrical tradition rather than to any cinematic tradition. Stephen Holden, for example, compared the film to Chekhov's *Three Sisters* (1900) and *The Cherry Orchard* (1903): "The Langrishe property, like the estate in *The Cherry Orchard*, is in debt, and the mansion Imogen shares with her sisters [. . .] will eventually have to be sold" (n.p.). Similarly, in his interview with Harold Pinter, Jack Emery suggested that the story was "an Irish *Cherry Orchard*," to which Pinter replied: "Oh, yes. I know exactly what you mean. The collapse is imminent" (83). And in his critical biography of Pinter, Michael Billington describes the film as "neo-Chekhovian": "*Three Sisters* constantly comes to mind. As with Masha's passion for Vershinin in Chekhov's play, nothing is overtly said by the sisters about Imogen's relationship with Otto" (269).

Billington also suggests that the play that Otto brings Imogen to see in Dublin is Strindberg's *Miss Julie* (1888)—"another work in which a member of the gentry is dragged down by her passion for a social inferior" (268). In fact, in both the screenplay and in the film, this production is simply referred to as "a Swedish play" (screenplay 584), although in the original novel it is more precisely identified as *The Father* (1887) (Higgins, *LGD* 115), Strindberg's domestic tragedy about an estranged couple fighting for possession of their child. This is a subtle but significant point. Firstly, as Morris Beja notes, the intertextual reference helps evoke the Oedipal undercurrent of the novel, which explains, in part, Imogen's attraction to the cold and overbearing Otto:

> Otto [. . .] becomes the mirror image of her father, squatting on the land and taking on the education (in more ways than one) of his daughter. That process includes—and this may seem a bit much—an excursion to Dublin to see a production of Strindberg's *The Father*, as well as seduction: [. . .] "Why did I? . . . Because I liked his manner; because I desired him to be happy; because I wanted to give him something; because he had father's eyes . . ." [Higgins, *LGD* 104] (Beja 168).

Secondly, the reference to *The Father* also evokes the bitter end of Higgins's novel, where Imogen conceives a child by Otto which she later aborts—a scene that is significantly absent from either the screenplay or the film (I will return to this particular point later on).

In all of the film reviews though, the influence of classical European theatre is emphasized at the expense of the many intertextual allusions to the cinema, which to my mind are far more important to our understanding of both the film and the novel. Take, for example, the reference near the beginning of the screenplay/film to the Hollywood melodrama *Forbidden Heaven*, which I quoted in my opening epigraph. Again, the reference here is subtle but resonant: in *Forbidden Heaven* (dir. Reginald Barker, 1935) a young man

(1930s heartthrob Charles Farrell) saves a distraught young woman (Charlotte Henry) from drowning herself during the Great Depression. Afterwards, they take refuge with a group of homeless people in London's Hyde Park, where they miraculously find employment, hope and love along the way—a stirring contrast to the paralysis and inertia of the "four human derelicts" in *Langrishe, Go Down*, and an ironic counterpoint to Otto's callous abandonment of Imogen.

It is important to note that all of the cinematic references in the screenplay and film are taken verbatim from the original novel, e.g. "Helen bent to read the cinema poster. Forbidden Heaven, featuring Charles Farrell and Charlotte Henry, was showing at the Electric Picture House, Newbridge. Romance and pathos among four human derelicts" (Higgins, *LGD* 33). These references fulfill a naturalistic purpose (they help situate the drama in a particular time), as well as a symbolic function (they mirror the underlying themes of the novel), and a dramatic function (they tell us something about the characters' fears and desires, and their conscious and unconscious motivations).[6] An excellent (and revealing) example of this intertextual process comes at the very end of the screenplay/film, where Imogen reads a newspaper in her late sister's bedroom:

[IMOGEN'S] P.O.V. THE PAPER.
ANSCHLUSS!
FINAL DOWNFALL OF AUSTRIA
GERMAN TROOPS POUR IN

[. . .] *Imogen turns the pages until she reaches:*

DUBLIN ENTERTAINMENTS:

and (in boxes)

Grand Central:
DR SYN
with George Arliss.
Pillar Picture House:
THE GOOD EARTH
With Paul Muni.

Imogen throws the paper to the floor. (Pinter, screenplay 659)

Again, this insert is taken verbatim from the original novel (which is even more expansive in terms of its detailed movie references):

Imogen lay resting on Helen's bed, reading the entertainment section of the evening paper, four days old. *Dr Syn*, with George Arliss, was still playing at the Grand Central. *The Edge of the World* ('Selected as one of the best pictures of the year'), starring Niall MacGinnis and Belle Chrystall, was coming to the Pillar Picture House. [. . .] *It's Love I'm After* was still showing at the Savoy. Leslie Howard, Bette Davis. A photograph of the German cameraman Karl Freund holding up a reel of film to the light. Noted for the great attention he pays to detail . . . will be remembered for his brilliant work filming *The Good Earth*. (Higgins, *LGD* 247–48)

Yet again, these references fulfill naturalistic, dramatic and symbolic functions. *Dr Syn* (dir. Roy William Neill, 1937) is a British adventure yarn about a country vicar who is also a pirate captain. Syn (George Arliss) uses the profits from his smuggling ventures to support his impoverished parishioners, and at the end of the film his daughter—significantly named "Imogene" (Margaret Lockwood)—finds happiness with the handsome son of the local squire. *The Edge of the World* (dir. Michael Powell, 1937) is a romantic drama about the struggle to survive on a remote Shetland island. Significantly, in terms of *Langrishe, Go Down*, the character played by Belle Chrystall becomes pregnant with an illegitimate child (like Imogen at the end of the novel). What's more, the film is told almost entirely in flash-back: in the opening scene we see that the island is long deserted (a fate which also awaits the Springfield estate). *It's Love I'm After* (dir. Archie Mayo, 1937) is a screwball comedy about a temperamental couple (Leslie Howard and Bette Davis) who have postponed their marriage eleven times. In order to deter a rival, Bette Davis pretends that her fiancé has had children by another woman (thus mirroring the lascivious and feckless Otto Beck in the novel). *The Good Earth* (dir. Sidney Franklin, 1937) is a drama about a poor Chinese farmer (Paul Muni) who leaves his wife and child for a younger woman (again, shades of Otto deserting Imogen and her unborn child for Molly Cushen). And Aidan Higgins's close attention to detail is reflected in the comment about the "German cameraman Karl Freund," who was indeed noted "for the great attention he pays to detail" (it also evokes Otto, and his pedantic attention to facts).[7] Finally, this newspaper insert also serves a structural function in the novel, whereby advertisements for contemporaneous movies frame the opening and closing sequences of the narrative, thereby linking Helen and Imogen on an intertextual, vertical plane.

"JUST A SIMPLE LITTLE LOVE STORY":
ALLEGORY AND INTERPRETATION

You heard about Aidan Higgins teasing Harold [Pinter], "Ah well, it's just a simple little love story"? Maybe people will see it just as that. (Dench; qtd. in Emery 83)

Taking all of these elements into account—the retrospective star power of the actors, the atmospheric mise-en-scène and the fluid montage, the resonant intertextual allusions and the thematic motifs—what does the film of *Langrishe, Go Down* actually tell us about the parent text (and vice-versa)? How does the screenplay/ film differ from the novel, and what can these differences reveal about the whole process of translation and interpretation?

Throughout the critical reviews of the film, there is a general feeling that some kind of inner mystery remains, some hidden core of meaning that eludes rational analysis. Stephen Holden, for instance, noted how the "resonant screenplay is full of veiled allusions and meaningful pauses," but reluctantly concludes that it is "far too refined and introspective a film to expect box-office glory" (n.p.). Jessica Winter was puzzled by the seemingly listless relationship between the two central characters—"not a rapport but a fascinatingly robotic mutual affect (Otto pontificates pretentiously; Imogen stares into space intoning 'Oh are you?' and 'Is that so?'), they fall in love, they fall out" (n.p.). Manohla Dargis's assessment was scornful but shrewd: "What precisely should be gleaned from the Langrishe sisters, however, and their slide into indigence remains shrouded in mystery, though it may have something to do with English-Irish relations or perhaps fascism" (n.p.). Dargis goes on to note how Maureen Layde "rains down abuse on Imogen for being of Anglo-Irish heritage," while in another key scene "Otto tells Imogen that Irishwomen are 'pure' in ways that German women no longer are, which seems Pinter's attempt to draw a line between two of his favourite themes, sexual repression and political oppression" (n.p.). Dargis is surely correct here; in fact, in order to reinforce this latter theme—which Dargis wittily refers to as "the Bavarian at the family gate"—Pinter repeats Otto's comment about the "essential purity" of Irishwomen at two distinct points in the screenplay:

level, Otto could be said to liberate Imogen's unclaimed sexuality; on another, he is a moral monster whom you could easily image joining the SS. As well as a love letter to Ireland, the film is also an exploration of Pinter's complex feelings about the German psyche. (268–69)

Pinter himself would be the first to acknowledge this political preoccupation. Indeed, it may well have been the reason he was attracted to the novel of *Langrishe, Go Down* in the first place; as Morris Beja points out, Jewishness is an important theme in Higgins's oeuvre as well (174). As Pinter stated in an interview: "While, on one level, [*Langrishe, Go Down*] is a love story, a story rather of discovery, on another level lots of things were going on in the world during the 30s outside of Ireland, in which very little was going on" (qtd. in Emery 80).

"Before the invention of the camera": Representing Women

Joyce, Beckett and Flann O'Brien put women aside. Irish writing on women puts one in mind of paintings and drawings of horses (galloping or still) before the invention of the camera. (Higgins; qtd. in Beja 167)

By way of conclusion, what I would like to propose here is that Pinter's political interpretation of the novel, although perfectly valid, pushes itself forward to the detriment of other possible interpretations, most notably the more personal—but equally political—story of Imogen and her unborn child. In possibly the most perceptive and sensitive review of the film, A. O. Scott begins by quoting Otto's abstruse comment made during the drunken debauch in Dublin: "It was a German who discovered parthenogenesis in bees" (screenplay 603). As Scott writes: "I have not corroborated this assertion—to be perfectly honest, I'm not altogether sure what it means—but it is one of the many tantalizing non sequiturs uttered in the course of [the film]." Scott then goes on to quote Paul Schrader (who directed Pinter's adaptation of *The Comfort of Strangers*): "'Pinter's characters are always saying one thing and meaning something slightly different,' and that remark about the bees would seem to be a case in point" (Scott n.p.).

It is worth noting that while Otto's strange comment about bees might seem typically Pinteresque, once again it is lifted verbatim from the original novel (Higgins, *LGD* 117). What is the purpose of this gnomic comment? Is it entirely meaningless or does it actually gesture towards other semantic possibilities? Parthenogenesis—from the Greek "parthenos" ("virgin") and "genesis" ("creation")—"is an asexual form of reproduction found in females where growth and development of embryos or seeds occurs without fertilization by males. The offspring produced by parthenogenesis almost always are female in species" ("Parthenogenesis" n.p.). This seems to tie in to the ending of the novel, where Imogen is left pregnant by Otto: "She looked down in horror at her stomach. That had put the lid on it. In a little while she climbed slowly out of the bath, holding her burden with one hand" (*LGD* 230). Consequently, she begins to drink excessively and the unborn child—a daughter—is miscarried: "I hadn't killed it because it had already ceased to move, it was already without life, and I not knowing whether it was dead or not within me" (*LGD* 232). Afterwards, Imogen tells her sisters "a cock and bull story to the effect that I had German measles, a rash on unspecified parts of me" (*LGD* 233).

None of this appears in the screenplay/film, and this is undoubtedly the greatest alteration to the original novel. Instead, as Linda

Renton notes, "Pinter creates an intense loss by intercutting images of the sisters' golden childhood. [. . .] The screenplay ends, as it began, with the sense of loss as, alone in the wintry present, Imogen contemplates the death of Helen, the lost Otto and those eternally lost summers" (Renton 32–33). All in all though, Pinter's stripped-down version is more outward looking, and emphasizes its anti-fascist credentials. However, it seems to me that something else is lost in this particular act of transposition.

At the end of novel in 1938, Ireland is not only closed off to the outside world but it is also closing down on the inside as well. Between Imogen's affair with Otto in 1932 and her subsequent decline in 1938, the very role of women in Ireland has changed dramatically with the introduction of de Valera's 1937 constitution. Formally inscribed in Article 41.2 of this sectarian constitution is the Catholic, nationalist ideal of the perfect family, a microcosm of the State where the role of woman is entirely defined in terms of her "duties in the home" (Bunreacht Na hÉireann 138). In this context, Otto's abandonment and Imogen's abortion take on a greater allegorical weight, mournfully reflected in Imogen's final thoughts: "Hide away here, let the days pass and hope that things will change" (*LGD* 253).

Throughout *Langrishe, Go Down*, Aidan Higgins is as much concerned with memory as he is with history. As Imogen muses, "The memory of things—are they better than the things themselves?" (*LGD* 67). For Imogen, the answer is an emphatic "yes," as she re-edits her memories in the cinema of her imagination. In this regard, film, not literature, remains the dominant ontological metaphor in this most cinematic of novels.

Works Cited

Bair, Deirdre. *Samuel Beckett: A Biography*. London: Jonathan Cape, 1978.

Baneham, Sam. "Aidan Higgins: A Political Dimension." *Review of Contemporary Fiction*: Special issue on William Eastlake / Aidan Higgins 3.1 (Spring 1983): 168–74.

Beckett, Samuel. *Film*. Dir. Alan Schneider. 1965. YouTube Web Video. 4 August 2008. <http://ie.youtube.com/watch?v=5keZfirB8gE>.

Beja, Morris. "Felons of Our Selves: The Fiction of Aidan Higgins." *Irish University Review* 3.2 (Autumn 1973): 163–178.

Billington, Michael. *Harold Pinter*. London: Faber & Faber, 2007.

Bunreacht Na hÉireann/Constitution of Ireland. 1937. Dublin: Government Publications Office, 1980.

Buñuel, Luis, dir. *Un Chien Andalou*. 1929. YouTube Web Video. 4 August 2008. <http://ie.youtube.com/watch?v=5cKVZ6pkeEk>.

Clarke, Donald, dir. *Pitch 'n' Putt with Joyce 'n' Beckett*. 2001. YouTube Web Video. 4 August 2008. <http://ie.youtube.com/watch?v=p856CfM64w8>.

D'Angelo, Mike. Review of *Langrishe, Go Down*. *Time Out* (New York) 18–25 July 2002: 103.

Dargis, Manohla. "There's little worth digging up in the recently exhumed *Langrishe, Go Down*." *L.A. Times* 18 July 2003. Web. 4 August 2008.

Ebert, Roger. Review of *Cries and Whispers*. *Chicago Sun-Times* 12 February 1973. Web. 4 August 2008.

Eliot, T. S. "T. S. Eliot reading *The Waste Land*." YouTube Web Video. 4 August 2008. <http://ie.youtube.com/watch?v=3tqK5zQlCDQ>.

Ellmann, Richard. *James Joyce*. Oxford: Oxford University Press, 1982.

Emery, Jack. "Just a Simple Little Love Story?" Interviews with Harold Pinter, Judi Dench, and David Jones. *Radio Times* September

1978: 80-83. Rpt. *The Unofficial Chronology of Dame Judi Dench's Career* 26 November 2006. Web. 4 August 2008.

Fox, Ken. Review of *Langrishe, Go Down*. *TV Guide* 2002. Web. 24 June 2008.

Gale, Steven H. *Sharp Cut: Harold Pinter's Screenplays and the Artistic Process*. Lexington, KY: 2003.

Garfitt, Roger. "Constants in Contemporary Irish Fiction." *Two Decades of Irish Writing*. Ed. Douglas Dunn. Cheadle: Carcanet, 1975. 207-241.

Higgins, Aidan. *Donkey's Years* (1995); *Dog Days* (1998); *The Whole Hog* (2000). Rpt. *A Bestiary: An Autobiography*. Champaign, IL: Dalkey Archive Press, 2004.

—. Introduction. Samuel Beckett: *Photographs by John Minihan*. London: Secker & Warburg, 1995. 1-21.

—. "Killachter Meadow." *Felo de Se*. London: John Calder, 1960. Rpt. "North Salt Holdings." *Flotsam & Jetsam*. London: Minerva, 1997. 79-100.

—. *Langrishe, Go Down*. 1966. London: Paladin, 1987.

—. "*Sommerspiele*, Munich, 1972." *Ronda Gorge & Other Precipices: Travel Writing 1956-1989*. London: Secker & Warburg, 1989. 93-105.

Holden, Stephen. Review of *Langrishe, Go Down*. *New York Times* 14 July 2002. Web. 4 August 2008.

Imhof, Rüdiger, and Jürgen Kamm. "Coming to Grips with Aidan Higgins: 'Killachter Meadow'—An Analysis." *Études Irlandaises* 9 (December 1984): 145-160.

Joyce, James. "James Joyce 'Anna Livia Plurabelle' Poem Animation Movie." YouTube Web Video. 4 August 2008. <http://ie.youtube.com/watch?v=TUS7HgyouSI>.

Langrishe, Go Down. Screenplay by Harold Pinter. Dir. David Jones. Perf. Judi Dench, Jeremy Irons, and Annette Crosbie. BBC2 Play of the Week, 1978.

Mahon, Derek. "We Shift About: The Blithely Subversive Aidan Higgins." *Times Literary Supplement* 9 May 2007: 12.

Murphy, Neil. "Aidan Higgins: The Fragility of Form." *Irish Fiction and Postmodern Doubt: An Analysis of the Epistemological Crisis in Modern Irish Fiction.* Lewiston, NY: Edwin Mellen Press, 2004. 37–101.

"Parthenogenesis." Wikipedia, n.d. Web. 5 November 2009.

Pinter, Harold. *Langrishe, Go Down* screenplay (1987). *Collected Screenplays 1.* London: Faber, 2000. 561–660.

—. "Mac." 1966. *Various Voices: Prose, Poetry, Politics 1948–1998.* London: Faber & Faber, 1998. 26–33.

Renton, Linda. *Pinter and the Object of Desire: An Approach through the Screenplays.* Oxford: Legenda, 2002.

Roche, Anthony. "Pinter and Ireland." *The Cambridge Companion to Harold Pinter.* Ed. Peter Raby. Cambridge: Cambridge University Press, 2001. 175–191.

Sarris, Andrew. "A Dench-Irons Flashback." Review of *Langrishe, Go Down. New York Observer* 28 July 2002. Web. 4 August 2008.

Scott, A. O. "A Foolish Affair in a Frustrated Life." Review of *Langrishe, Go Down. New York Times* 17 July 2002. Web. 4 August 2008.

Skelton, Robin. "Aidan Higgins and the Total Book." *Mosaic* 19 (1976): 27–37. Rpt. *Celtic Contraries.* New York: Syracuse University Press, 1990. 211–223.

Sterritt, David. Review of *Langrishe, Go Down. Christian Science Monitor* 19 July 2002. Web. 4 August 2008.

Welles, Orson, dir. *The Lady from Shanghai.* Columbia Pictures / Mercury Productions, 1947. Film.

Welles, Orson, and William Vance, dir. *The Hearts of Age.* 1934. YouTube Web Video. 4 August 2008. <http://ie.youtube.com/watch?v=pXKIMag5hHE>.

Winter, Jessica. "Vive L'amour." Review of *Langrishe, Go Down*. *Village Voice* 16 July 2002. Web. 4 August 2008.

Yeats, W. B. "Yeats reads from 'Coole Park and Ballylee,' 1931." YouTube Web Video. 4 August 2008. <http://ie.youtube.com/watch?v=-Tyc5DfK9_o>.

NOTES

1. By "contrapuntal viewpoints" I mean the way in which the author-narrator sometimes comments on—and often contradicts—what his characters are doing, saying or thinking. For example, in "Killachter Meadow" (from *Felo de Se*, 1960), the ur-text template for *Langrishe, Go Down*, we get the following parenthetical intrusion: "Swept towards it by an unbearable wind, courage and endurance (she never had either) ceased to matter" (100). Something similar occurs in *Langrishe, Go Down*: "Slow and shallow (her life depended on it) she breathed in the faint scent of herself, her clothes: a fading odour of mountain fern" (13). As Neil Murphy has argued, "The stories of *Felo de Se* [Latin for "felon of oneself," an archaic legal term for suicide] expose the barren condition of passivity by presenting surreal, linguistic instances within which the perceptive eye of their creator carries more import than that of the creations themselves" (41). This narrative flickering between *mimesis* (showing rather than telling) and *diegesis* (telling instead of showing) is fairly common in self-conscious, metafictional texts such as Beckett's *Murphy* (1938) or Flann O'Brien's *At Swim-Two-Birds* (1939). However, this contrapuntal viewpoint also features in certain types of European cinema as well, such as the director's omniscient voiceover in the British version of *The Third Man* (dir. Carol Reed, 1949) or the director's parenthetical intrusions in *Bande à Part* (dir. Jean-Luc Godard, 1964).

2. In *The Whole Hog* Higgins presents a list of the films that "seemed to reveal [to him] something of that strange threatening life, the life that other people led": "*Un Chien Andalou* [dir. Luis Buñuel, 1929], *Extase* [dir. Gustav Machatý, 1933], *Blood and Sand* [dir. Rouben Mamoulian, 1941], *Bahama Passage* [dir. Edward H. Griffith, 1941], *The Brothers* [dir. David MacDonald, 1947], *The Lady from Shanghai* [dir. Orson Welles, 1947], *The Outcast of the Islands* [dir. Carol Reed, 1952], *Knife in the Water* [dir. Roman Polanski, 1962]" (522). Interestingly, Higgins's favorite star, Rita Hayworth, stars in two of these films, the bullfighting melodrama *Blood and Sand* and the baroque *film noir* classic *The Lady from Shanghai*. As Higgins wrote of *Blood and Sand:*

> Tyrone Power had to swim across a river and in the blue moonlight of day-for-night photography fight a bull, so that he could ascend to the castle where Rita slept, and climb up the side of the creeper and enter, to find her preparing for bed, her wide mouth decorated with a slash of lipstick like blood, as if she were a vampire, which was all extremely exciting and mysterious when I saw it at the age of fourteen at the Savoy Cinema in Dublin. (*The Whole Hog* 671)

Throughout his memoirs, Higgins refers to Orson Welles—and especially *Citizen Kane*—with obvious affection and awe (e.g. *Dog Days* 356; *The Whole Hog* 726). However, in the short chapter he gives over to a discussion of *The Lady from Shanghai*—tellingly entitled "The Shapely Flanks of Rita Hayworth"—Higgins makes no mention of the fact that Welles's screenplay was adapted from the Sherwood King novel *If I Die Before I Wake* (*The Whole Hog* 527–29). Instead, his analysis focuses almost exclusively on the off-screen/on-screen relationship between the two stars, Welles and

Hayworth, who divorced shortly after the film was completed. This cineaste approach epitomizes Higgins's love of the cinema as a vehicle for desire. As Michael "Black Irish" O'Hara (Welles) says of Elsa Bannister (Hayworth) in the opening voiceover of *The Lady from Shanghai*: "If I'd known where it would end, I'd have never let anything start, if I'd been in my right mind, that is. But once I'd seen her, once I'd seen her, I was not in my right mind for quite some time . . ."

3. Jeremy Irons first made his name as a screen presence in the 1981 Pinter adaptation of *The French Lieutenant's Woman*, while Judi Dench—although well established on the British stage—did not become a fully-fledged movie star until her Oscar-nominated role as Queen Victoria in *Mrs Brown* (dir. John Madden, 1997). Dench later won an Oscar for her supporting role as Queen Elizabeth in *Shakespeare in Love* (dir. John Madden, 1998), while Irons won the Oscar for Best Actor in 1991 playing Claus von Bülow in Barbet Schroeder's *Reversal of Fortune*. As A. O. Scott has argued, "The chief fascination of *Langrishe, Go Down* [. . .] is that Otto and Imogen are played by Jeremy Irons and Judi Dench, who were great English actors long before they came to personify Great English Acting" (n.p.).

4. A. O. Scott argues that Jeremy Irons "has done some of his best acting in Continental European accents," citing his turns as "a deracinated Danish socialite in *Reversal of Fortune* and a migrant Polish carpenter in Jerzy Skolimowski's *Moonlighting* [1982]." As Scott concludes, "His deep Englishness—the glum stoicism of his face, the stiff diffidence of his posture—works best when it seems put on, revealing what a sly comedian he can be" (n.p.).

5. Very few reviewers mentioned the textured use of color in the film. Manohla Dargis wrote that: "Unearthing even the roughest gems serves a programming purpose, but in this case it has also led to a theatrical release of a movie that looks like a muddy second-

generation Xerox and contains all the emotional and intellectual appeal of cold tea and soggy toast" (n.p). Ken Fox was more sympathetic: "And while time and the transfer process has not been kind to the quality of the print, the washed-out palette adds a suitably gloomy patina to the general aura of decay" (n.p.).

6. Throughout Higgins's autobiographies, he frequently describes himself and others in terms of characters from classic movies, e.g. Maureen O'Hara and Robert Young in *Sitting Pretty* [dir. Walter Lang, 1948] or Deborah Kerr and Robert Donat in *Perfect Strangers* [dir. Alexander Korda, 1945] (*Dog Days* 274); Clarke Gable and Claudette Colbert *It Happened One Night* [dir. Frank Capra, 1934] or Pierre Batchef in *Un Chien Andalou* [1929] and Dita Parlo in *L'Atalante* [dir. Jean Vigo, 1934] (*Dog Days* 310–11).

7. Karl Freund worked as director of photography on over a hundred films, including *The Last Laugh* (dir. F. W. Murnau, 1927) and *Metropolis* (dir. Fritz Lang, 1928). He later won the Oscar for Best Cinematography for his work on *The Good Earth*.

Aidan Higgins

PATRICK O'NEILL

Programmatically entitled *Felo de Se* (1960), Aidan Higgins's first published volume contains some of his best and most characteristic writing and introduces almost all of the themes that will dominate his later work. The collection of six stories is prefaced by an epigraph from the Austrian poet Hugo von Hofmannsthal's unfinished novel *Andreas*: "Wenn die Sonne tief, leben wir mehr in unserem Schatten als in uns selbst" (7)—"When the sun is low we live more in our shadow than in ourselves." The epigraph, like the title, prefigures the fascination with self-estrangement and the shadow side of human nature that informs not only each of these stories but each of the later works as well.

"Killachter Meadow," the opening story, focuses on the failed life and successful death of Emily Norton Kervick, whose remains are committed to the grave in the opening sentence, "one cold day in March of 1927" (9). Emily, a misfit all her life, comes into her own on her deathbed: "It did not seem that she had died and escaped them; on the contrary, dead, she had come to stay" (10). Emily is the eldest of four aging sisters, "unprepossessing and unmarriageable" (11), who inhabit an increasingly dilapidated Irish country house in Higgins's native Kildare—and who will reappear (with a new surname) as the central characters in his next work, *Langrishe, Go Down* (1966). Each of the sisters inhabits her own hermetically sealed universe; on the rare occasions when they attempted to establish contact with each other "each had to rise to the surface in order to say what they had to say, after which they sank again to their respective depths" (13). Emily's life is one of "constant and virtually unrelieved embarrassment" (15). Outwardly she is a comically awkward figure, inviting ridicule, inwardly she "had run out of enthusiasms early on in life, and in the halls of her spirit, so to speak, toadstools grew" (15). Her sister Helen, herself a recluse whose favorite reading is Burton's *Anatomy of Melancholy*, writes of her on one occasion: "The pattern of a final retreat runs through her like a grain in rough delf" (19). Emily, a non-swimmer, finds her main solace alternately in overeating and in floating naked in the river, one foot cautiously maintaining contact with the bottom. One cold March day—not entirely surprisingly, perhaps—the trailing foot fails to find any further contact, and Emily, a sadly grotesque Ophelia, blue with the cold, floats "weirwards towards extinction and forgetting" (30f.).

"Killachter Meadow" strikes that characteristic note of alienation and even desperation that echoes through the rest of *Felo de Se* and Higgins's entire subsequent output. Sevi Klein, for example, in the story "Lebensraum," German, thirty-nine years of age, with a "small crucified face" (36) and a highly promiscuous nature, travels from Cologne to London in 1947, where she strikes up a liaison with "a Mr. Michael Alpin, late of Dublin, the doubtful product of Jesuit casuistry and the Law School" (35), twelve years her junior, and about whom everything "suggested furtive through arrested flight" (36). Their cohabitation is superficial: "He did not attempt to touch her, for there were depths into which he did not care to penetrate" (38). Sevi is a traveler, "had travelled all her life and would probably continue to do so until the day of her death" (39), and, in a statement which applies to all of Higgins's fiction, "the traveller is perpetually in the wrong context" (39). She is beyond reach, both for Alpin and for herself as well, victim as she is of a profound "disgust with the Self" (*Asylum and Other Stories* 43). One day, without any particular reason, she simply disappears as quietly as she had once appeared, walking out of sight along an Irish beach, the advancing tide obliterating any trace of her onetime presence. She has a counterpart in Ellen Rossa-Stowe, "of Irish extraction, but licentious" (154), in the story "Tower and Angels." Ellen "kissed as though determined to be lost: a touch bitter as quassia" (154), and "matching her bitter kiss was an embrace which had a wild recoiling quality of the bolting horse biting on its snaffle" (155).

The long centerpiece of the collection, "Asylum," more a study for a novel than a short story, balances the ambiguous rise of one man against the ambiguous fall of another. Eddie Brazill endures the average vicissitudes of a young and impoverished member of the rural Irish lower classes: menial work in Ireland, followed by menial work of various kinds in England, followed by near total destitution. "Alone and miserable beyond words, Brazill walked out along a high parapet of hunger" (74), a prey to hallucinations and sudden irrepressible bouts of unmotivated laughter. His luck turns when he accidentally runs into Ben Boucher, a well educated alcoholic who employs Brazill as a golfing companion in an attempt to cure his addiction. As Boucher's mind deteriorates with increasing rapidity Brazill is correspondingly free to explore the increasingly available charms of a music hall actress whose person he had once thought entirely unattainable. Each pursues his own happiness—or, at any rate, asylum—success in Brazill's case, failure in the case of Boucher, for whom "the established failure who in his rashness or wisdom has put himself outside the beneficial scheme of things—he is the happy man" (113). Both achieve their goal, and simultaneously: as Brazill finally succeeds in climbing into bed with the object of his desire, Mr. Boucher, quite mad, is busily setting fire to the curtains of his hotel room and flinging pieces of furniture out of the windows. The hastily summoned Brazill can muster only one partly understood thought, a confused reflection on the disorder that lurks quietly just beyond the edges of all civilized discourse: "He has gone to the madhouse, I have come from the poor home" (129).

Willie Bausch, the central character of "Winter Offensive," and an appalling character at that, is the first of a line of ruthless predators running through Higgins's fiction. Bausch is a grotesque straight out of a George Grosz drawing: "his features squeezed themselves together in a veritable snout, on each side of which were arranged little bloodshot eyes" (131). A self-made man about town in the Berlin of the thirties, he is the epitome of a totally ruthless capitalism allied with an equally ruthless militarism, and his compulsive love-making—for preference with married women—is only one further outlet for his insatiable aggression: "Rolling on his femur as if adjusting his aim, he bore down, heavy and inflexible, until safely embedded in still-living subject female flesh" (137). "Nightfall on Cape Piscator," the final story of *Felo de Se*, strikes quite a different note, for Mr. Vaschel, its central figure, unlike many of the characters in this collection, is a rather ordinary sort of man, a mild-mannered and mildly eccentric dealer in antiques, whose life is admittedly blighted by the obesity of his wife, but who seems on first acquaintance to have very little in common with the tortured borderline worlds of the Sevi Kleins and Ellen Rossa-Stowes. Ordinariness is no guarantee of contentment or safety, however. On a holiday at the seaside Mr. Vaschel undergoes a revelatory experience—reminiscent of that of Aschenbach in Thomas Mann's *Death in Venice*—and is led by the contemplation of a decomposing shark on the beach to intuit "the impossible extent of his own decay" (178). "Mr. Vaschel stood . . . in the light of the open door, his shadows enormous behind him" (185). Recurring dreams of sexual orgies drive him to the bed of an alluring colored servant girl, where his unexpected success completely surprises him—and later dissolves into bitter disappointment. "Looking for wild oats then, had he found garbage? He felt nothing" (190f.). Success can sometimes be indistinguishable from failure: as he furtively returns to his own room "the jackasses let loose their atrocious bray, derisive and as though pre-arranged" (191).

The emphasis in *Felo de Se* is far less on what happens than on the kind of character who causes or allows such happenings to occur. Almost all of the characters verge in one way or another on the grotesque, unaccommodated men (and women) out of kilter with the comfortable everyday world of their more fortunate, less threatened fellows. Typically they emerge abruptly out of nowhere, are subjected to a portrait painter's penetrating scrutiny, and disappear again equally abruptly into the darkness from which they came. The technique is not unlike that attributed to the painter Irwin Pastern in "Tower and Angels": "He first laid down a foundation of black and out of this primeval bog, in a month or two of excavating, a misted scene at last emerged—grey, bled off, revolving slowly within the frame, colourless as a dream, an image of the caul itself, a thin piping out of utmost darkness" (158). There is an edge of extremity and self-destructiveness to almost all the inhabitants of this fictional world, these "felons of themselves" whose lives are nothing more than an intolerable burden to them. The tone is occasionally not too far from the hysterical, and there are definite stylistic echoes of Beckett in places, but nonetheless Higgins emerges in this collection with a clearly individual and authoritative voice and the occasional flash of brilliance.

Langrishe, Go Down, his first longer text, situates itself firmly in the tradition of the Irish Big House novel. However, for Higgins, the

Big House theme is clearly not just a realist portrayal of the decline of a passing age of grace, beauty and culture—though it certainly *is* that—but also a symbol of the inevitable dissolution of all order, all form. The narrative is concerned in the first place with the love affair of Imogen Langrishe, at thirty-nine the youngest daughter of a once flourishing, now genteelly decayed family of Kildare landed gentry, and a ruthless German graduate student at Trinity College, Dublin, one Otto Beck. Beck—modeled on the very minor character Klaefisch in "Killachter Meadow" and to some extent Bausch in "Winter Offensive"—is for Imogen "an outlandish, a legendary figure" (91), another manifestation, in fact, of the outsider figure so frequently encountered in *Felo de Se*, and his maleficent influence is certainly a contributory factor of some importance in the decline of the Langrishes. But it does not instigate it. That process has begun long before Otto Beck puts in an appearance on the scene. He is a symptom, not the illness.

The narrative opens with Helen Langrishe, the middle sister of three aging spinsters (a fourth sister, Emily, the eldest, had already died several years before, in 1929), fighting off nausea as she returns from Dublin by bus to the ironically named Springfield House in County Kildare. Against the gathering darkness outside the windows "a white face that never seemed to turn away was watching her in the glass," until in the growing "stench of perspiring and unwashed bodies" and the "poisons breathed out by two-score labouring lungs" the windows cloud over, "drops of moisture began to condense, wet lanes of it trickled down; the face broke up and vanished" (9). Here the fatal blend of qualities that categorize the Langrishes is crystallized: introspective self-fascination, distaste for the great unwashed, inability to survive. It is 1937, and in the "world of crush and sunder" (12) the Italians are arming, Madrid has just been bombed again—pointlessly, from a military point of view—by insurgent artillery, and the Dublin welder who recently killed his girl friend is pleading insanity. "Brief life, she thought, brief life, breathed on for a while, allowed to live, then blotted out" (16).

Springfield House, once a symbol of grandeur, is overrun with weeds and brambles, the countryside around it is filled with ruins, graveyards, creeping bogs, and the equalizing wind that blows coldly and impartially over all, the living and the dead alike (36). Springfield is rooted in the past, in the romance of history, Swift and his Vanessa, Grattan and Speaker Connolly and Buck Whaley. Helen, "the recluse" (100), at one point intends to write a history of the whole area, but she is unable to bring any coherence to her scattered notes. "In the course of years the evidence itself was disappearing back into the ground, like the headstones in the graveyard. The landscape, so indifferent to its history, the bloody wars waged upon it and for it, still turned its back upon the living" (39). The family is no more capable of dealing with the present than is the house. The Langrishes are characterized by a pervasive vagueness, an inefficiency, a will to dissolution: Major Langrishe, weak and ineffectual, lets the practical affairs of the estate go to rack and ruin in his last years while he devotes himself to his increasingly nebulous researches (51); Helen has lived in her country village all her life but has no idea what the timetable or the route of the local bus may be (16), cannot remember where the family plot is in the cemetery (35); her two sisters blandly refuse to face the brutal reality she brings from her discussion with the lawyers in Dublin that "the old impossible life was ending" (18); Imogen "living in a daze" (58) until she meets Beck, afterwards increasingly finding solace in alcohol, "slurring her words, swallowing vowels, whole sentences trailing off into silence" (25). Otto Beck, scholar and poacher, hunter, trapper, fisherman, smoking his collection of pipes in strict rotation (85), and prepared to take ruthless advantage of any weakness, is characterized on the other hand precisely by sharpness, decisiveness, accuracy, relentless and precise marshalling of endless facts and figures.

Beck, like Sevi Klein, is a traveler, physically and intellectually; the sisters have rarely moved beyond the walls of the estate. Imogen is very soon fascinated with his otherness. Otto is an exotic, a taste of the outside world of adventure and romance that she has never known. Otto has strong and confident opinions on a wide variety of subjects; for example, "He talked of 'culturally inferior nations' and of 'culturally insignificant' individuals" (166). He "blandly" cuts a wasp in two with a pair of nail scissors: "Very hard to resist the temptation not to stamp on certain shapes, put an end to them" (200). He has little time for "disorganised minds" (167) and "stale old tales no one believes in any longer, full of morals and impossible virtues" (167), such as Imogen's pious notions about the habits of Ireland's medieval saints (170). Otto, in short, like Willy Bausch, is a natural predator—"A hawk; *Habicht*, in suspended motion, hovering" (170)—while Imogen is equally one stamped by nature as a prey. "In life, Otto said, man has [the] choice in life of being either hammer or anvil, as the divine Goethe would have it" (181). Woman, presumably, has no such choice: Imogen, indeed, is consistently associated with the small animals that Otto kills for sport or for the stewpot.

Otto, amateur anthropologist, studies Irish history and its peculiarities, "going on about place-names and how they changed, how new ones were formed from corruptions of the old names" (175). Imogen, only half-listening to all of it, *is* one of those peculiarities. Predictably, she sets out to tame him; predictably, she fails. Imogen is a natural victim, and for Otto she eventually becomes a mere object of contempt, infuriating in her vulnerability, like "some soft spineless insect that's been trodden on" (227). Imogen, "his slave and doormat" (211), knows what the liaison with Otto, who already has a son somewhere else as the result of another such affair, is likely to do to her, in spite of her occasional references to marriage. "All fairy tales end in violence" (215), says Otto, who sees a "cruelty . . . at the root of things" (215) and is indeed about to leave her for a younger competitor for his favors. All the predictable stages are gone through, rage, jealousy, despair, a half-hearted murder attempt on her part, desertion by Otto, a stillborn child. But in the end, and this is typical of the tone of the novel, she is essentially beyond caring, unsurprised. "We are like figures come loose out of a frieze" (239).

In one sense the main character in *Langrishe* is disintegration itself, an entropic degeneration: Part One concentrates on the accelerating decay of Springfield House and its owner, Major Langrishe; Part Two focuses on Imogen's ill-starred affair; Part Three centers on the funeral of Helen. At Helen's funeral Imogen looks into the grave, and "it dropped away before my eyes until the pit was bottomless and all I could see was this dark awful hole in the earth opening up and out of the darkness down there a dank wind blowing" (255). Soon the earth "was subsidizing into place once more, and nothing would ever change again" (260).

Langrishe is a tale of the passing of an era. Their affair takes place in the Ireland of 1932: "They lay in bed together" in Imogen's bedroom in Springfield House "in a high-ceilinged room facing south, admiring the fires that burned on the hills as though they would go on burning there forever, celebrating the Eucharistic Congress" (184). The fires would not burn forever, even in Ireland. Even in Ireland the stability of the old order was rapidly disintegrating, the trees of Springfield House were being cleared and sold for firewood, and on the not too distant European horizon new forces were gathering their strength and would soon be on the march. "The teeth of the dogs in the side of the hare, pulling it apart" (190). Otto Beck, a student of Husserl and Heidegger, ostensibly rejects Hitler and Nazism but is clearly associated by the narrative voice with the power and ruthlessness of Nazism, even to the grotesque touch of his ferret, which rejoices in the name of Nazi. Beck uses Nazi on his rabbit-poaching forays on the crumbling Langrishe estate, forays which are soon extended to the youngest daughter of the house, and Higgins impressively extends the range of reference of the novel by suggestively fusing the collapse of the Irish Big House and the fall of Austria in 1938. The second-last chapter, immediately after the death of Helen, is devoted to the Anschluss and the "final downfall of Austria" (262), as the "small portion of what remains of the mighty Empire of the Habsburgs" falls to the Nazi invaders (262). Beck, ironically, is working on a graduate thesis on the literary relations of Ireland and Germany: the influence of Ossian, and through him the Gaelic world, on Goethe and the Grimms (213).

The account of the ill-fated romance occupies by far the greater part of the book, but it is framed by an opening section and a closing section which together serve to provide it with a wider interpretive context. The opening section takes place in 1937, the central section in 1932, and the conclusion in 1938. The entire story of the love affair, that is to say, is an extended narrative flashback, serving, as is the nature of flashbacks, to explain the narrative present of the opening section, which continues implacably on in the final section as if nothing had intervened between the action described as belonging to 1937 and that ascribed to 1938. Realistically, of course, on the level of the story that is told, that is exactly the situation. In terms of the narrative discourse, *how* that story is told, however, the reader's perception of the narrated events of

1938 is inevitably very different in quality from his or her perception of the narrated events of 1937. As we read the final pages of
the novel, in other words, the love affair is in one sense very keenly
in the forefront of our mind; in another sense it is as if it had never
happened at all. This suggestion of the immutability and indifference of things, the essential existential irrelevance of human beings and their concerns, is repeated throughout the narrative in
the attitudes of the Langrishe sisters. "All was as it had always been,
variations apart (the passing of her parents, the death of Emily), in
the immutable order of events" (23), Helen typically reflects. Imogen muses in similarly fatalistic tones: "the trees fall, the palings are
sold, nothing changes, the house stands; we depart" (58).

Langrishe, to a much greater extent than *Felo de Se*, is characterized by a wide variety of narrative styles, omniscient narration
continually alternating with reported monologue and narrated
monologue, focalization continually shifting. Part One is focalized
largely through Helen Langrishe, Part Two largely through a more
or less objective narrator, though colored by Imogen's altitudes,
Part Three very clearly through Imogen herself. The telling phrase
of realist description is still in evidence—"the inner calves of their
legs mottled brown, like burns on pancakes" (20)—but there is a
new emphasis on modernist symbologies: Imogen, for example, "a
sort of specimen of a bygone world" (92), is consistently associated
with water imagery, Otto, the predator, "eyes blazing" (94), with
fire. In *Felo de Se* Higgins had established himself as a writer of
undeniable authority, in *Langrishe* his abilities as a self-consciously
experimental writer become much more apparent. In the later
novels this movement towards narrative experimentation becomes
even more marked.

Subtitled "Diary (1956–60)," Higgins's next book, *Images of Africa* (1971), is a documentary evocation of the different faces of

South Africa (where Higgins spent those four years). The text, only seventy pages long, beginning with "the plunge over the equator" (11) and ending with the eventual return to "grey Tilbury" (71), is made up of a series of short, numbered sections—the "images" of the title—each focusing on a single character, event, scene, or action. The collection consequently has something of the evocative character of a photograph album, each of the constituent sections reflecting shrewd powers of both observation and presentation. The technique is in some ways a practice run for *Balcony of Europe* (1972), Higgins's lengthiest work to date. Its central narrative thread, as in *Langrishe*, concerns a relatively unhappy love affair. The protagonist this time is the first-person narrator, Dan Ruttle, an Irish painter in his mid-forties, and his narrative focuses on his brief affair in an Andalusian coastal town with the sultry Charlotte Bayless, fresh "from the dark plains of American sexual experience where the bison still roam" (77).

The narrative is divided this time into five parts, but again centered on a long flashback in a manner reminiscent of *Langrishe*. The centrality of this analeptic narrative is underlined by the proportions: the long central section of roughly 150 pages is symmetrically flanked by four parts which are each roughly half that length. Part I opens in Autumn 1961 in Dun Laoghaire, introduces Ruttle's family, once well-to-do country gentry but now much reduced, his nagging mother and weak father, and focuses on the deaths first of a much admired younger cousin and then on that of his mother, following which Ruttle and his wife Olivia leave to visit some acquaintances in the south of Spain. Part II is set eighteen months later in Spring 1963 in Andalusia and portrays the end of his affair with Charlotte (who is married). Part III reverts to Winter 1962 in Spain, and recounts the early stages of the affair, while Parts IV (Summer 1963, Andalusia) and V ("Autumn 1963 and after," by which time Ruttle and his wife, uneasily reconciled, are back in Ireland again) continue the chronology interrupted by the central part.

The affair itself is not at all unusual, any more than it was in *Langrishe*: for Charlotte, whose physical appetite is insatiable, it is just one of a continuing series of more or less casual marital infidelities; for Ruttle it is of considerably more importance, but in the end he too gets over it relatively quickly and apparently without any very major trauma. "In five years it would mean less, in ten, less again. In twenty years it would be forgotten" (444). Much indeed, as Imogen Langrishe gets over her affair. And just as the love affair in *Langrishe* is only one symptom of a potentially fatal disease rather than the disease itself, so too in *Balcony of Europe*, as the title might suggest, the role of the central affair is essentially symptomatic. The pervasive tone of both novels, in short (and indeed at least implicitly of *Felo de Se* as well) is essentially threnodic, a lament for the crumbling of order—"the Jesuit fiction of the world's order and essential goodness" (43)—and the irreversible encroachments of entropy. But there are clear differences in the way in which this central theme is handled in the later novel.

Balcony begins with two pages of epigraphs and ends with a further four pages of "Rejected Epigraphs," which between them effectively conjure up both the pervasively elegiac, disillusioned tone of the narrative and a concurrent overt fascination with what one might call a relativizing and self-reflecting intertextuality. One epigraph, for example, (allegedly) quotes, in translation, a Prado catalogue description of Hieronymus Bosch's painting "the Garden of Delights": "It represents sensuality and lubricity behind which runs [sic] so many mortals that resemble beasts" (8). The ostensible catalogue is further quoted (in Spanish) as interpreting the title of Bosch's painting as an "ironic title referring to the world," supported by a (quoted) quotation (again in Spanish) from the seventeenth-century poet Quevedo that "Bosch did not paint pictures as strange as those that I have seen" and a further quotation from Jeremiah 5.8 that "They were as fed horses in the morning: everyone neighed after his neighbour's wife" (8). *Balcony*, in other words, is not just a surprisingly old-fashioned and realistic story about the futility of earthly passions in a world where all is transient (though again it can certainly be read in that way on its most accessible level); it is also, and overtly, a highly modernist *text*, a way of presenting that world and a way of presenting its own discourse. "A picture of a picture by Magritte" (463), as one of the "rejected epigraphs" has it, quoting the poet Howard Nemerov writing on a picture by the painter Magritte, whose subject is the interrelationship of the painted reality and its (painted) representation.

The representation of the love affair of Ruttle and his Charlotte is on one level entirely realistic and realistically motivated; on another its essential fictivity is underlined even by the fact that it allegedly takes place in the town of "Nerka." The real Andalusian town which serves as a model for Nerka—and whose historic and spectacular promenade, long nicknamed the Balcony of Europe, gives the novel its title—is actually called Nerja, but this spelling occurs in the narrative only on one occasion, when the epitaph of the characters, the Spanish barman Miguel Lopez Rojas, is quoted from the tombstone in "Nerja cemetery" (459). The novel is also dedicated "to the memory of Miguel Lopez Rojas" (5), whose name thus serves as a link between the world of lived reality and the world of textual reality—as thus that of Brendan Behan in the last section of the narrative, as Ruttle moves homeward from the brandy of Nerka to the Guinness of Davy Byrne's.

Dan Ruttle is a painter, and all the members of the Anglo-American circle in which he moves in Andalusia are likewise

text (228)—giving the word a spurious "Russian" appearance. The foreign, the other, the extraordinary in all its manifestations is one of the central preoccupations of Higgins's Garden of Delights, and the affair with Charlotte is in one sense little more than a narrative string on which to hang a veritable gallery of grotesques in the manner of *Felo de Se*—though the somewhat portentous tone of the earlier work has given way to a tone rather of wry humor. In early 1963 Europe and the world briefly poised on the verge of nuclear war, and it is against this potentially apocalyptic background, à la Bosch, that the characters of *Balcony* are painted. "Anything is permissible and possible in a world in which no one any longer believes in anything," as one of them puts it (136): Baron Alex von Gerhar, for example, is—or at any rate claims to be—a completely unrepentant Nazi who holds that Hitler was a great man and his attempted annihilation of Jews a completely sane and defensible solution to the problems of Europe. The Baron spends his waking hours alternately drinking, boasting, and vomiting, "sickened," as Ruttle puts it, "by the brute world that we are smiling with" (115). God is far from in his heaven—"Our Father who art not in Heaven, hollow be thy name" (92)—and all is certainly not well with the world, held together only by "the dear normality of contingency, the healthy ingenuousness of custom" (163). For many of the characters in *Balcony* this is finally not enough—the self-obsessed Rosa Munsinger, for example, "anaesthetized to the world that was there in flagrant opposition to her way of looking at it" (173), the obstreperously virile Roger Amory, who "enjoyed life as a cannonball enjoys space, travelling to its aim blindly" (315), or Ruttle's (and Higgins's) fellow countryman Brendan Behan, suffering from "a kind of success that is indistinguishable from panic" (414). "As I grow older my hopes get less and less. Like rotting fruit, we rot down to a hard stone" (90), a saying attributed by the narrator to

Behan, becomes the ground bass of the narrative and its various characters, lost in the private worlds of their desperate imaginings, "crawling in and out of each other's beds like slugs" (232).

One of Higgins's most characteristic traits as a writer is his ostentatious use of various forms of what one might call cultural intertextuality, and *Balcony of Europe* is the most striking example of this. The narrator continually situates between his own narrated world in the context of other worlds, historical, geographical, and linguistic. "Mountains older than Marathon when the world was young, older than the first battles in Europe, Salamis, Plataea, older than Sparta or Jericho . . . River of unknown name, river older than Garavogue . . . A boulder bigger than the Split Rock from the ice age on the roadside near Easkey on Sligo Bay . . . The debris of the centuries" (356f.). Very obviously fascinated by the foreign, the other, the non-Irish, not-now, not-here, and very consciously anti-parochial, Higgins continually incorporates scraps of foreign languages—individual words, phrases, excerpts from poems and the like—in the fabric of each of his books, and here again *Balcony* leads the way. Irritatingly frequently these scraps are given quite incorrectly, it must be said—but to be irritated at this is perhaps to miss the main point, which is the essential *foreignness* of this extraneous matter in the body of the text. Travel—an overt metaphor for the interior journeys covered by his characters—obviously plays as important a role in the lives of his characters as it does in his own. *Balcony of Europe*, his most demonstratively international work, boasts a multiracial and multilingual cast of characters, Irish and Spanish settings, frequent use of Spanish, French, German and Irish phrases and tags (not to mention occasional scraps of Latin, Greek, Old English, Italian and various Slavic languages) and allegedly "rejected epigraphs" from Violette Leduc, Djuna Barnes, Husserl, Kafka, Yeats and Marcus Aurelius among several others. The final "rejected epigraph" is appropriately a quotation from H.A.L. Fisher's *History of Europe*: "Purity of race does not exist. Europe is a continent of energetic mongrels" (463).

Higgins's play with intertextuality in *Balcony* represented another interesting experiment in narrative presentation—the boldest one yet. For intertextuality in one sense, as the ultimate interrelatedness of all things, is clearly only another name for the calm of total entropy, the stillness of death. All of Europe is an "ancient bone-heap, where every grain of earth has passed through innumerable bodies" (101). The "underlying theme of the overlying earth" (59), so apparent in *Langrishe*, is equally overt in *Balcony of Europe*, which symptomatically opens with the death of Dan's mother and closes with Miguel's epitaph. In another sense, however, intertextuality is equally the answer to death, the negation of entropy, and its name is not only life but art as well, for to live is to order, and the most complex form of ordering known to the human animal is precisely art. "Art from the Bulls of Altamira to the Horrors of War has sought to limit the scope of what is beyond our capacity to order, and comes in the end to be a desperate attempt to disturb the equilibrium of the most harmless objects" (332), to establish an order, in other words, even if by necessity a fictive one, through imposing *our* order on a natural order completely impassive to our needs.

Scenes from a Receding Past (1977) which appeared five years after *Balcony*, recreates Dan Ruttle's childhood and adolescence in County Sligo and fills in the gaps in the story up to his meeting and marrying Olivia. The "scenes" of the title is an accurate description of the technique, which has much in common with that of the similarly titled *Images*. Thirty-seven brief chapters are arranged in two parts, the first taking us from the "Distant Figures" of the very young child's perception to "The End of Innocence" of the schoolboy, the second taking us from his days in secondary school to the relationship with Olivia and the miscarriage of their first child. The major stylistic innovation of *Scenes* in Higgins's work is its attempt in the first part to recreate the past through the eyes of the protagonist as he then was rather than as he later came to be, employing only the mental, emotional and expressive resources of the young child as it accumulates experience and develops in psychological complexity. The experiment is both interesting—developing the technique of the opening pages of *A Portrait of the Artist*—and risky. The negative aspect is that it is a difficult technique to sustain effectively, and the text can indeed occasionally tip over into preciousness, occasionally push the reader to the point of boredom or irritation. Its positive aspect is its nuanced ability to portray progressively the development of the protagonist's mind and character, seen from within rather than described from the outside.

There are few surprises in store for the seasoned reader of Higgins's work as regards the details of Dan's youth. Rather we quickly experience something of a sense of (directed) *déjà vu*, a transposition of old songs into new keys. An author's note makes it clear from the beginning, spinning an intertextual web woven equally of autobiography and fiction, that "the Sligo Town mentioned here is (or was) Celbridge, Co. Kildare, the River Garavogue therefore the River Liffey; Lissadell House being Killadoon House in the latter county, and Slish Wood—Killadoon Wood. Nullamore was Springfield where I was born" (10). Many of the details, such as the zealous brutality of the National School teachers, the conditions in factories in London, or the golfing Ben Boucher, are familiar from "Asylum," others from "Killachter Meadow" and *Langrishe*—the description of Dan's misfit brother Wally playing tennis, for example, is prefigured in detail in the earlier descriptions of both Emily Kervick's and Emily Langrishe's performances.

Scenes from a Receding Past, as the title suggests, is a lamentation for the relentless dissolution of what was once the vibrant present into an increasingly dimly remembered, increasingly fictional past. "C'est ainsi que je fons et eschape à moi," Higgins quotes Montaigne in an epigraph, "Thus do I dissolve and take leave of myself" (104). Dan is a "dreamy reserved unhappy sort of boy," for whom "the things that make the life seem far away and quite beyond . . . reach, not in the country at all perhaps, not in Ireland" (39). Bouts of determined masturbating alternate with "bouts of erratic piety" (85). He is intimidated by Protestants. He is unpopular at school. His father is a "passive, evasive man" (125), his brother and then his mother suffer nervous breakdowns. "College is not a time I myself look back upon with any pleasure" (132). He moves to Dublin to a job with an insurance firm, meets his future wife, Olivia, nicknamed Billy, moves to London and a job in an ice-cream factory, consorts occasionally with a vaguely "literary" set. As the narrative draws to a close they are saving hard for an Adriatic cruise, an escape made all the more necessary when Olivia loses her baby in her fifth month of pregnancy. The novel itself, in accordance with its narrative strategy, comes most vibrantly to life in these closing pages under the pressure of grief, as the sorrowing Dan finally acquires the contours of a present rather than a remembered character. Lost in the rain somewhere in London in a taxi, he attempts to sum up the situation so far: "Long ago I was this, was that, twisting and turning, incredulous, baffled, believing nothing, believing all. Now I am, what? I feel frightened, sometimes, but may be just tired. I feel depressed quite often, but may be just hungry" (204).

There are writers who devote their resources to the invention of new and gripping situations in every book, and there are those who prefer to return again and again to what is essentially the same situation. Higgins is clearly one of the latter kinds. *Bornholm Night-Ferry* (1983), his latest major narrative to date, recounts the story of yet another ill-fated love affair, but the account has become even more oblique, more complex, more technically risky. In *Langrishe* the protagonist was the victimized woman, in *Balcony* it was the victimized man. In *Bornholm* both participants are victims, and this time the story is presented impartially from both of their points of view through the (old-fashioned) device of the epistolary narrative. Two writers, an unhappily married Irish novelist named Finn Fitzgerald and an equally unhappily married Danish poet named Elin Marstrander, fifteen years his junior, meet and fall desperately in love during a brief meeting in the south of Spain, where Finn lives, in 1975. The story of their stormy relationship emerges through the five-year exchange of letters that constitutes the book, fleshed out with Finn's diary entries. The narrative opens with his diary account of a reunion on the Danish island of Bornholm in 1980, the third such reunion that has taken place over the intervening five years of their increasingly uneasy relationship, which drifts interruptedly but inexorably from ecstasy to crisis, suspicion, resentment, recrimination, and something close to despair. The few pages devoted to this brief and joyless meeting lead into the story of the affair, related chronologically through their exchange of letters over the years, and the book ends with the proposed visit to Bornholm and the hoped-for revival of their flagging love still in the future.

The structure of the narrative is therefore implicitly circular. Bornholm, which in the course of the account comes to represent the hypothetical possibility of an eventually achieved idyll, an almost mythical *ultima Thule* where the lovers might eventually come together in some sort of shared happiness, despite all their own misunderstandings and the multiple problems presented by the outside world, reveals itself as an illusion even before the reader is permitted to begin reading of the course of their doomed love. They do in fact meet on three occasions during the course of the narrative, spending some six weeks or so together in all, in Spain, London, Copenhagen, Bornholm, in the course of the five years, patched together out of fugitive weekends hurriedly snatched from the demands of their respective spouses and families and the demands of their respective professions. These meetings regularly end up in a misunderstanding followed by a quarrel—as indeed had happened even during the brief course of their first intoxication with each other. Subsequent letters are then filled with bitter mutual recriminations and self-reproach, accusations and psychoanalysis, renewed declarations of love and half-hopeful plans for another meeting, which in its turn proves to be equally hopeless.

Higgins's preoccupation with travel functions as the central metaphor of *Bornholm Night-Ferry*, and it is a metaphor for desolation. The lovers, Finn sometimes in the south of Spain, sometimes in London, Elin mostly in Copenhagen, both under continual jealous observation by their increasingly frantic spouses, write continually and with growing desperation to each other—"notations in the void," to quote a chapter heading—planning their next putative meeting in Galway or Donegal, Copenhagen or Málaga, London or Greece. European geography, which in *Balcony of Europe* still serves essentially as an intertextual link between here and there, then and now, serves in the later novel as a metaphor underlining the essential and unbridgeable separation of the lovers. *Bornholm Night-Ferry*, as the title already suggests, is a novel about the possibility of communication, the possibility of researching one place from another, reaching one person from another. Or more accurately, it is a novel about the impossibility of such an endeavor, a theme already familiar from Higgins's earlier work, but nowhere portrayed with such painful intensity as in his last novel.

Bornholm is the most overtly self-reflexive of Higgins's works, and language, appropriately, remains very much in the foreground, though in a rather different fashion. *Balcony of Europe,* whose lovers are both English-speaking, is generously sprinkled with shards of various European languages, as we have seen. Finn and Elin—much more obviously than Imogen Langrishe and Otto Beck—are at home in different languages. Writers both, dealers in language, the lovers devise a secret language, a "bogus Deutsch" (24), an invented language that does not depend on the rules of grammar or the rules of the real world, and thus provides the lovers, à la Tristan and Isolde, with a linguistic grotto of love, a fairytale retreat in language, a "dream of opposite life" (109) safely cut off from an unsympathetic world and its importunate problems. It is moreover a "neutral" language, neither Finn's English nor Elin's Danish, an Esperanto of the heart. The pressures of the real world are not permanently disarmed by this fairytale solution, however, and the solidarity underwritten by the fantasy language soon emerges as illusory too: the lovers speak not one language but two, not a unitary common territory after all, but rather, as is the way of the world, a competing and conflicting "Fitzish" and "Elinish."

Higgins's work as a whole, as will have emerged from the foregoing, is essentially lyric rather than narrative, static rather than dynamic, paradigmatic rather than syntagmatic in structure, returning again and again as it does to a single central preoccupation verging on obsession, painting again and again in varying but intimately related and finely nuanced tones the essential and inevitable failure of communication among human beings, especially those who love each other or at any rate wish to think they do so. For all his formal experimentation, much of it very interesting from a technical point of view, it is also fair to say that

Higgins is most essentially a realist writer, one whose primary concern has always been the fictional portrayal of real human beings and their usually unavailing efforts to make sense of their more or less unhappy lives. Higgins's people, from *Felo de Se* to *Bornholm Night-Ferry*, are deeply and desperately lonely people, attempting always to reach out and touch another human being who might allow them to forget or ignore that loneliness, and always failing to do so. There are no happy endings, no rainbow's end, no sunset glow of contentment in Higgins's fictional universe. Finn and Elin, endlessly circling around their own inability to find each other, are in the end the characters most typical of Higgins's fictional world as a whole. Love, the ghost center of this dead universe, is the name of an absence rather than a presence, yearning rather than fulfillment, question rather than answer, and hunger rather than solace.

WORKS CITED

Baneham, Sam. "Aidan Higgins: A Political Dimension." *Review of Contemporary Fiction* (Spring 1983): 168–174.

Beja, Morris. "Felons of Our Selves: The Fiction of Aidan Higgins." *Irish University Review* 3.2 (1973): 163–178.

Higgins, Aidan. *Balcony of Europe*. London: Calder & Boyars, 1972.

—. *Bornholm Night-Ferry*. London: Allison & Busby, 1983.

—. *Felo de Se*. London: John Calder, 1960; as *Killachter Meadow*, New York: Grove Press, 1961; as *Asylum and Other Stories*, London: John Calder, 1978; New York: Riverrun Press, 1979.

—. *Images of Africa*. London: Calder & Boyars, 1971.

—. *Langrishe, Go Down*. London: Calder & Boyars, 1966.

—. *Ronda Gorge & Other Precipices*. London: Secker & Warburg, 1989.

—. *Scenes from a Receding Past*. London: John Calder, 1977.

Imhof, Rüdiger. "*Bornholm Night-Ferry* and *Journal to Stella*: Aidan Higgins's Indebtedness to Jonathan Swift." *The Canadian Journal of Irish Studies* 10.2 (1984): 5–13.

—. "German Influences on John Banville and Aidan Higgins." *Literary Interrelations: Ireland, England and the World*. Ed. Wolfgang Zach and Heinz Kosok. Vol. 2. Tübingen: Gunter Narr Verlag, 1987. 335–347.

Imhof, Rüdiger, and Jürgen Kamm. "Coming to Grips with Aidan Higgins's 'Killachter Meadow': An Analysis." *Études Irlandaises* (December 1984): 145–160.

Kreilkamp, Vera. "Reinventing a Form: The Big House in Aidan Higgins's *Langrishe, Go Down*." *The Canadian Journal of Irish Studies* 11.2 (1985): 27–38.

Lubbers, Klaus. "*Balcony of Europe*: The Trend towards Internationalization in Recent Irish Fiction." *Literary Interrelations: Ireland, England and the World*. Ed. Wolfgang Zach and Heinz Kosok. Vol. 3. Tübingen: Gunter Narr Verlag, 1987. 235–247.

Rauchbauer, Otto, ed. "Aidan Higgins, 'Killachter Meadow' und *Langrishe, Go Down* sowie Harold Pinters Fernsehfilm *Langrishe, Go Down*: Variationen eines Motivs." *A Yearbook of Studies in English Language and Literature* 3 (1986): 135–162.

Skelton, Robin. "Aidan Higgins and the Total Book." *Mosaic* 10.1 (1976): 27–37.

Felons of Our Selves:
The Fiction of Aidan Higgins

Morris Beja

The fiction of Aidan Higgins—who is surely one of the most important Irish novelists writing today—presents to us a world that is insistently claustrophobic. We are made aware of that at the very start of every one of his books. The first sentence of the first story in his first book, "Killachter Meadow" in *Felo de Se*, tells us that "the remains of Miss Emily Norton Kervick were committed to the grave one cold day in March of 1927" (9). The title of the second story is "Lebensraum," of the third "Asylum"—and its first sentence reads, "All the leaded windows of the house had blind views" (51). At the start of Higgins's second book, the novel *Langrishe, Go Down*, Helen Langrishe feels oppressed and crowded by her fellow passengers in a bus, till in defence—as if "her life depended on it"—"she breathed in the faint scent of herself, her clothes" (11). In the first entry of *Images of Africa: Diary (1956–60)*, Higgins reflects that the ship on which he is a passenger is "a kind of prison" (11). Prison imagery also begins Higgins's second novel, *Balcony of Europe*, with its description of a cold, depressing flat into which "a barred window admitted some light" (15).

Ireland, people are always saying, is a small country. *Felo de Se*, *Images of Africa*, and *Balcony of Europe* all roam far beyond the Irish boundaries to which *Langrishe, Go Down* restricts itself, and Higgins himself has traveled as widely as such books would lead one to expect; indeed, as John Hall observes in his account of an interview with Higgins, "travel seems to be an important component of his aesthetic" ("Beckettwise" 8). But although travel can help to alleviate some of the symptoms of claustrophobia, it cannot ultimately cure us of the basic sickness arising from our imprisonment within ourselves.

Or, rather, our selves—two words: not merely my self, for example, but my selves. Like the Yeats whose words he quotes in one of the "rejected epigraphs" of *Balcony of Europe*, Higgins tends "to see things double—doubled in history, world history, personal history" (462)—above all in "personal history" and in personal make-up. His people are, in several senses, divided, dissociated: each is a victim, to one degree or another, of that age-old malady which nowadays tends to be referred to (in R. D. Laing's term) as "the divided self." Although there are subtler and deeper evidences of this malady as well, Higgins's fiction is replete with *doppelgängers* and the experience of seeing or sensing one's double, from Sevi Klein's encounter with her mirror reflection in a bar in "Lebensraum" (*Felo de Se* 35), to the "avatars" of Charlotte in *Balcony of Europe* (257–59). In a dream Higgins records as his own in *Images of Africa*, he cuts himself on both wrists: "I am weakening; it's I who have done this, yet I seem to be standing outside myself. I watched 'myself' do it: 'him' I take for myself" (62). Earlier, Higgins's reflections on "years dreams return" seem reminiscent of Stephen Dedalus's thoughts on entelechy: "I am another now, and yet the same" (59).[1] In *Langrishe, Go Down*, Imogen seems similarly cut off from her own self as she thinks about her past, "How many years ago, and was it I?" (196).

In the epigraph to his first volume and its depiction of varieties of relentless experience, *Felo de Se*, Higgins evokes the classic image of dissociation, the Shadow, in a quotation from Hofmannsthal: "Wenn die Sonne tief, leben wir mehr in unserem Schatten als in uns selbst." Frequently too, Higgins employs that other dominant image for such self-division, that of the "mask" (31); not surprisingly, both those images recur importantly in the work of R. D.

Laing—whom, incidentally, Higgins has not read,[2] but to whom I shall occasionally refer here for what I hope will be a helpful context for important points I would like to raise.

A key element in Laing's study of the "ontologically insecure person" is his stress on the "unembodied self," as in people who feel themselves to be "detached from their bodies" (Laing 65–66). In *Felo de Se* Higgins speaks of "the unrelated head and unrelated body"; the reference is to a man whose "touch was more an experiment than an act of possession," yet who could not be pitied "because he could not be found, could not find himself" ("Lebensraum" 46–47). A more important figure who goes through a similar state is Eddy Brazill, in "Asylum": "fainting with real hunger and fatigue he felt the whole weight of his hot oppressive flesh hanging down . . . His own past, with its absurd pretensions intact, blew before; the body of Brazill dropped downwards like a stone between them." Wandering through Camden Hill in such a condition, he encounters his double:

> Behind the dark trunks, sunken in an opaque light, he saw the outline of a seat. There, under overcoats and sacks, a down-and-out slept his thin troubled sleep. As Brazill drew close to this mound, the sleeper rose up in a terrifying manner, still sleeping, struggling with a nightmare and the damp coverings, then fell back again. An indescribable feeling of loss took hold of Brazill. To the end of his life that scene, that helpless gesture, would be repeated. It seemed then that the only acknowledgement one could offer to another human being, once life was over, would be in the form of an embrace. He would have to lie under the sacks himself to be at peace. (76–77)

But Brazill does not embrace the man, and indeed the usual pattern of the disintegrated self involves a failure to connect with others. So later, as Mr. Boucher's mind goes, Brazill remains unaware of what is happening, oblivious of the devastating experience through which another human being is suffering—although at the end a glimmer of a realization of his own involvement with Mr. Boucher's fate does come to him, as "all he could say in wonder was, *He has gone to the madhouse, I have come from the poor home,* over and over again" (129).

Inevitably then, dissociation entails not merely a dissociation from and within oneself, but leads as well to dissociation from others (or comes out of it); of many of Higgins's characters it can be said, as it is said of Mr. Vaschel by his wife in "Nightfall on Cape Piscator," that "he doesn't fit in, it's a speciality with him that he doesn't fit it" (184). The sense conveyed is sometimes one of mere solipsism, as when Irwin Pastern observes in "Tower and Angels" that "for every human being on earth life ends in themselves" (167); more frequently, as in Eddy Brazill, the retreat from others is a defence. Unfortunately, psychological defences, as Freud and Laing and so many others have shown, can easily be more destructive than what they are meant to protect us against—the world, for instance. Or if at times the world seems to us dangerously intrusive, at other times it and its people abandon us to ourselves, ourselves alone. The epigraphs to Part One and Two of *Images of Africa* are both from *Robinson Crusoe*, and Michael Alpin of "Lebensraum" is typical of Higgins's characters in having "emerged out of a past barren as Crusoe's as far as passionate attachments went" (*Felo de Se* 36).

Given that sort of sense of the human predicament, it is no wonder that much of Higgins's work features an exploration of love and its role in our existence. At best love is an "illusion . . . that others can participate in one's life" (*Langrishe* 250), and at worst it is a "kind of curse"—though a curse for which we all long (*Balcony* 327). It becomes a curse when, as is usually the case in Higgins, it is destructive, of others or ourselves or both. Yet love ought to be life-giving; it should help us either to survive or to create a new self out of our mutilated selves, and at times it does so even in Higgins's world: in *Felo de Se*, notably for Brazill and for Mr. Vaschel. And so, too, in *Langrishe, Go Down*, Imogen feels at the start of her affair with Otto Beck that "henceforth her life would be entirely different," and at the end of it she recalls that "I was not myself, yet never have I lived more in my senses" (129, 179).

On the surface, *Langrishe, Go Down*—a re-working of the first story of *Felo de Se*, "Killachter Meadow"—is in the tradition of the Irish novel of the Big House. But although the house is big, the claustrophobia remains, and even intensifies; no house is big enough to get rid of that, especially one that is falling apart, breaking up: "the rockery and main garden grow wild; shrubs and grass hide the pathways; weeds proliferate everywhere," while "indoors too there is neglect and decay" (81–82). The Langrishe house, then, is like Gerontion's, a decayed house. But the entire land is a waste land as well, as a number of pointed allusions to *The Waste Land* help us to realize (121–22, 149). The Langrishe big house is in "the townland of Ballymakealy Upper, which is in the Parish of Killadoon, which is in the County Kildare, which is in the province of Leinster" (27). Which is in Eddy Brazill's "defunct Ireland" (*Felo de Se* 54). Ireland of course is not defunct, but the Ireland of the Langrishes is. Imogen thinks of herself, with at least some accuracy, as "a lady who is now a sort of specimen of a bygone world" (92), but Higgins devotes little space to nostalgic clichés about a romantic Ireland that is dead and gone. Nevertheless, the Ireland of the past is constantly evoked: Helen thinks of writing a history of the area, and quotations and epigraphs from historical accounts of Ireland are sprinkled through the novel, counterpointed with headlines from the contemporary European history of the 1930s—accounts of speeches by Franco, of the bombardment of Madrid, of the invasion of Austria.

Yet despite the way in which the sense of place and the sense of history pervade *Felo de Se* and *Langrishe, Go Down*, few of the characters in the two books display either. For all her half-hearted desire to write history, Helen's sense of the past is limited and faulty (like, indeed, her sense of place: although she takes the omnibus from Aston Quay to Springfield numerous times, it never occurs to her to wonder where the bus goes after she leaves it); her only genuine moment of a measure of communion with her "place" and its "people" comes among the dead, in the local churchyard (*Langrishe* 35). Imogen's communion with the area and its past is even more restricted, as her conversations with an exasperated Otto reveal. For that matter, Otto's own relationship to history—especially contemporary history, as we shall see—is hardly a model. In the end, perhaps the most notable interaction between history and Higgins's character is one of mutual abuse.

The title of *Langrishe, Go Down* seems to hint that the Langrishes' decline is the result of a categorical imperative, but I suspect that we must be wary of the easy and in a sense too comforting assumption that history is to blame. If Helen is right in feeling that "for the distressed . . . life is just a scourge" (10), too often the scourge is administered in a process of self-flagellation. From the title page of Higgins's first volume, a controlling image of his work has been that of self-destruction. Each of us is inevitably a felon of himself, his selves. The Langrishe sisters are, as Helen knows, "human derelicts" (32), but their decay is largely their own doing. Certainly the decline of their fortunes is shown to have been avoidable: as Otto observes in perplexity, "Why fail? . . . I don't understand it. You have seventy-four rich acres of land, ten of that in tillage. You had a herd of cattle once, a supply of eggs, pullets, a vegetable garden, a fruit garden, an orchard. You did not live riotously; so why had it to fail?" (189). Again and again we are shown the failure of the sisters to exert themselves against their "destiny." "Here I languish under blankets and eiderdown" (73), Helen thinks—and indeed, in *Langrishe, Go Down*, languishing, they go down: victims, we are perhaps meant to feel, of what Higgins calls in *Felo de Se* "the classical feminine languor" (85). Elsewhere in that volume, we are told how "the disgust with the Self, total and languishing no more, is transmitted to inanimate objects—sinless as well as free in space and time—and the dead person freed at last from the responsibility of feeling" (43).

As such a passage suggests, nothing in Higgins's world is so difficult as to love, yet nothing is so difficult to avoid. Higgins has observed that the journeys in his books—and there are many—are "journeys towards 'love,'" and he wonders if any other Irish writer has attempted to portray the role of love in our lives in quite the same way—and, especially, if any has attempted to present the love that *women* feel: "Joyce, Beckett and Flann O'Brien put women aside. Irish writing on women puts one in mind of paintings and drawings of horses (galloping or still) before the invention of the camera." He dismisses the most famous figure who might immediately seem to be an exception as "Molly Bloom with her knickers and period, an Earth Mother and also a kind of monster."[3] Although one may not go along with the suspicion that Higgins's attempt to portray women in love is quite so unique in Irish literature as all that, it is arguable that the company he keeps in this regard is a small and select group; the boldness of his presentation becomes even more striking when we learn that the models for the Langrishe sisters were in fact Higgins's own brothers. The transmutation from male to female sensibility seems (at least to one male reader) so impressive that one would be tempted to assume that whatever autobiography originally lay behind the Langrishes must have disappeared in the process, but in fact Higgins has more than once insisted that "all" his work is "autobiographical."[4]

The sisters do not display—or feel—much love for one another, and they don't make up much of a "family" in any positive sense; instead, they variously display the characteristics of two unhealthy family patterns described by Laing: the "series" (the members of which keep together as a result of social pressure, say, rather than affection) or the "nexus" (where the controlling forces tend to be fear and guilt).[5] Interestingly, the only sister to feel an active and healthy need for sexual love is the one whose love-relationship with her father might have seemed so devastating. Imogen constantly recalls her "handsome father" and half seems to understand why, "as a growing girl, when she had sat on his knee, she had sensed his resentment at her putting her hot bottom there." Once "he had surprised her naked in the bathroom admiring her figure in the long glass." The eyes that had thus beheld her—"pale blue eyes that tended to water" (*Langrishe* 50)—are the features that she later most connects with her lover, Otto, who becomes the mirror image of her father, squatting on his land and taking on the education (in more ways than one) of his daughter. That process includes—and this may seem a bit much—an excursion to Dublin to see a production of Strindberg's *The Father*, as well as seduction:

> *Why did I? . . .*
> *Because I liked his manner; because I desired*
> *him to be happy; because I wanted to give him*
> *something; because he had Father's eyes . . .*

. . . She had joyfully agreed to go. Had with misgiving agreed to go. Because she liked his manner, because she wanted to know him better, wanted to be happy, because, in fine, he had Father's eyes. (108–09)

Otto Beck is probably the most complex and interesting character in the novel, perhaps in all of Higgins's fiction thus far; certainly he is a much more formidable figure than his counterpart, the "pallid youth named Klaefisch," in "Killachter Meadow" (*Felo de Se* 12). Beck is one of the very few strong people in Higgins: at least on the surface, *his* self is not divided (like his name, he is the same front and back, coming or going, here or there). As a result of such strength, he is more destructive than destroyed; if others are victims in part of their sensitive solipsism, his self is preserved—for what it is worth—by his cruder selfishness. No more considerate of the "property" of others than the "tinkerman" who takes over his hut after he has gone (*Langrishe* 271), his relationship with the world around him is that of the exploiter to the exploited, the rapist to his victim. It is in that sense alone that he is close to nature, his participation in which is that of the man who feels free to fish in it, hunt in it, kill in it, at will:

> Taking a pair of nail scissors Otto cut the wasp in two. It arched its back, darting its sting. He gazed blandly at it. Black and yellow transverse stripes. Narrow-waisted. Blinkered eyes.
> – The human eye cannot allow certain shapes, Otto said. Very hard to resist the temptation not to stamp on certain shapes, put an end to them. (200)

That scene inevitably reminds us that Otto Beck is a young man in his thirties from the Germany of the thirties, and an admiring product of his culture ("Higher education in Germany is beyond criticism. Excellent, really excellent" (218)). Not that he is a Nazi; instead, he is "indifferent to politics, absolutely indifferent" (148). He himself is not a Nazi, and indeed observes that "you would have to read *Mein Kampf* to appreciate what a claptrap it all is" (149). He himself is no Nazi, even if he can talk of "'culturally inferior nations' and of 'culturally insignificant' individuals" (166). By no means is he a Nazi, although his response to the Germany emerging under Hitler is a callous "I am well out of it" (209). To such a man, as to the Nazis, people are mere things, mere objects; Laing speaks in terms of the distinction between one's relation to "a person" and one's relationship to "an organism" (Laing 21). To Beck, women are merely prey, and sex is the weapon with which you bring them down: after he and Imogen make love (as it were), Otto is "at peace," for "once again he had run his quarry to earth" (163). His compatriot in "Winter Offensive," Herr Bausch, rolls on his femur during sex "as if adjusting his aim," bearing down "until safely embedded in still-living subject female flesh" (*Felo de Se* 137). But in the light of the self-destructive tendencies in most of Higgins's characters, it is not surprising that Imogen does not mind Otto's attitude all that much: "I wouldn't mind being his trollop. Him to be cruel to me, as such men are reputed; he could do anything he likes with me. What else is my soft white useless women's flesh good for? What else?" (91).

The fact that Otto Beck is probably the least sympathetic important figure in all Higgins's fiction makes his portrayal a key element in the presentation of love in that fiction, for even in the face of his monstrous character, Imogen feels the better for her encounter with him—and we tend to agree. However unworthy the beloved, she at least has had the love. It is here that, for example, we begin to understand why the novel begins with Helen, only to have our attention shifted to Imogen, for Helen displays Imogen's alternative, a life without any man entering her being, a life without sex, without love. Someone—even an Otto Beck—is better than no one. It is not that he makes Imogen happy—that would seem rather more than one can legitimately expect, at least for very long—but he does make her feel alive.

Yet when Imogen overhears a woman mutter, "it's a fact, people can never get enough of what's bad for them" (228), she wonders if the woman is talking about her—as well she might. Otto has been good for her, but finally the terms of their affair are demeaning and destructive for she remains a mere object to him, in effect an instrument with which he may masturbate. So she ends their affair. Nevertheless, when "the illusion . . . that others can participate in one's life" is "shattered for good and all" (250) it is far from clear that Imogen is truly better off, that the end of the affair is less destructive than its prolongation. It is as if we must be felons of ourselves no matter what. The felony of course takes various forms. The masochism of Imogen's relationship with Otto has been a feature of Higgins's earlier fiction, and was to go on to be a feature of the characterization of Dan Ruttle in *Balcony of Europe*—as would the death-wish felt by so many of Higgins's characters.

One especially interesting manifestation of the self-destructive tendencies of Higgins's people is their impulse towards what Laing terms "petrification," a Bartleby-like retreat into stasis or even catatonia which is one of those modes of self-preservation by which we are accomplices in our self-destruction.[6] But of course Higgins does not use Laing's term; rather, he favors a word which has significant connotations for an Irish writer: "paralysis." Paralysis is as pervasive a danger in Higgins as it is a key term in Joyce, as in Joyce's famous declaration that he intended in *Dubliners* "to betray the soul of that hemiplegia or paralysis which so many consider a city" (55). In the earlier version of *Langrishe, Go Down*, "Killachter Meadow," the dissociation of Emily-May is pondered by Helen, who imagines her sister's self-effacing life as one in which she "could be seen lurking in the background in a succession of family snapshots": "Until at last she came to resemble that other person trapped in the snapshot, a version of herself perpetuated in some anxious pose and unable to walk forward out of that paralysis" (*Felo de Se* 17–18). Within *Langrishe, Go Down*, it becomes clear that *all* the sisters are victims of a languor which paralyzes them; it is not Imogen's father's presence alone, surely, which "paralysed her" (54).

I am not trying to argue that there is necessarily a Joycean "influence" at work in Higgins's presentation of paralysis (or languor, or petrification). Nor would it be necessary to cite such correspondences in order to show the obvious—that Joyce's impact on Higgins's fiction has been a major one. Allusions to Joyce and his work are so numerous and persistent in Higgins that there would be no point in pursuing them here. And anyway Higgins is undoubtedly correct in remarking that he does "not write like Joyce," although even that denial occurs in the context of his saying that "in my beginnings as a writer I spent seven years reading Joyce, and maybe another four forcing myself *not* to imitate him" ("Tired Lines" 58). Obviously, Higgins's work is the better for his care on this score: great writers tend to be much more dangerously oppressive models than merely good ones. In Higgins's case, another major Irish writer has provided "the great corrective" for the Joyce influence: Samuel Beckett ("Beckettwise" 8). Of Beckett's effect too, for that matter, Higgins uses ambivalent terms, remarking that *Felo de Se* was, he supposes, "under the shadows of Beckett and [Djuna] Barnes."[7] Conceivably, the influence of Beckett could be even more straitening than the influence of Joyce, whose danger is that he "offers too many possibilities to the young Irish writer" ("Beckettwise" 8); Beckett could lead to the opposite risk—the restriction of possibilities and even the sense of a dead end. But neither influence has distorted the power of originality of Higgins's own vision. In any case, it is interesting that, an expatriate himself—Ireland, he says, does not feel "like home" any more, or it is the home he "cant breathe in"[8]—the major influences on Higgins's work should be those of the two great expatriates of modern Irish literature.

One of the lessons any writer can learn from Joyce and Beckett is not to fear experimentation. *Balcony of Europe* came six years after *Langrishe, Go Down* and marked a radical departure from Higgins's earlier work. To be sure, some of the most notable features of *Felo de Se* and *Langrishe, Go Down*—such as the use of autobiographical elements—appear here as well, but they are carried to greater extremes, while even more notable are approaches which in Higgins are quite new. Thus, for the first time we have a continuous first person narrative and a restricted point of view. And in his earlier work Higgins had practiced a scrupulous meanness, concentrating on the well-wrought artifact; in *Balcony of Europe* he permits himself to sprawl, to be expansive—even to the extent of occasionally leaving himself open to the danger of being loose or repetitious. The method now is neither that of the well developed "plot" nor that of the fluent "stream," but rather one of isolated tableaux, each Joycean "fadograph of a yestern scene" (20). "The form," Higgins has said, "is a spider web of cross references": "I wanted to dispense with a plot, do it that way: tenuous associations that would ramify, could be built upon, would stay in mind better than the plotted thing—all lies anyway."[9]

One of the chief unifying elements in *Balcony of Europe* is *not* new in Higgins: his magnificent ability to evoke the sense of place, which is once again inextricably involved with the sense of time and history. Bob Bayless urges the narrator-protagonist, Dan Ruttle, to think "about time": "Not space. Not space-time either. I don't mean space-time at all. Fuck space-time. I mean just time, all by itself. Just try it some day" (229). But on the evidence of *Balcony of Europe*, it can't be done.

The novel begins and ends in Ireland, with dream-like images of the Aran Islands especially prominent. Early in the book, Ruttle sees an advertisement for "the Aran Isles, that *Tir na nÓg* occupied by the old, the embittered, the sea-enclosed" (28). Otto Beck had seen such an ad almost thirty years before, and he is rather improbably remembered when Ruttle does visit Inishere at the end of the book. In between, the bulk of the novel takes place in Spain, where Ruttle acts out his role as a middle-aged playboy of the west end world of Europe, although Aran remains in Ruttle's consciousness as a refuge, the place he would go to in the event of the expected cataclysm of a new world war. Not surprisingly, Ireland seems to Ruttle "the country I had never left" (340)—partly because it occupies inner space, but also because of echoes of each land in the other:

> Six waves of invaders, centuries of occupation, the expulsion then Civil War, in Catholic Ireland and Catholic Spain. One cut off from Europe by the Pyrenees, the other by the Irish Sea. Both on the outer fringes of Europe, both saved from two world wars by their long-nosed leaders; neither part of Europe. (338)

Most of the novel takes place in Nerja (or Nerka), on the coast of Andalusia. The title refers to the name of a hotel which, in the copy of Fodor's *Spain* that I consulted, is listed as "*Balcon de Europa* (B), own beach, dancing"; but those who assume from such a setting that *Balcony of Europe* provides light holiday reading about packaged tours on the Costa de Sol will no doubt be disappointed.

Ruttle informs us that "King Victor Emmanuel named this *paseo* the 'Balcon de Europa' because of the view" (68); from this balcony we see something of the world, while at the same time we see displayed upon it numerous tableaux, incidents, people, and relationships. The effect, then, is that of a stationary picaresque—like that of *The Magic Mountain*, the sanatorium of which also provided a balcony of Europe. Here, our Castorp is Dan Ruttle, and his Clavdia is Charlotte Bayless. As in Mann's novel, for a long time we are distracted by a dazzling display of secondary characters who occupy much of our attention, but increasingly we perceive that our fundamental interest is in our hero, such as he is. But although most of the novel takes place in Nerja, it is always fully clear—and here we have a contrast to Mann's mountain—that Nerja is merely a way station for a miscellaneous group of restlessly peripatetic people. Indeed, just about all the characters convey, like Amory, the impression of enjoying life "as a cannon ball enjoys space, traveling to its aim blindly (and spreading ruin on the way?)" (315).

Once again, however, most of Higgins's people are less notable for the ruin they inflict on others than for the devastation they bring upon themselves. Dan Ruttle, a middle-aged Irish painter married to an attractive and admirable woman, Olivia Grieve, places himself in the cliché-ridden and potentially ludicrous position of having an affair with Charlotte Harlan Bayless, a beautiful twenty-four-year-old American. The names are suggestive. Ruttle is in a sexual rut, which leads him to abandon Olivia (called "Livvy"—Liffey, life), only to be entrapped by Charlotte's web. Olivia may grieve, like Anna Livia before her, but she will outlast them all. The desiccated connotations of Charlotte's married name, Bayless, are perhaps overly harsh on her husband and marriage, while the connotations of her maiden name—Harlan, harlot—are perhaps not fair, although she is treated sympathetically.

Charlotte's web is love, and Ruttle enters it willingly and eagerly. "I should like you to ruin me," he thinks as he watches her, providing one of the answers to his own later question, "Why is the spider considered a sexual symbol?" (133, 355). Higgins has written a *Liber Amoris*—the book Ruttle says the Baron is wrong to expect him to be reading (92). But if Higgins's novels are stories of love, they are also about people who have what will seem objectively (that is, of course, to other people, like us) inordinate love or passion for someone who does not strike us as worthy of so much emotional excitement. Charlotte, while she is no Otto Beck, is nevertheless the recipient (and victim, as well as beneficiary) of a love that cannot but appear to others as disproportionate or obsessive. Moreover, if one of the suspect elements in Imogen's love for Otto had been his identification with her father, one of the troubling aspects of Ruttle's erotic dependence upon Charlotte is her identification with his mother. The two women even share the same nickname, "Dilly." As his mother is dying, and then after her death, Ruttle hears music from *Sundays and Cybele*, and asks, "But who was Cybele?" Cybele was of course the Great Mother, whose involvement with Attis led to his self-castration (and to his annual mutilation of himself in rites performed by emasculated priests). Cybele is the devouring mother: "an Earth Mother and also a kind of monster," to adopt the words we have seen Higgins use for Molly Bloom. Ruttle, however, answers his own question by connecting Cybele in his mind with "the Jews of Thessalonika and Amsterdam" who "kept the keys of their lost Spanish houses" (61, 166).

For Cybele is Charlotte, who is not only his mother, but a *Jewish* mother. This time round, the Jew among the American expatriates seeking refuge in Spain is not Robert Cohn, but Brett Ashley herself. The interest in Jews shown in Higgins's earlier work becomes here almost obsessive. Even in *Images of Africa* the insistence on identifying every Jew he encounters as a Jew—including the "pampered Jewish children" who look forward to the later group of "pampered over-fed Jewish children" (22, 54)—goes beyond the tendency which foreigners often note in Irishmen to identify everyone in terms of religion or religious background. The sense of Jewishness that one gets in Higgins is complex; pampered some Jews may be—Charlotte is, surely—but even more pervasive is the sense of their victimization. As in *Langrishe, Go Down,* but more centrally, the Jewish experience comes to stand for the horrors of all human history. The long conversation between Ruttle and the Baron, spiritual disciple of Martin Bormann, is one of the most fascinating sections in the novel, and provides Ruttle with a chilling and frightening sense of his *own* danger. But a sense of communion with victims can turn such victims into threats; if the expatriates from Ireland and America are like the exiled Jews of Thessalonika and Amsterdam, that is an association with which those expatriates are uncomfortable. Still another element contributing to our sense of Jews as threats in *Balcony of Europe* is their otherness: the Jews are seen by the non-Jews in the novel as different, alien, exotic, if fascinatingly so. Sort of like Durrell's Justine. And like Justine—although Ruttle's words refer to Joyce's Bloom—Charlotte is "the invention of a Christian" (156). Higgins pins it down more accurately in his own words, when he speaks of Ruttle's "dream about the *pseudo*-Jewess."[10] For Charlotte does strike one as a Jewess less in the tradition of either Molly or Justine than in the "Jewish" tradition of, say, Ali MacGraw.

At one point, a doctor warns Ruttle not to "play with American girls . . . it is *unsafe*" (300)—but by now we know enough about people in Higgins's world to realize that such danger can be a major source of appeal. Actually, one may be excused for wondering if Charlotte is any the less Ruttle's dream about the pseudo-American than his dream about the pseudo-Jewess. Certainly Ruttle gets numerous things about America all wrong; to cite all or many of them would be to risk pedantry, but a few will make my point. California is by no means "the only wine growing region in the United States" (257). Charlotte, we are told, is nicknamed Dilly after Dillinger, the facts of whose death are not right (77). She is also said to have gone to Samuel Gompers High School in New York, a fact made improbable but not impossible by its being a "vocational" school from which a student would be unlikely to go on to such a college as Antioch: what does make it impossible is that Gompers is an all boys' school. And Antioch, although recognized as a liberal arts college in Ohio, is placed "on the east coast" (329). The sense of American slang is shaky: a boy "by the fire hydrant" would be unlikely to call Dilly "dicey"; relatives would not speak of having sons "in trade" (268, 318). Other things also strike me as questionable, although reactions to them would be more subjective—such as the way in which the various Americans seem, in late 1963 and 1964, to think less about John F. Kennedy's death than about Brendan Behan's.

It is probably not uncharitable to assume that at least some of the debatable conceptions are Higgins's rather than Ruttle's.[11] On the other hand, it is probably not overly charitable to say that if they are Higgins's, they may be distracting but ultimately do not matter all that much. If, however, they are most of them Ruttle's, they fit in with certain elements in the presentation of Ruttle and his narrative that are especially intriguing. Ruttle's narration is like Marlow's in Conrad, in so far as he feels free to wander, to digress, to reflect, to discuss. But unlike Marlow, Ruttle rarely insists on ambiguity and mystery, on how much he does *not* know about the people he describes. Therein lies the trap, for Ruttle and potentially for us. As we read *Balcony of Europe*, our confidence in Ruttle's ability to comprehend the full dimensions of his own tale, in his role as

Perhaps surprisingly, however, the world does not end, for us, for Ruttle, for Charlotte, for the others. And Ruttle's affair with Charlotte is no more totally negative than was Imogen's with Otto. If both affairs seem to involve a distorted passion for people it is hard for us to get excited about, obviously we are not the ones who count, and anyway logic is irrelevant in such matters. It is not so much the beloved that people need, as the love. It may break them up, but it is also what makes them whole. If a controlling image of Higgins's fiction is, as I have argued, the process of self-destruction, then it is notable that in relatively few of his characters is the process completed, for not many of them end up totally annihilated. "Farce must survive, Brazill!" insists Mr. Boucher as he and Eddy watch a clown at the theatre, "Farce must survive!" (*Felo de Se* 97). Later, however, he tells Eddy about physical pain that can lead to "the entire organism's unwillingness to continue with the farce much longer" (114), and we perceive still once more a sense of the unembodied self, the dissociation between one's self and one's body; shortly afterward, Mr. Boucher does in fact attempt to kill himself.

Obviously, then, Higgins is hardly one to forget the remark he quotes Joyce's sister as having made about hope: "It's not very fattening" ("Beckettwise" 8). In *Balcony of Europe*, the doctor attending Ruttle's mother tells the family that they "could but hope. (He meant there was no hope)" (41). Yet the farce does survive, most of the organisms feel it worthwhile to continue, and if Higgins is not deluded by hope, neither does he meekly succumb to despair. In that, he is like most of his Irish literary contemporaries, with whom he otherwise seems to share surprisingly few characteristics.

It is to be sure a common assumption that all the contemporary Irish fiction that is worth serious consideration describes human existence as at best crushingly tragic—and at worst irredeemably dark, horrible, futile and, we must not leave out, absurd. Readers who make this assumption do so from various critical vantage points, but—ignoring these who are merely trying to be fashionable and who gather that this is how books are being read this year—they fall generally into one of two categories, depending on whether or not they approve. First, there are those who endorse such despair as, after all, reflecting things as they are. Many of them are older critics of all ages, as it were, who have been weaned on Irish writers like Joyce and Beckett, to say nothing of such non-Irish figures as Kafka and Faulkner—at least some of whom, in fact, they have oversimplified when they have not actively misread them. These readers and critics recall the fellow in Graham Greene who feels "the loyalty we all feel to unhappiness—the sense that that is where we really belong" (Greene 180)—a loyalty which they extend by assuming that (in Ireland in a troubled time; i.e., an Ireland of any time) that is where literature really belongs.

Directly opposed to them are the critics who attack twentieth-century Irish fiction as distorted repulsive, all wrong—or, even if they suspect that it is not all wrong, as unhealthy anyway, they are often, but by no means always, the positive thinkers of popular journalism. According to this perspective, the joy of Irish life is being assassinated, a victim of some sort of literary counterpart of the Provos, the solution to which would presumably be critical Internment, or an artistic Amendment to Offences Against the State Act.

A few decades ago, William Butler Yeats felt the need to complain about the "hysterical women" who were sick "of poets that are always gay." Nowadays the hysteria comes from those who seem sick of artists that are always somber—not suspecting that there may in fact be a "gaiety transfiguring all that dread" (291–92). The poem that Higgins quotes as the opening epigraph to *Balcony of Europe* is by Zbigniew Herbert, and begins:

It's good what happened
It's good what's going to happen
even what's happening now
it's o.k.

One of Higgins's heroes is Samuel Beckett, and his "Tribute" to him suggests that what he especially admires is Beckett's courage in the face of darkness, with "no edifying surroundings," "no air to breathe" (*Beckett at 60* 91). At the end of Beckett's trilogy, the Unnamable waits for the inevitable silence, knowing that he must go on, cant go on, will go on. At the end of *Balcony of Europe*, Dan Ruttle—a figure no more and no less reliable than the Unnamable—knows that "soon it will be dark," (458) but in his last words he reaches out, like so many of Higgins's people, in an attempt to attain the comfort of contact with another person: "The light begins to go. The light is going. Are you asleep? Answer me."

WORKS CITED

Calder, John. *Beckett at 60: A Festschrift*. London: Calder & Boyars, 1967.

Greene, Graham. *The Heart of the Matter*. New York: Viking, 1948.

Higgins, Aidan. *Balcony of Europe*. London: Calder & Boyars, 1972.

—. "Beckettwise and Unblooming." Interview with John Hall. *Guardian* 11 October 1971: 8.

—. *Felo de Se*. London: John Calder, 1960.

—. *Images of Africa*. London: Calder & Boyars, 1971.

—. *Langrishe, Go Down*. London: Calder & Boyars, 1966.

—. "Tired Lines; or Tales My Mother Told Me." *A Bash in the Tunnel: James Joyce by the Irish*. Ed. John Ryan. Brighton: Clifton Books, 1970. 55–60.

Joyce, James. *Letters.* Ed. Stuart Gilbert. London: Faber, 1957.

Laing, R. D. *The Divided Self: An Existential Study in Sanity and Madness.* Harmondsworth: Penguin, 1965.

"Questions of Origin." *Times Literary Supplement* 6 October 1972: 1185.

Yeats, W. B. "Lapis Lazuli." *The Collected Poems of W. B. Yeats.* New York: Macmillan, 1956.

NOTES

1. Cf. James Joyce, *Ulysses* (New York: Random House, 1961): "I am other I now" (189).

2. Letter to me, 15 December 1972.

3. The quotations are from the letter to me, cited above. Elsewhere, Higgins has suggested that he may regard two female Irish novelists as genuine exceptions to this criticism, Kate O'Brien and Edna O'Brien. See "Sitecast," Higgins's contribution to a series on "The Irish Novelist," in *The Irish Times,* 15 December 1972, p. 12.

4. Letter to me. Cf. "Beckettwise and Unblooming," p. 8.

5. See Peter Sedgwick, "R. D. Laing: Self, Symptom and Society," in Robert Boyers and Robert Orrill, eds., *R. D. Laing and Anti-Psychiatry* (New York: Perennial Library, 1971), pp. 14–15.

6. See Laing, *The Divided Self:* "It seems to be a general law that at some point those very dangers most dreaded can themselves be encompassed to forestall their actual occurrence. Thus, to forgo one's autonomy becomes the means of secretly safeguarding it to play possum, to feign death, becomes a means of preserving one's aliveness . . . To turn oneself into a stone becomes a way of not being turned into a stone by someone else" (Laing 51).

7. Letter to me.

8. Letter to me.

9. Letter to me. Cf. his praise of Joyce: "The exhibitionary needs of a fictional plot—what poet Montague has aptly called 'the fireside chattiness of most Irish story-telling'—did not seem to concern him at all (which was a relief); he wrote out his own life" ("Tired Lines" 57).

10. Letter to me, emphasis added.

11. Suspicions about Higgins's total grasp of American popular culture, for example, are not dissipated by a reference at the end of *Images of Africa* to "Gershwin's *Night and Day*," p. 71.

Questions of Travel:
Writing and Travel in the Work of
Aidan Higgins

GEORGE O'BRIEN

> Should we have stayed at home,
> wherever that may be?
>
> —Elizabeth Bishop

To think of Aidan Higgins as a travel-writer is not merely to register the distinctive perspectives and heterogeneous observations which distinguish, for example, the pieces that make up *Ronda Gorge & Other Precipices*. And to use travel in his writing (*Balcony of Europe, Lions of the Grunewald, Bornholm Night-Ferry*) as a pretext for aligning it with the expatriate branch of twentieth-century Irish fiction is not the whole story, either. Travel is not just a feature of the Higgins *oeuvre*, supplying color, difference, exoticism, surface. Rather, it's a structural principle, or rather the ground upon which an aesthetic articulating the absence of any such principle in experience, is established. This ground is delimited not merely by the disjecta it contains, the flux of cultural, economic and historical flotsam and jetsam which denotes the material conditions of the present day—and not just merely the present day, but the moment of the traveler's apprehension of it. For, in addition, the terrain in question is besides being itself is also matter to be regarded, scrutinized, seen through and registered by a subjectivity which both resists and absorbs what it sees, and which avails of the given conditions less for their own sake than as a scrim against which more necessary and fundamental human exigencies may be played out. The title of *Ronda Gorge & Other Precipices* draws attention to faults besides the geological, and the book's subtitle, *Travels and Autobiographies 1956–89* hint, with familiar Higgins dualism, at an autobiographical dimension to travel and a place-based mediation of self, although the volume itself significantly complicates any assumption that the space-time relations suggested amount to a continuum. If Higgins's dualism may be familiar, it is never facile, and the emergence of the complications mentioned is one gloss among many in his work on the state first addressed in the personage of Sevi Klein:

> Sevi too was a woman never at rest . . . . If sleep and death, as we are told, bestow on us a "guilty immunity," then travel does too, for the traveller is perpetually in the wrong context; and she was such a traveller.[1] ("Lebensraum" 39)

The "rightness" of this "wrong" or, if such a vocabulary is inapt, the interplay between location and dislocation, is a marked feature of the aesthetic of travel in Higgins's work.

Before going on to consider the enactment of this aesthetic, some further sense of the traveler's identity may be outlined. The earliest piece collected in *Ronda Gorge & Other Precipices* is *Images of Africa* (whose full title,[2] incidentally, draws attention, through "images" and "diary" to the link elaborated in much of Higgins's subsequent works between travel and the autobiographical, between the worldly data supplied by Africa and the inevitable—though arrestingly honest—sketchiness of a diary's subjective response, the link itself mediated through the aesthetic instrument of the image). The diary is divided into three parts, the initial two of which deal with, first, the travels of Higgins and his wife through South Africa and Southern Rhodesia as members of the John Wright Puppet Company and, second, with living and working in Johannesburg. The subject of the diary's third part is the return voyage to England.

The first two parts are accompanied by epigraphs from *Robinson Crusoe* (Part Three doesn't have an epigraph), and while they are certainly suggestive in the localized context they are also noteworthy for not only their textual relevance but for drawing attention to "bold Robin Crusoe"[3] (*A Bestiary* 243) himself, a figure whom Higgins has accorded a certain illustrative status, particularly, though by no means exclusively, in *A Bestiary*. It should be noted at once that this status is not very prominent: as a writer not given to interpreting, Higgins is not likely to supply interpretative devices. Nor is Crusoe to Higgins's Dan Ruttle what Odysseus is to Joyce's Bloom. In keeping with the unmythic disposition of his imagination, with his work's focus on the body as exemplifying both the limit and range of experience, and with the way ahead as unredeemably disintegrative and fragmentary, Higgins is not interested in either treating Crusoe as systematically as Joyce treats Bloom or as presenting him as an occasion of comedy's reintegrative ethos. And of course Higgins's Crusoe is nothing so determinative as a father figure or an avatar to mimic.

Nevertheless, for author and reader alike, there is something about this figure which makes him a useful rhetorical spar to cling to. And among those uses are the beginnings, at least, of a way to discern the traveler's identity—in other words something of the nature of the Higgins narrator, protagonist, double, presence. Indeed, from the standpoint of Higgins's biography, the appeal of "the marooned one" (*AB* 305) is perhaps no surprise. From that point of view the sinking of Springfield House, and the abandonment and abject isolation following in its wake, as recapitulated not only in *A Bestiary* but in *Balcony of Europe*, where it is expressed as a prelude to travel and expatriation (father- and motherland proving no longer viable, fated only for one final disintegration), has the force of a primal scene. It need hardly be said that resonances of wreckage richly inform *Langrishe, Go Down* and "Killachter Meadow," the latter complete with aquatic undertow leading to ineluctable terminus:

> Under wet hanging branches she was carried, dropping her keel, touching nothing but water. By fields, by grazing cattle, by calm estate walls, Emily Odysseus Kervick drifted, the last of her line, without issue, distinction or hope. (*FDS* 30)

The passive voice here ("steered by no passing bell . . . . The river carried her on . . .") finds its equal and opposite in the impersonal imperative of "go down," a locution which evokes both the irresistibility and indifference of an anonymous and unknowable (uninterpretable) down-thrusting agency.

Emily-May Kervick is no Odysseus, obviously. And she's no Robinson Crusoe either, not merely by virtue of the physical facts of her case but by the inability she has in common with her sisters to understand their deteriorating plight, a failure expressed by sister Helen in the following terms:

> "Listen, have you ever considered this: that Crusoe's life could only cease to be intolerable when he stopped looking for a sail and resigned himself to living with his dependents under a mountain—have you ever thought of that?" (*FDS* 25)

No member of the Kervick household is capable of answering this question, including Helen herself, and certainly not Emily, who in all senses of the word is not part of the conversation. Yet by virtue of the very silence in which it is received, the question introduces a view of Crusoe as an emblem of making good loss, specifically when in full consciousness of what that loss signifies.

This view persists through many variations and alignments over the course of Higgins's work. If Crusoe is one who has been "lost in a sea of waters" (Joyce 168), he also discovers, as a direct consequence, his own worth. Swimming goes on in the shadow of sinking. Retrieval presupposes wreckage. The place of the littoral—point both of landfall and embarkation—in the *oeuvre* comes to mind. And in *Images of Africa* the *Crusoe* epigraphs preface the parts of the story dealing with getting to know the territory and then setting up house there, and with indications that the former is echoed in the latter, united here, perhaps, by a shared emphasis on working for a living. Itinerant and settled are not conditions opposed to each other. Rather, they seem complicit, as transition and temporariness declare themselves the main characteristics of the life lived. Time and space are experienced in fluid, provisional relation, instead of constituting the mausoleum of the affections encasing the existences of Kervicks and Langrishes.

Crusoe, then, may be seen as something of a touchstone for such central Higgins preoccupations as loss, recuperation, difference, integrity, autonomy and return. An image of the problematic son, and of problematic heritage and inheritance, Crusoe also exists with equal, or even more, compelling plausibility as an image of possibility, of all that is released and must be confronted in the aftermath of shipwreck. Further, his utility as a thematic repertoire does not quite exhaust his interest. A more suggestive aspect of his status as a Higgins "prototype" (*AB* 305) is his having traveled, not simply in the geographical sense but in the sense of his having completed his journey. Travel entails limits, returns, endings. In Crusoe's case the return, due as much to its very unlikeliness (his rescue) as to the conditions from which it arose, becomes his warrant for writing. His narrative takes the form of "the life," to the full possession of which he is now entitled, and in terms of which he fashions a property more durable than the island home on which it is based. The act of acknowledging the raw material for what it is also relieves it of the obduracy and recalcitrance of direct experience. Everything is rescued. There is nothing that is not a ground to build on. The protocols of story-telling construct the ultimate in defensive compounds.

But it is at this point, where the Higgins persona might appear to be most closely and most tellingly associated with that of his prototype—in their both being travel-writers, in their both fusing travel with life story, in their both making something of being castaways—that the differences between them become most obvious. Crusoe becomes the self-made man the conventions of "the life" vouchsafe. The Higgins persona remains unmade, landless, stateless, stubborn, a figure immersed in a text that has no teleology rather than the author of a life. Ultimately, the differences are essentially aesthetic, and bear on questions of form, which in turn concern the significance of the return, its finality, completeness, terminus. For it is arguably with regard to this particular area, the sense of an ending, that Higgins's work emerges most clearly into its own light. The set of circumstances established in a Higgins novel—novels which, coincidentally, make use of the material, documentary quiddity of their settings in a thoroughly Defoe-like manner—and the personnel encountered in those circumstances are not brought together in order to achieve oneness, or to stage rescues.

Dan Ruttle and Charlotte Bayless in *Balcony of Europe* do not live together happily ever after. Instead, their landfalls are on other balconies—Connemara for Ruttle, New York City for Charlotte. Both these locations are home, but in Ruttle's case at least the return does not reintegrate him with a former way of life. "Odours from my youth; soft verbena-scented evenings"[4] (*Balcony of Europe* 456) are here, no doubt. But this is no Ithaca, and the sensory evanescences of "Lennane" (*sic*) are no prompts to Proustian indulgence. Their momentary evocation of a lost world cannot, and is not intended to supplant, the Andalusian world recently lost, the world of "transient friends which events bring and events take away" (*BOE* 455). Both realms of experience have been displaced, and both have been retained. Both have equal narrative standing, having attained to that state of perceptual grace existing beyond what Finn FitzGerald, another beached, becalmed but not by any means finished Higgins voyager, calls, "the this and the that, all hazy, that is to say, unwritten"[5] (*Bornholm Night-Ferry* 132).

Rather than concluding in the conventional sense, Higgins's novels break off, drift towards silence, isolation, withdrawal, departure—"Of all that remains, what residue is there, I ask you, trapped in vertiginous Time?" (*LG* 301). The intervening interlude passes, its passing inevitably tending towards fragmentation and dispersal, flotsam and jetsam, its character and trajectory inevitably reproducing, understandably yet unreasonably, the lineaments of the primal misadventure, cornerstone and millstone of the Higgins biography, the tide of things that landed the family on the rocks. As it was in the beginning—certainly, but also, not quite. The primal dislocation has been temporarily displaced, perhaps, by subsequent facsimiles, but it has also been, in a sense, placed, objectified, ratified in its inevitability by its participation in the fate of all things to decline, even (or especially) those most dear. So, Dan and Charlotte part; Finn and Elin part; Weaver and Hannelore, victims and celebrants of the "fugacious nature of life and time,"[6] (*Lions of the Grunewald*) have no hope of lasting either, and not merely because of Lore's pregnancy. Genteel Imogen Langrishe's stillborn child by feral Otto Beck offers an uncharacteristically dark-toned, emotionally stark, finality in which is recapitulated the wreckage of the novel's 1930s historical context, the decay of the Langrishe family's lands and spirits, and the immediate locality with its freight of "human derelicts"[7] (*Langrishe, Go Down* 32)—all of these elements images of each other, and all brought into unavoidable collision by the transitory presence of Otto Beck, "a travelled man" (*LGD* 159).

And yet, what time erodes, mind retrieves. Writing actualizes what is missing, supplies a local habitation and a name to what is lost, declares itself a resource against the vanished years. And one of Higgins's singular artistic accomplishments is to see the written word as a means both of attesting to and arresting all the slippage. If Derek Mahon's addition to Wittgenstein—"The world, though, is also so much more—/Everything that is the case imaginatively"[8] ("Tractatus" 23)—then Higgins's is an *oeuvre* in which it is possible to observe that claim taking shape. That participle is worth noting. Rather than confine experience to the prefabricated norms of "the life," Higgins conveys the ongoingness of experience, its tidal races, its eddies, its doldrums, which in their presentness, their unexplained and inexplicable singularity, are more true to life than genre can hope to accommodate. And as Higgins's *oeuvre* evolves and he abandons even the comparatively slight hold on the commonplaces of fictional form evident in *Langrishe, Go Down*, the resulting identity—his narrating persona—presents himself, in what its unadorned prose suggests is at least a facsimile of all honesty, as being seduced by what happens in the course of the experience of travel—"All converge, all disperse; reassemble only to disperse again. Figure me there"[9] ("Berlin Days and Nights" 80).

As in a painting, the identity in question embodies many perspectives all present at once in the same field, each having the status of an occurrence in its own right, each a vector of a certain energy and tendency, each a color or tonality, smear or arabesque contributing to an overall image which persuades us of its authenticity by how difficult it is to regulate its activity. We see in combination the writer traveling, the traveler writing, the living moment and the lived moment, the full tide and the ebb tide, the wreck and the aftermath. While Crusoe can be a pointer to this identity, in his abandonment, his expatriation, his improvisations, in his existence within a wreck-age-and-retrieval modality, as a pilot travel writer, he is also a point of departure, a history to be acknowledged by resisting, a rescue to be repudiated, a return that is beside the point. Higgins is Crusoe and anti-Crusoe, both—although it is also possible that the doubleness is itself one of the prototype's legacies: "In an ingenious technique of survival Crusoe had to multiply whatever meager resources lay to hand, *multiply himself* . . ." (*AB* 243; italics in the original).

■

If the traveler is more complicated than one might conventionally expect, so too is the nature of the travel which he documents. Through immersion rather than by guidance—travel as a way of life—is how the reader experiences the travel site. The second paragraph of "Autumn in Cómpeta" reads:

> Insects rise; all is calm; a breeze blows from the right hand, the olive trees shiver, exposing their silvery undersides. Now a mule is led past by an old man with head lowered, a small dog standing on the saddle like a circus

act. I hear the robin in the valley, a repeated series of high
fidgety twitterings. (*RGP* 109)

(This follows an introductory disquisition on local headgear.) The
sensorium supplants the inventory. Immediacy of effect replaces
sense of direction, cardinal points, numbers and names and the
measurable world of roads and habitations. Here and now couple
in the act of apprehension. Presence is registered by sensitivity to
atmosphere, color and so on, not by a preciosity of recapture—and
the ludicrous, too, is allowed its part. To judge such moments, to
incorporate them in a schema is to ignore both their tacit rebuke of
taxonomy (the guide's friend) and their simpler and more important expression of what might be called a felicitous adequacy.

The foreignness, or travel-worthiness, of landscapes and cityscapes are represented not as cartographical spectacles, possessing
contours and colors noteworthy for their peculiarity—or rather,
since it is impossible to overlook this or that striking feature of a
given location, what comes across tends in the activity of describing to undercut mere description:

> The land climbs into the *campo* and from there by stages
> into the sierras; ascending ranges scarred by fire-breaks
> and crowned with lowsized savin and pine. The village of
> Maro is situated on higher ground up there by the caves.
> In summer the nearer ranges of the sierras stand out clearly,
> the back ranges diffused and hazy. In winter this changes
> and far and near alike all the ranges stand out with an
> equal and vivid clarity. A windbreak of cane grows on the
> region lying alongside the narrow shore, its high plumes
> waving in whatever winds that blow. The terraces descend
> from the broken table-land (*tablazo*), shale mixed with
> granite and calcite, where in prehistoric times a great river

came down, carrying all before it. Of this all that remains is a small stream that dries up in grass and moraine before it reaches the sea. Sedimentary rock occurs further along, the stains of fishermen's fires and dried human excrement. Where a gulley or ravine comes, gaps open out, there in former times the wide river forced its way past this delta into the sea. (*BOE* 323)

Thus, Burriana beach and thereabouts. The rock-solid material of the view, sharply composed and represented with a certain spatial scrupulosity, retains its place while also giving rise to a series of substantial seasonal and geological and workaday temporal shifts. The spatial scene may appear, in the moment of apprehension or in keeping with descriptive principles, to be immune from, or raised above, temporality. Instead, time and space are shown to be complicit. The primordial river flood provides the destructive and creative connection. Other matters may be glossed also—the inevitability of the human stain, the precision of the language, the painterly terracing of the visual field (Dan Ruttle, the implied perceiver, the writer, is a painter). The overall effect, however, is that of detached intimacy, blending an objective appreciation of the lay of the land as a matter of geographical fact with an imaginative engagement with the forces that went into the making of such massive ostensible stability, forces whose cataclysmic trace is still to be observed, is not to be written out of the picture.

This blend amounts to a form of knowledge, deriving partly from discovery and partly from domicile. Travel obviously gives rise to discovery, the awareness and, often, pleasure of things not previously seen. Domicile establishes a structure for domesticating the novelty of the foreign, installing it in a round of familiar tasks, obligations, practices and expectations. (Thus, again, venues whose signatures may be seen as time and space are interdependent, opposed, merge and maintain their differences. For this duality of discovery and settlement *Images of Africa* suggests itself as something in the nature of a preliminary sketchbook.) In a word, the form of knowledge is that of "living in" rather than the more typical travel experience of "passing through"—or, more accurately, the combined registers of observation, allusion, historical data, intertextuality, learning and imaginative improvisation which gives Higgins's prose its sense of a known world, the form of knowledge is passing through as living in.

Detachment maintains the observer's integrity, articulates the distinctiveness of his presence, authenticates his travel-writer identity by demonstrating how little of the foreign scene is lost on him, substantiates the value of the outsider (the traveler). But it is also intimacy's mask:

> The old rheumy-eyed breadwoman stands stupefied with cold at the foot of the stairs that I have forbidden her to climb. She waits at the foot of the glacier, calling up *Pan!* drawing a deep shuddering breath, wheezing again *Pan!* Her voice summons me from deep sleep. I put on a raincoat and go down. Her gnarled hands and wrists are knotted like wood, the knuckles shiny; long arms deformed with age, thin and scraggy as branches, hair the colour of sea-grass. Her hooded eyes are filmy like a bird's, the *arcus senilis* has spread; she speaks close to my face, and from her breath I smell decay. She touches my hand, trusts me, her semi-paralysed hands fumble at the purse and presents me with bent *centimos* deformed as her own extremities. (*BOE* 164)

A Goyaesque crone? The figure may indeed be regarded in such a light. Or is she the historic sister of the old milkwoman who troubles Stephen Dedalus's morning in the opening of *Ulysses*? Or perhaps Ruttle is particularly sensitive to the decaying one what with his having recently witnessed his mother's death. Whatever interpretative interest the representation may be called upon to serve, there is also in the material the sheer act of looking, the attentiveness, the patience, the shaping of a perspective through focusing on the hands, the acknowledgment of infirmity, that conveys the impression of nothing being overlooked and of the subject being thoroughly held while at the same time not being relocated in either a Goyaesque or other framework.

Other locals are treated with comparable degrees of absorption, none more so than Miguel Lopez Rojas, proprietor of the Balcony of Europe bar, whose dignity and civility Ruttle holds in special regard, the ultimate expression of which is a reproduction of his headstone in Nerja cemetery on the novel's closing page. Clearly, foreign is not alien. Foreign is its own reality, recognizable and admissible, but also shaped by unknowable historical twists, its own tides of action and reaction. This is a foreignness in which home partakes, as Dan Ruttle recalls from his Sligo childhood and his brother's withdrawal into mental breakdown, as well as from sitting with his "pal,"

> meaning the old man who sits on a bollard on the Mall all day long. I am often with him . . . Smelling of tobacco, old clothes, he makes all seem both far away and near, both perfectly formed and twisted, both exact and forlorn. With him I feel at peace. (*Scenes from a Receding Past* 54)

To remain a local is a special destiny, a matter of fascination to Higgins from the Kervicks of Springfield House ("Killachter Meadow") or the Brazills of the gate-lodge ("Asylum"), on to the grotesque Kinsalers of "Sodden Fields"[10] ("Sodden Fields" 41–82) and the servants and schoolmates of childhood in, particularly,

Donkey's Years. All these are also framed within the traveler's dual perspective of distancing difference and detailed closeness, all images not merely of the joint past but of a country of somebody who is, as Finn FitzGerald writes to Elin Marstrander, "so Irish I cannot live there, can't live anywhere" (*BNF* 45). The destiny is not one the Higgins persona partakes of, obviously. As the vignette of Ruttle and his pal indicates, the peace the local makes available is sufficiently rare, and odd, to merit frank avowal, not the kind of thing the child is used to. As time goes attritionally by, the familiar scenario of a disintegrating family structure asserts itself. Dan moves on, lives here and there, this way and that, in Dublin—"In the dead part of that year, one of those pallid onyx-and-opal days that descend so frequently on the grey capital, I was making my way with no particular purpose towards the Rotunda" (*SRP* 138)—and in London, where the "Arctic scene" (*SRP* 176) of the ice-cream factory he works in is an apt image of the emigrant life.

Yet here again—or for readers inclined to place a strictly autobiographical construction on Higgins's work, here for the first time—departure is a prelude to onset, drift reveals itself as the mask of desire. In meeting Olivia, Dan rehearses the phrase with which Finn FitzGerald concludes his statement about his inability to live anywhere—"except perhaps in you" (*BNF* 45). A similar thought, invoking ideas of embarkation, safety, destination and an acknowledgment of dual presence, occurs in an emblematically aquatic image from the early days of Olivia and Dan. They are in a boat, Dan rowing:

> I pulled, facing Olivia, just a nose and hair now emerging from the seersucker. Water and air were cold, the tide on the turn. Such opaque peace. (*SRP* 155)

Some sort of stay against wreckage is implied, some sort of course to steer, though following the course of Olivia and her various spousal surrogates throughout the Higgins *oeuvre* will reveal the fragility of such peace and the seeming inevitability of their relationship running aground.

Like the Higgins persona, Olivia has a variety of embodiments—variations on the theme of *wieb*. Her one constant is her foreignness—usually South African, but a New Zealander in *Scenes*. She is first among equals in attesting to the truism that to travel is to embrace opposites. And the history of the Higgins persona is essentially the history of that embrace. That history's key component is, of course, physical. But it also has a marked linguistic strand within it, indicative of the degree of intimacy Higgins attains with the host culture, how willingly he gives himself to, and avails, of differences in phrase and allusive repertoire, and even, in *Bornholm Night-Ferry*, in idiolect, not only in the publication of Elin's imperfect English but in the acknowledgment of that unique language of hers as indispensable and integral to the character of her epistolary exchanges with, and the quality of her attachment to, Finn, who applies a context for it: "Do you know Swift's Journal to Stella [sic]? It has an invented love-language in it" (*BNF* 41). Here, the loved one's language is an inimitable code of intimacy, even when it documents commonplace events in Elin's daily life and work in far-off Copenhagen. It's a code whose embrace both dissolves and accentuates distance. But, in general, to be immersed in the linguistic code of the foreign expresses a desire for cultural intimacy, a desire never to be fully satisfied, since the traveler cannot be a native, though on that account all the more a psychological reality.

Another sign of the embrace's remit is a type of residential savvy, a kind of conversancy with the foreign surroundings that seems to reproduce linguistic familiarity. This know-how, yet a further expression of knowledge as a form of intimacy, is particularly evident when cityscapes are being negotiated, as though to allay Dan

Ruttle's admission, "I hate my rustic ignorance" (*SRP* 38). London, Berlin, Málaga, are not so much explored as ingested, or rather drunk down, another facet of absorption.

> Weaver, a great walker, took to rambling about the Rehweise or took the path that traversed the Joachim-Klepper-Weg; for could you find anything pleasanter than emerging from the shadowy wood to espy just ahead the blue neon sign for Schultheiss Bier welcoming the drinkers in, and Wieland far away in the vaults of the bank on the Bundesallee! (*LG* 11)

Weaver is not lost. He is making his own, apparently uninformed, way, forging ahead, sticking to the path, where he does not meet any dangers or distractions. He proceeds unchallenged, ends up in a place indicating the city's hospitality, can begin to discourse freely about the city's other reaches. Angst does not attend his going forth. His venturing step yields pleasure. The passage's various landmarks signify Weaver knows what he's doing, he has learned to function, to appear in his confident navigation to be as a Berliner—although the native would not necessarily consider his perambulation either an accomplishment or a pleasure. Weaver's jauntiness conveys both, from which one possible conclusion, at least, may be said to follow—he knows that his getting to know the city is achieved by some intimacy with it.

Both the linguistic and the domiciliary aspects of the embrace of opposites also has a degree of reciprocation in it (he speaks, he is spoken to; he walks the street, the street leads him). And obviously in the physical character and conception of the embrace reciprocation goes without saying (he loves, he is loved). Reciprocity and complementarity even has a geographical dimension in these relationships—Olivia, as noted, comes from the far side of the world;

which side, precisely, is beside the point, since there are two and since, more importantly, the loved one is, to some necessary degree, an imagined one. Charlotte Bayless has arrived in the south of Spain from San Francisco. And the same general area of Spain, focusing on Compéta, is the venue for trysts with both Hannelore and Elin, the latter a native of what's called "The Opposite Land" (*RGP* 163–175). In one way or another, these lovers are also travelers, venturers, fetching up on unexpected shorelines, in unanticipated circumstances, birds of passage, figureheads of the strangeness that is in any case characteristic of their temporary resting places, a temporariness made more explicit by their own restlessness, their own capacities for desire, for intimate knowledge.

The joint, mutual articulation of desire—the discovery of one another, the "knowing" in the Biblical sense, the appreciation of difference and its difficulties which the discovery discloses—focuses and intensifies the detachment and intimacy intrinsic to the travel experience. Not only is it important that Dan Ruttle's, Finn FitzGerald's and Dallan Weaver's affairs are in their different ways affronts to conventional morality, in view of each persona's being himself married and the lovers, too, being unfit due to their own family circumstances. Under such conditions, the risk that the primacy of desire will culminate in wreckage seems highly likely. It also seems necessary that the women in question are unknowable, that they possess some fundamental and irreducible core which keeps them at a distance even as intimacy flourishes. Thus Charlotte, even if her name has been chosen to emphasize elective affinity,[11] is also colored by her Jewishness, not only through its American form but in the traces it bears of an old European history, a narrative which cannot, after all, be extirpated. In Elin's case, her Danish life is something Finn can observe and enjoy but cannot enter into: "We take a train from Østerport Station to Humlebæk. . . . It is not as I had imagined it. But what ever is? I am with you" (*RGP* 171).

Yet, just as the affairs themselves, by virtue of clandestinity in Charlotte's case and because of distance in Elin's, require a good deal of scheduling, mapping out, itineraries, rendezvous, alternative arrangements, delays and other recognizable elements from the formal framework of travel, so internally they also permit imaginative improvisation, speculation, dreams, fantasies, memories and similar departures common to the activity of writing. The latter phase is indispensable from the first. It is certainly arguable that in their recurring scenarios of love in a warm climate, Higgins's works comprise an erotics of place, and that by doing so an emotional and psychological truth of travel is asserted. Yet, the journey inward which such an erotics also engenders, has perhaps a greater reach, facilitating not only a necessary inventiveness—"Of course I invent you," Finn writes Elin (*BNF* 94)—but that departure out of oneself into another realm which is the traveler's ultimate goal, the attainment of a Rimbaud or a Conrad, the realization of that state expressed in an epigraph attributed to Montaigne in *Scenes from a Receding Past*—"C'est ainsi que je fons et eschape à moi" (translated, in the text, as, "Thus do I dissolve and take leave of myself"). This is the spirit of travel, to trust to the buoyant, wilful tide without direction or landfall, but simply for the sake of being sustained by its force, sink or swim. Or both.

> Ortega says that in loving we abandon the tranquillity and permanence within ourselves and virtually migrate towards the objects of our desire; this constant state of migration is what it is to be in love—a constant state of migration. ("The Bird I Fancied" 180)

The external form of this state is travel. Its internal form is writing.

Works Cited

Higgins, Aidan. "Asylum." *Felo de Se*. London: Calder, 1960.

—. *Balcony of Europe*. London: Calder & Boyars, 1972.

—. "Berlin Days and Nights: Letters from Lindermann, 1969–70." *Ronda Gorge & Other Precipices*. London: Secker & Warburg, 1989.

—. *A Bestiary*. Champaign, IL: Dalkey Archive Press, 2004.

—. *Bornholm Night-Ferry*. Dingle: Brandon, 1983.

—. *Images of Africa: Diary (1956–60)*. London: Calder & Boyars, 1971.

—. *Langrishe, Go Down*. London: Calder & Boyars, 1966.

—. "Lebensraum." *Felo de Se*. London: John Calder, 1960.

—. *Lions of the Grunewald*. London: Secker & Warburg, 1993.

—. *Scenes from a Receding Past*. London: John Calder, 1977.

—. "Sodden Fields." *Helsingør Station & Other Departures*. London: Secker & Warburg, 1989.

James Joyce: Occasional, Critical and Political Writing. Kevin Barry. Oxford: OUP, 2000.

Joyce, James. "Realism and Idealism in English Literature (Daniel Defoe—William Blake)." *Occasional, Critical, and Political Writing*. Ed. Kevin Barry. Oxford: Oxford University Press, 2000. 163–182.

Mahon, Derek. "Tractatus." *The Hunt By Night*. Winston-Salem, NC: Wake Forest University Press, 1982. 23.

Notes

1. Further references to this work *(FDS)* will be made parenthetically in the text. This book appeared in an American edition as *Killachter Meadow* (New York: Grove, 1961) and in a revised edition

as *Asylum and Other Stories* (London: Calder, 1978); the story also appears in Higgins, *Flotsam & Jetsam* (London: Minerva, 1996).

2. Originally *Images of Africa: Diary (1956–60)*.

3. Further references to this work (*AB*), which contains Higgins's autobiographical trilogy—*Donkey's Years* (1995), pp. 5–252; *Dog Days* (1998), pp. 253–448; and *The Whole Hog* (2000), pp. 449–742—will be made parenthetically in the text.

4. Further references to this work (*BOE*) will be made parenthetically in the text.

5. Further references to this work (*BNF*) will be made parenthetically in the text.

6. Further references to this work (*LG*) will be made parenthetically in the text. For another treatment of some of this novel's wreckage-strewn and terminal events see Jill Anders, *McDaid's Wife* (London: Marion Boyars, 1988).

7. Further references to this work (*LGD*) will be made parenthetically in the text.

8. This poem is dedicated to Higgins, and opens by quoting Wittgenstein's well-known dictum, "The world is everything that is the case."

9. Further references to this work (*RGP*) will be made parenthetically in the text.

10. Higgins, "Sodden Fields," in *Helsingør Station & Other Departures* (London: Secker and Warburg, 1989): 41–82, a piece relevant to the nature of "the return" for the Higgins persona.

11. The allusion is to Goethe's novel, *Elective Affinities*, whose leading female character is called Charlotte, a name with distinctively passionate reverberations for Goethe. Here is a complicated illustration of Higgins's densely intertextual fictions, indicative of his extensive travels in the European canon and beyond.

Despair and Desire:
Langrishe, Go Down and a Poetics of the Body

ROBERTA GEFTER WONDRICH

After decades of what has been a nearly unchallenged postcolonial critical orthodoxy in which the "literature of the Big House" has not always been at the fore of the most avant-garde critical speculation, it may be tempting to see how *Langrishe, Go Down* can be re-read as a seminal novel in the context of Irish literature today. That is to say, of an internationalized, well-established Irish contemporary literature that, nonetheless, at the beginning of the new, globalized century's first decade still dwells on its identitarian preoccupations.

Since Higgins's *Langrishe* is perhaps the most Irish novel of this purportedly European-Irish writer, it makes sense to examine some aspects of this work which branch out and connect to some crucial literary contexts. Richard Kearney places the novel in his Counter-Tradition of Irish fiction, and its acknowledged Modernist affiliation eschews a clear-cut collocation within the Irish canon, much like its Joycean indebtedness, since Higgins made use of a crucial and specific feature of "the Irish matter" such as the Anglo-Irish decline and the world of the Big House in order to question it and inherently remythologize it on a wider, European and international scale.

Langrishe, Go Down is in fact, *also* a Big House novel or, better, a radical reworking of the genre which revives its basic formal and thematic conventions, set in Celbridge, Co. Kildare, and centered on two Anglo-Irish aging sisters, Helen and Imogen Langrishe and their aimless, miserable life in the family mansion, Springfield House. The narrative structure is tripartite, beginning in 1937 with a powerful portrait of Helen's anguished reconsideration of her life and followed by a second section, set in 1932, which recounts the destructive, doomed love affair between Imogen and a younger, thirty-five-year old German would-be scholar, Otto Beck, living in a lodge on the estate, who eventually abandons her. The final and shortest part, set in 1938, describes Helen's death and burial and Imogen's growing awareness of her unhappiness, solitude and impending death.

This *début* novel, still Higgins's most famous work to date, has often been critically paired with another groundbreaking and subversive Big House novel, Banville's outstanding *Birchwood* (1973) and the coverage it has received over the decades (Beja, O'Neill, Imhof, Kreilkamp, Murphy) has focused mostly on its radical renovation of the genre and its formal and stylistic choices, indebted to High Modernism and aimed at dispensing with the realism and naturalism of the contemporary Irish mainstream. In this regard, it could be argued that the intertextual echoes, allusions and reminiscences are sometimes so self-consciously paraded as to suggest an underlying ironic, self-conscious skepticism; this is also the case with the many Joycean echoes,[1] which include the interior monologue technique, the piling of names, topographies and historical references, and several motifs. The Joycean strand is traceable through a great deal of allusions, from Imogen's aimless roaming of Dublin city on the aftermath of her squalid sexual initiation, to the epigraph from *Finnegans Wake* in chapter 10, and so is the tribute to T. S. Eliot, which is made explicit by the reference to *The Waste Land* when Otto Beck tells Imogen that the Starnbergersee is his homeland, and is crucial to the whole imagery of the novel, as it will be shown.

While the historical plight in which the characters find themselves is sketched through Helen Langrishe's gloomy meditations in the opening section of the novel, the social scope covered by the narrative is essentially no exception to the rule of the genre, as it merely glances at the Catholic and socially inferior Irish people, opting instead for marginal, semi-bohemian and petty bourgeois figures. As Vera Kreilkamp remarks in her extensive study of the Big House novel, "Even the most successful novels do not offer the double narrative [...]: the Big House and the cabin, Protestants and Catholics, Ascendancy and peasant culture, the conquerors and the dispossessed" (*The Anglo-Irish Novel* 265). With *Langrishe, Go Down*, Higgins seems to have actualized one of the most important and fascinating aspects of "Big House fiction in Ireland"—"the fact that it reflects cultural ambivalence and self-irony. It defines Anglo-Irish experience as doomed from the start" (ibid.). It remains to be argued, instead, on what terms he actually engages with another thematic asset of the novel; the counterpart to the awareness of Anglo-Ireland's disintegration which constitutes that "doubleness"—a hallmark of the Big House novelistic tradition: "the vision of a lost ideal and a failed cultural purpose—of social responsibility, enlightened landlordism, or personal dignity" (*The Anglo-Irish Novel* 268). The bleakness of tones with which the whole family saga, and the descriptions of the house itself are presented, disclose a radical skepticism that obfuscates any residual vestige of an idealized, Yeatsian world of the Big House, and rather reveal an essential mediocrity and inadequacy. There are, in fact, in the sisters' reminiscences, only vague references to a pristine life, prior to the dystopic fall of Springfield House, much like there seems never to have been a true family tradition, because the Langrishes were Catholics who bought the property, only to let it go over the years.

Thus Helen, in the opening section, broods over the present in sort of ominous *cupio dissolvi*:

> The world was in a bad way. Full of calamities, real or im-
> aginary, impending or completed [. . .]. Let it, she thought,
> let it be. Let it all happen, and, as violently as possible—
> with the utmost ferocity. Let it snow, too. She would not
> live to see another war. (*LGD* 12)

In other words, in Higgins's vision there is, ostensibly, very little
at work of that ambivalence in the writer's stance which is one of
the sources of the prolonged vitality and complexity of the genre.
There seems to be very little worth praising and idealizing even in
the original version of the Langrishe estate, never a truly aristocratic mythological place. Helen Langrishe, the eldest sister and
the true critical conscience of the family, is well aware that "the old
impossible world was ending" (18), but it is doubtful whether that
world was ever truly blissful and harmonic. The fact that the Langrishes, the sisters' parents, were actually Catholics who acquired
the house in recent times, is decisive to the Anglo-Irish pedigree of
the estate: while they are somehow diminished in their prestige and
authenticity as Ascendancy members, they appear to be interesting
precisely because of the even greater hybridity and indeterminacy
of their social and cultural status.

Higgins thus is resolute in his rejection of any residual Yeatsian
idealization of the (autobiographical) world of Springfield House.
There isn't the vaguest hint, in the depiction of the estate, of that
aura, that uncontestable fascination which Elizabeth Bowen defined as "the inner force of its style," referring to *Bowen's Court*,
very little of what she called an "aesthetic of living."

Rather, there are many instances in the narrative where the
memory and representation of the past at Springfield House are
informed by a bleakness of tones, as Helen, in particular, is aware
that there is no way out of the Langrishes' existential dead end. In
a brilliant scene, where Helen contemplates her condition while in

In this regard, it is also interesting to consider that Higgins re-elaborates the gender issue, problematizing the role of the daughters—for the Langrishe heirs are all women—and hence of Anglo-Irish patriarchy, without subscribing to the trope of the feminine nature of Ireland and Anglo-Ireland in a cliched, oppositional fashion. Rather, he re-contextualizes the socio-political and historical connotations in such a way as to privilege metaphors over tropes, cultural allusiveness over stereotypical links with the literary antecedents of the genre and a more general Irish "canon." Although the Langrishe sisters were actually modeled on Higgins's brothers, their psychological depth and consistency as characters is quite relevant to the overall conception of the novel, and so is their sense of and quest for identity as women. Far from merely complying to the trope of the violated, "conquered," subjected nation, both Helen and Imogen self-consciously interrogate their identity and destiny, acknowledging what is also a physical bond with their place in the world, their crumbling "home."

On the whole, though, what appears to be the true hermeneutic key to the complex texture of the novel is an all-pervasive concern with the imagery and the rhetorical uses of the *body*, to the extent that this polysemic reality, conceived as a cultural, epistemological entity rather than as a biological one, emerges as a structuring feature.

Apparently, the centrality of the body and of the physical, corporeal dimension is no novelty to the tradition of the Big House novel in which, as Neil Corcoran succinctly puts it, "the fall of the house is frequently a matter of literal, physical depredation" (Corcoran 36). Vera Kreilkamp in her study of the genre underlines that "[t]he hypocrisy, self-delusion, or drunken improvidence of Edgeworth's Rackrents, Lever's Martins, Somerville's Prendevilles, and Keane's Swifts are presented to the reader in detailed account books, as it were, of physical decay and social irresponsibility" (*The Anglo-Irish Novel* 268). Higgins, however, thematizes the idea of a social, historical and cultural decline, and physical disintegration, by means of a powerful pervasiveness of the body as both metaphor and metonym, replete with explicitly Modernist literary allusions and intertextual echoes.

All the different sections which form the family narrative of the Langrishe sisters are dominated by images of the aging, decaying or sick body, and by a deep discomfort bred by its spectacle. Such is the case—only to mention some of the most significant instances—with Helen's sense of revulsion at having to face the proximity of other bodies in the very opening pages:

> In a great stench of perspiring and unwashed bodies, they were there, all about her. In the stuffy, smoke-laden atmosphere others more robust than she experienced no discomfort, giving off their warm bands of heat and well-being. (11)

But there is also the picture of Helen's "abject" aging, Imogen's recalling of the agony and death of her father, focused on his "flaccid, wrinkled" and "intolerably cold hands" (55), and again, Helen's self-conscious agony in the house "languishing" and "freezing," "dead with cold" (71).

In the first section, dated 1937, the sisters are, by now, entrapped in their own bodies and reduced to a kind of disabled condition, while the house itself is fleetingly represented as a body, as a massive, ailing body now grim and unkempt, doomed to barrenness and sterility, the orchard neglected, the trees felled and sold. As in other Big House novels, the "physical fall from grace is the outward sign of an inward catastrophe" (Corcoran 36).

It is through and upon their own wasting bodies that Helen and Imogen Langrishe face the slings and arrows of their being in the world, the senseless wasteful existence of their class, the downfall of a small world that will soon end, darkened by one of the most grim moments of Western civilization.

The corporeal perception of the domestic spaces and the tendency to personify the house itself is actually a relevant feature of the Big House novel imaginary, and it could be equated to what Gaston Bachelard considers a "body-space" in his idea of the house as a kind of body. If, according to Bachelard, the rooms and corridors of a house articulate "the topography of our intimate being" (Bachelard xxxii), Springfield appears to be in the grip of an un-romantic cold:

> In the airless study a coal fire was burning wastefully up the chimney . . . In this small library permeated with a dry heat they had spent most of the winter, hardly talking at all, the inner calves of their legs mottled down, like burns on pancakes. They could not leave the fire on cold nights. (21)

> Night comes. The darkened house is breathing . . . windy, bronchial. (71)

Even the cat's body is affected by the same decay that permeates the estate and its inhabitants ("His body, stiff as a board, had resisted all contact with her" [23]), and the pets are connoted by the repulsiveness of the life-cycle, as from time to time they bring home "dismembered rats, thrushes and robins, disposing of them in a semi-masticated condition about the bed" (24).

The centrality of the body as essentially sick, decaying, degraded and somewhat disabled, especially when gendered as female in relation to the Langrishe sisters, becomes apparent from the very first description of what remains of the family, when Helen's *toilette* reveals an aging, toothless woman shedding hair, soon to be followed in physical collapse by the other sisters, Lily, and Imogen who is "moulting" in her turn. Aging for women is never graceful in the novel, as the parodic echo of Yeats's "Scholars," "bald heads forgetful of their sins," foreshadows: "Soon they would be bald as old men, sitting around the fire at night, holy shows" (25). And, again: "Soon we will be old. Old, ill and poor; and when we die no one will mourn for us, or afterwards remember us" (71).

The sense of impending death, as the physical annihilation of being, affects all the sisters, who turn to what surrounds them in search of answers. Imogen interrogates the household objects, the memories of the family romance gone sour, and finds no answer to her dismay:

> The inheritance had not come. Offers of marriage had not come. The money they had, it had dwindled away. Where had the fine life gone to, and what would they do now? With fingers pressed to her cheek she stared at the rusted paraffin lamp, which told her nothing. (48)

Ultimately, like the female uttering voice in *The Waste Land*, a willing Philomel, she knows she can connect nothing with nothing.

Helen, the eldest, is, in a way, the true critical conscience of the novel, and in her interior monologues she is shown questioning the history and the memory of her class, her place, revealing that she once had the ambition of writing "a history of the whole area." Helen thinks of "all the Langrishe *moribundi*" (33), visits an old church at Donycomper and meditates gloomily, Bloom-like: "Dusty roots, a piece of oxidized metal, brown bones of dead animals, the scant dropping of the living. Alenscourt: what did that name mean to her?" (34). All of Helen's attempts at interrogating the past and its symbols, its testimonies and ghosts, are ultimately vain: to her, Lear-like, nothing seems to come of that nothing which communal and personal history represent and have always been to her and her sisters. Significantly, both Irish history and landscape, the celebrated, culturally and historically resonant landscape of Ireland, are utterly unyielding to her, as if frozen in a mutual deadlock of indifference. In front of a spectacle of "picturesque Irish antiquity," Helen muses:

> But nothing had come out of this. It all lay in bits and pieces in three big green notebooks. Her grasp of history was poor. She could not assemble the material she had collected, no, not in any coherent way. In the course of years the evidence itself was disappearing back into the ground [. . .]. The landscape, so indifferent to its history, the bloody battles waged upon it and for it, still turned its back upon the living. (39)

This notion of a landscape indifferent to history, rather than in some ways consubstantial with it, is a crucial element in the "un-Irishness" of Higgins's revised version of the Big House novel and its pastoral subtext, and, even more importantly, of his very personal engagement with some of the most important tropes of Irish literature, such as, in this case, the sense of place and the idea of landscape as place/space always inscribed with the historical past, the idea, to quote Terry Eagleton, that "in Ireland Nature becomes history" (11). On the whole, as Vera Kreilkamp remarked, "in its most powerful moments *Langrishe, Go Down* is about the loss of historical memory, and even more painfully, about living in a world where history itself has been transmuted into the debris of civilization. For Stephen Dedalus history is a nightmare; for Helen Langrishe, history consists of the dead monuments of a dead culture" ("Reinventing" 210).

The Big House novel has often been classified as a predominantly feminine genre, both by virtue of the feminization of the house itself, of its having been largely woman-authored and also because its main characters are most often women. *Langrishe, Go Down* complies with this tendency, although the character of Otto is—though entirely disagreeable—extremely dominating.

And the gender issue too appears to be informed by a dominant imagery of the body. On the one hand the novel entails the feminization of the Big House in the person of its daughters (not exactly the colonizers' daughters, though, to quote the title of a book on the topic,[2] for the Langrishes are Catholics, not Protestant Ascendancy). On the other, femininity is always deeply troubled in the narrative, whether because of the lack of fulfillment or excess of desire, the two sides of the same coin for many repressed Irish and Anglo-Irish literary characters in modern Irish fiction. This, in fact, has long been a foremost theme in the Irish fictional imagination among authors as diverse as Edna O'Brien, Brian Moore, John McGahern, Jennifer Johnston, Mary Morrissy, to name a few.

Furthermore, the feminization of the land/nation may also be seen to surface in a sort of willing surmise of the feminine essence of the Big House as a kind of attempted survival which is dramatized in Imogen and Otto's love affair.

Those who remain of the family are besieged by doubt and anxiety: while Helen has "never known the love of the body or of the heart" (76), Imogen chooses to give herself up to Otto because she does not want to become another living corpse, like her sisters. Helen clings to her despair, Imogen to her desire.

Thus, the centrality of the body in the novel also connects to the issue of taboo and transgression in modern Irish writing, which figures in a remarkable tradition that aligns names such as Joyce, Edna O'Brien, John McGahern, Pat McCabe among many others.

Imogen can thus be seen as an interesting representative of the thwarted, impaired true nature of an idealized Irish and Anglo-Irish womanhood, signaled by Otto's ironic and hypocritical reference to the "essential purity of Irish women" (211); and to "Irishwomen as being so pure and so clean . . ." (210). The irony lies not only in Otto's ruthless and exploitative male chauvinism, but also in Imogen's basic persuasion that she exists primarily as a desiring, corporeal creature, as shown by her yearning to debase herself with Otto: "I wouldn't mind being his trollop. Him to be cruel to me, as such men are reputed; he could do anything he likes with me. What else is my soft white useless woman's flesh good for? What else?" (91).

Significantly, Imogen is aware of Otto's predatory nature and attitude to her, as is evident when she bears witness to an act of sheer sadism on his part which symbolically foreshadows her own tragic physical undoing at his hands, when Otto, trout-fishing, makes a display of his cruelty:

> A knifeblade flashed. He had cut the fish open on the grass. Its stomach. Roes. Pathetic mouth. A little trout— female this time. Holding in his cupped hand the helpless larvae, half an inch long, twitching in the palm of his hand, he extended them to her. [. . .]

His lips found mine, his hands my breasts. How he sta-
red at me with famished eyes! He treats me as if I were
meat. His seed burns me. Bonemarrow. The firm pressure
of another's body in the cling of the embrace. Gentle and
then not gentle any more. (196–97)

In *Langrishe, Go Down*, the body is primarily Eliotian, not Joycean, or, rather, consonant with *Dubliners* rather than *Ulysses*, despite the many intertextual hints: the female body, most significantly, but the male body as well, is marked by, inscribed with decay and loss, indifference and senselessness, almost anesthetized
on the eve of its final undoing.

It is remarkable, I guess, that what is perhaps the most strikingly
direct Joycean allusiveness, disseminated through the text and
anticipated from the beginning with Helen's meditations, should
be of an explicitly funereal character, and that it also pairs significantly with the pervasive sense of spiritual and cultural *paralysis*
that entraps the lives of the Langrishe sisters. *Dubliners* looms large
over many pages of the novel.

This is a crucial feature of the novel's cultural critique with regard to Irish tropes: even while Joyce had achieved the most outstanding celebration of the human body in its physicality and actuality—at the same time exploiting its metaphorical and symbolic
implications to the utmost—his many representations of it had
almost invariably been tightly bound up with the issue of religion
and religious culture, hence also with Catholic Ireland's obsessive
denial of the primacy of the body. Molly's and Bloom's unrestrained
physicality ultimately exceeds the confines of the Irish dimension,
with Bloom being a Hungarian Jew and Molly an Anglo-Spanish
Jewess. Unlike Joyce's bodies, T. S. Eliot's ones, instead, at least as
far as the explicitly quoted *Waste Land* is concerned, are the "living

corpses," the lost, violated shells of the whole Judeo-Christian/ Western civilization, de-contextualized while actualized through the juxtaposed temporalities of the Mythic method.

The sexed, gendered body also figures in Higgins's radical re-definition of a recurring theme of the Big House novel, the misalliance between the Ascendancy and the alien world; as Kreilkamp notes: "The insecurity of Ascendancy society before the native Irish expresses itself just as frequently in sexual anxiety about—or fascination with—misalliance" (*The Anglo-Irish Novel* 20). But, while Higgins imbues Imogen and Otto's sexual affair—and hence their bodily identity—with a historical and political connotation in his conspicuous emphasis on physical decay in its lowest manifestations, from illness to depravation, he focuses primarily on a *cultural* idea and representation of the body. More precisely, he offers a figuration of the body that engages with many tropes of Irish culture (repression and taboos, the thwarted awakening, illness and unhappy motherhood) while being part of a wider imaginary of decay and decline. The Langrishe sisters' ungracefully aging bodies and Otto's sturdy, vicious ugliness are ultimately *figurae* of a decaying civilization of which both Anglo-Ireland, Catholic Ireland and Western Europe are part. Bodies fall apart, the center cannot hold, mere ugliness is loosed upon the Big House world.

It is primarily through Imogen's body that the structuring and unifying imagery of the body unfolds in the novel: it is her previously suffering, repressed and later awakened body that acts and functions as an Eliotian unifying consciousness of the tripartite narrative, Tiresias-like. Yet the protagonist's self-awareness proves inadequate to withhold both the destructive emotional pressure of her affair with Otto and the final family disgrace. Quite explicitly, Imogen's restless and frustrated inexperience—sexual and psychological—mirrors her cultural ignorance and identitarian indeterminacy, a kind of original sin which affects her family and people, the blemish of the Anglo-Irish.

This is dramatized in Imogen's masochistic submissiveness to Otto, as she becomes "the abject slave of his foreign conqueror" (160) who constantly belittles and humiliates her, priding himself on his greater culture and intelligence: "He established his intellectual superiority. Namely that she accept the role that had been given her: that of being unable to contribute anything" (217). Furthermore, she is trapped in her unequal gender role; just like her sister, Imogen is haunted by a sense of bodily helplessness, a physical annihilation of being, and by the foreboding and the anxiety of her own death. Her anguish finds an outlet in the semi-grotesque Christ-like self-identification of her dream, and, most notably, her body is finally revealed as the sacrificial body of the story, and as a sacrificial body in history and in the history of Ireland:

> Such a strange dream, Imogen said, passing her hand across her face several times. I dreamt that Christ's body was discovered in the Ural Mountains outside a town called Vlannick, which I don't suppose exists. But later on in the dream it was me they had unearthed. I mean I was Him, two thousand years buried under the earth. (26)

In keeping with the frequently circular patterns that sustain the narrative texture of the novel, the motif of the unearthed dead body returns towards the end, in the grotesque burial of Helen's corpse, when Imogen falls into a kind of trance, a fantasy of being entombed, falling in the bottomless pit of the grave. It is a vision of her forthcoming death:

I went through the hole with increasing difficulty . . . in
dread of the mass of stone over me . . . attempting it alone
I was held fast, not being able to move forward or back,
caught between two spurs of stone . . .

Lying there in the dark among the woodlice and other
ground insects, in my mouth the taste of fallen mortar
and weeds, I heard the wind in the woods and the noises
that begin there at night, a prey to curious fancies. (240)

When she comes to her senses she is horrified to see that the coffin
will not fit because the grave has not been dug long enough. The
tragic grotesque of this botched burial is masterly attuned with
an authentically elegiac, humane note, at once far from pathos
and black humor, as if here Higgins were exploring the mystery
of the death of the body, combining a touch of "Hades" and "The
Burial of the Dead," and striking a very personal note which is
noteworthy in the rich array of Irish literary funerals, from Joyce
to McGahern.

The threatening, deathly overtones which permeate the natural
imagery of the novel are also implicitly and explicitly allusive to the
Gothic strand of the Big House tradition, in a way that suggests its
displacement onto nature itself and the body. The natural scenery,
and especially the animals which people the mansion and its surroundings while the "whole house creaks and groans" (71), are all
either dead or under threat, doomed as prey to other animals or
predators, like Otto, the human predator, the poacher who sponges
his living out of what remains of the Langrishe household. Animals
are associated with a potential danger even in their harmlessness,
as when Imogen bathes in the river and fears being eaten alive by
"scores of minnows," in a scene that evokes a multiple intertextual
allusiveness which ranges from *Hamlet*'s drowning of Ophelia to

Ulysses ("Proteus"),[3] in a *mise en abyme* of Joycean echoes from the Shakespearean sea-change in *The Tempest*, along with a parodic hint to Joyce's Anna Livia, to whom Imogen is compared in the epigraph to chapter 10:

> Imogen (a confirmed non-swimmer) in her underclothes, watched her pale body under the brown water. Down in the partial darkness of the stream. [. . .]
>
> She removed her underclothes, hung them on the bough, sank again to the full stretch of her arms until the river was up to her chin. Close to her ears she could hear its murmur. Running river, running river, carry me away with you. Sensation of drift, being of water. Quite soon she felt all over her minute sucking mouths, scores of minnows, a touch impersonal, insistent, soft, sucking. She looked down and saw them. Attracted by white flesh, darkly against her, tugging at her. Down below there her white limbs stretched. Touch. Down there being touched.
>
> – Otto . . .
>
> No response.
>
> – Otto! I'm being eaten alive by these damn minnows! Otto sitting near the hamper, examining his fly-case, ground his teeth in fury, ignored her, puffing at his pipe.
>
> Demolish a stray dog or a cat. Their toothless disagreeable little kissing mouths. Kissers. Down sink the white bones. Into smoke of settling mud. Carcass disappears. (*LGD* 192)

The white bones of the imagined disappearing carcass are yet another Eliotian echo, as the image is reminiscent of *The Waste Land*'s third section.[4] As in the fourth section, "Death by Water," Imogen's sexual parable does not prove to be a full awakening and metamorphosis into a lush, sexually fulfilled new woman, so much as the painful revelation of the end of hopes, youth and regeneration, to be followed by the same sad agony that befell her sisters. The densely textured semantics of the ailing body thus connects the house, the animal and human world alike, creating a repetitive pattern of correspondences, as when the repulsive description of the "carcass" of a cow, dead with calf (169) reads on second thoughts as an intimation of Imogen's "abject" miscarriage in late pregnancy, which signals her inner dying.

The contemporary philosophical and theoretical debate has extensively argued that the body is invariably inscribed with multiple discursive significance, but it has also emphasized how the body is, in a way, as a living entity, an essential bearer of subjective memory. As Neil Murphy reminds, one of Aidan Higgins's primary recurring epistemological concerns has always been the significance, and unreliability of memory, the difficulty of knowing one's existence, and the flood of transience that challenges such attempts to know one's life (Murphy 55). *Langrishe, Go Down* also contains a deep meditation on the meaning of the past in cultural terms, both beyond and at one with the subjective experience. As we have seen, the loss of historical memory is ultimately a radical questioning of its sense and meaning, which inevitably leads to a (subjective) reinvention of the past that is in itself an attempt to survive.

As a member of that second generation of the "Counter Tradition" of Irish fiction, to again borrow Richard Kearney's taxonomy, Higgins basically adopts a "Modernist narrative attitude to the past, memory and imagination, taking for granted the distance between the narrator's subjective consciousness and the historical world" (Kearney 98). As Imogen reflects, this Modernist gap between experience and memory can be deceptive, but necessary to survive, to cope with a half-lived life: "The memory of things—are they better than the things themselves?" (*LGD* 67), she wonders. This is certainly the case for Imogen, who recalls her love affair with Otto as a source of happiness and fulfillment, despite the humiliations she had to suffer at his hand, while Helen lacks this consolatory prop, and remains obsessed by the memory of her class, her people, her elusive history never to be traced down.

Again, in this crucial thematic and intellectual preoccupation of the novel—and of Higgins's entire output—with the subjective and historical past, the body holds a focal role, as it is always intrinsically bound up with the issue of transience, transformation, suffering and pain in the individual consciousness of the characters. The most striking instance, as seen, is when Helen in her interior monologue ponders how history begins and ends in her: her identity is resolutely corporeal, her decaying, ailing body a sick, collapsing old world in itself, a disintegrating civilization. All the more so, Imogen's memories cling to the body, her sensual nature having been revived by Otto. Her past, the memory of her past, is constantly marked by bodily images and sensations. She has existed as a desiring body, she is fading out and preparing to die as a violated, destroyed female body, as it becomes evident in the closing chapters of the book, where she begins to drink heavily, distraught by her loneliness, her pregnancy and its tragic epilogue: her fate spans from desire to despair, unquenchable, unassuaged.

Imogen's hazardous misalliance with Otto is melodramatically brought to a double climax, first in her attempted murder, then in the tragic miscarriage in late pregnancy which marks her final undoing by Otto: both episodes are, ultimately, a narrative of the body: the former, told in the third person, shows the woman while trying to shoot him out of jealousy in order to end "the mistake of a lifetime" (225, 227). But she is only partly aware of what she is doing *through* her body, when she perceives her act with her corporeal being as if in a distorted erotic fantasy:

There it was, in a split second, the mistake of a lifetime. The thick obscene feel of it and the kick, the sensation of the stock cushioned in her arms, the recoil . . . she heard and felt nothing more [. . .].

Trembling worse and worse, shaken and groaning (she was being torn bodily apart) her heart twisted in a vice. (227)

The unexpected pregnancy and birth of a stillborn child, instead, is lived as a sort of nightmare, a vision of horror and fear, and recounted in a deeply disturbing interior monologue that renders the distraught woman's thought-flow:

Three months of knowing . . . the drawstring didn't hold, muscle didn't hold . . . child came half out . . . had to be pushed back and muscle sewn up . . . it rotted in there . . . germs killed it . . . exposure to the air. After the thing, the cervix, had been sewn up . . . it didn't come away in a piece . . . decaying matter . . . six months old. [. . .] My stillborn child of that size, his child, turned over inside me and choked itself. The stitches undone . . . whole thing came away . . . flood of dead matter . . . he wouldn't let me see it . . . he said it was a little girl . . . he thought I never knew how it died . . . I knew well enough how it died. (233)

The birthing process, thus, marks the culmination of that visible, graphic "embodiment" of the characters of the novel. It is undeniable, then, that Higgins uses this emphasis on the female body and, in a way, on bodily abjection, in an essentially debunking sense, to demythologize the residual aestheticization of the Big House world and its literary survival. In a fashion similar to a later Big House novel, Molly Keane's *Time after Time* (1983), Higgins dwells on the organic consumption of a culture and a way of living, or, as Wolff claims of Keane's novel: "if Anglo-Ireland has a body [. . .] then stereotypical associations of Anglo-Ireland with 'civilization'—the ideological opposite of categories like 'nature' and 'the body'—do not hold" (Wolff 59–60).[5]

The Kristevian category of the abject looms large over the tragic epilogue of Imogen's life as a woman, which constitutes the culminating point of a dense semantic dissemination of recurrent images of suffering, maimed, ailing and, on the whole, almost repulsive human animal and bodies. The symbolism of the body at times becomes even too graphic and explicit, however, and especially Imogen's final miscarriage is described in pretty unrealistic terms, so as to highlight the "Gothic," morbid, strain that surfaces in the narrative.

Higgins thus shares in that remarkable propensity of modern Irish writing to emphasize images and themes of violation, illness and physical impairment in the representation of the female body. Irish modern and contemporary fiction in particular,[6] both by males and females, persistently display images of fragmentation, violence and abuse perpetrated upon the female body, which frequently lead to dissociation, collapse or—at best—to a questioning of identity and to an obsessive sense of lack and absence. This tendency can be considered a form of cultural discourse, as is always the case when representational practices of the body—and especially the female body—are at stake and comply to certain recurring patterns.

In Eavan Boland's words, the much disputed trope of the feminine nation entails "the powerful and secret meeting between a sexual trope and a historical assertion—a fusion of dominance and powerlessness" (Boland 142); *Langrishe, Go Down* engages with such a trope but does not completely subscribe to an aestheticization of the suffering female body, the "body in pain," to a "glamourized feminine passivity" (Boland). Rather, in this novel Higgins endows the imagery and the idea of the body with the extraordinary polysemic quality and turns it into a potent metaphor, metonym and allegory of desire, decline and despair which ultimately renders the fate of the Anglo-Irish a paradigm for the ambivalence and uncertainty of the modern world.

WORKS CITED

Bachelard, Gaston. *The Poetics of Space*. Trans. Maria Jolas. Boston, MA: Beacon Press, 1969.

Beja, Morris. "Felons of Our Selves." *Irish University Review* 3.2 (Autumn 1973): 163–178.

Boland, Eavan. "New Wave 2: Born in the 50s. Irish Poets in the Global Village." *Irish Poetry Since Kavanagh*. Ed. Theo Dorgan. Dublin: Four Courts Press. 1996, 136–146.

Corcoran, Neil. *After Yeats and Joyce: Reading Modern Irish Literature*. Oxford: Oxford University Press, 1997.

Eagleton, Terry. *Heathcliff and the Great Hunger*. London: Verso, 1996.

Imhof, Rüdiger. *The Modern Irish Novel: Irish Novelists after 1945*. Dublin: Wolfhound Press, 2002.

Joyce, James. *Dubliners*. London: Penguin, 1986.

—. *Ulysses*. London: Penguin, 1986.

Kreilkamp, Vera. *The Anglo-Irish Novel and the Big House*. Syracuse, NY: Syracuse University Press, 1998.

—. "Reinventing a Form: the Big House in Aidan Higgins's *Langrishe, Go Down*." *Ancestral Voice: The Big House in Anglo-Irish Literature*. Ed. Otto Rauchbauer. Hildesheim: Olms Verlag, 1992. 207–222.

Murphy, Neil. "Aidan Higgins." *Review of Contemporary Fiction* 23.3 (Fall 2003): 49–84.

Wolff, Ellen M. *An Anarchy in the Mind and the Heart: Narrating Anglo-Ireland*. Lewisburg, Bucknell University Press, 2006.

NOTES

1. Vera Kreilkamp, instead, states that "[w]riting with a Joycean particularity about place and time, Higgins creates a dense pattern of social contexts for his novel" ("Reinventing" 209).

2. Ruth Frehner, *The Colonizers' Daughters: Gender in the Anglo-Irish Big House Novel*. Tübingen/Franacke, 1999.

3. "Bag of corpsegas sopping in foul brine. A quiver of minnows, fat of a spongy titbit, flash through the slits of his buttoned trouserfly. God becomes man becomes fish becomes barnacle goose becomes featherbed mountain. Dead breaths I living breathe, tread dead dust, devour a urinous offal from all" (*Ulysses* 41–42). The reference is to the drowned man and to the watery sea-change on which Stephen repeatedly dwells.

4. "White bodies naked in the low damp ground / And bones cast in a little low dry garret, / rattled by the rat's foot only, year to year" (193–95).

5. There is no mention of Higgins's text in Wolff's analysis of Keane's novel.

6. Poetry is clearly another cultural context where this issue is most prominent, but I will only refer to fiction (the novel) for obvious reasons of space and topic.

"The Other Day I Was Thinking of You":[1] Love Remembered in *Bornholm Night-Ferry* and *Lions of the Grunewald*

NEIL MURPHY

> As to dream (perhaps the only word we
> cannot put quotation marks around) and
> "reality," whatever that may be, well they
> are for me one and the same.
> —*Bornholm Night-Ferry*

To discover a form that might accommodate his twin obsessions—love and the past—without denying them their full sweeping flow: Aidan Higgins's primary artistic challenge after *Langrishe, Go Down*. In the torrent of years since the extraordinary achievement of that first novel, Higgins has grown to view *Langrishe* as constrained and static[2] in contrast to what came afterwards. This is not least because the form itself, the re-vitalized Big House genre, has natural associations with a specific, linear historical focus. In addition, despite temporal variations, and highly skilled narrative shifts between the Langrishe sisters, as well as the presence of richly textured undercurrents that draw us in like quicksand, the plot remains firmly tied to the principle of sequential life, while simultaneously mirroring the broader sequences of European history. Compared with the ruminating, adventurous consciousness that emerges in the subsequent novels, it is clear that the search for a fluid form has as much to do with reflecting the inclinations of Higgins's perspective as it does with formal artistic design, and because the author's consciousness is firmly embedded in each of the post-*Langrishe, Go Down* primary narrators, (Ruttle in *Balcony of Europe* (1972) and *Scenes from a Receding Past* (1977), Fitzy in *Bornholm Night-Ferry* (1983) and Weaver in *Lions of the Grunewald* (1993)), the narrative perspectives of the novels are as close to Higgins's as is fictionally possible.

The two novels that Higgins published between 1983 and 1993, *Bornholm Night-Ferry* and *Lions of the Grunewald*, remain his most recent sustained long fictions and as such they represent his most mature fictional achievements, particularly in terms of his capacity to construct forms that might accommodate the multiplicity of living. *Bornholm*, Higgins's extraordinary epistolary novel (if that is what it truly is) was, from the outset, seen as an experiment in showing "how to make static figures flow" (Letter to Swainson, 1980), while the chapters in *Lions* are tellingly framed by titles like the "Fugacious Nature of Life and Time," and the "Fugacity of Pleasure, Fragility of Beauty," and the novel itself, a "missionary stew," in narrator-Weaver's words, is an elaborate collage of straight plot, historical gossip, anecdotes, memories, dreams, lists, selections of his children's writing (and a child's sketch), and a continuous spinning-top of circularity, return and echo.

Both novels represent different responses to the enormous difficulty of finding a form that is capable of accommodating the variousness of a mind that tries to operate outside the linearity of static temporal models—a difficulty that was later re-explored in the trilogy of autobiographies, in which the form is deliberately forced to the point of erasure in order to reflect the complex movements of a consciousness in pursuit of its own vanished past, only to repeatedly shift back into view—a now-you-see-it-now-you-don't playful response to the shards of past life. The concept of life-as-remorseless movement, and the parallel refusal to accept living as an ordered sequential set of coherent knowable elements, have always been present in Higgins's work. Almost forty years ago in the early travel document, *Images of Africa*, the sense of multifarious existence is already everywhere evident, including the "dream of living elsewhere . . . on St. Helena, in the Seychelles. Endless life, endless choice" (41). More recently, in "Sodden Fields,"[3] the narratorial voice acknowledges the deeply complex process involved in the transference of interior meaning to textual expression when he confides,

> I tell you a thing. I could tell it otherwise. A few pictures emerge into the light from the shadows within me. I consider them. Quite often they fail to please me. I call them 'pictures' but you kind readers suffering from an ideal insomnia, must know otherwise. What I mean to convey is: movements from the past. (*Helsingør Station* 44)

Experience is repeatedly expressed in terms that suggest intangibility, fragility and evasiveness, and it is in this context that the logic of his formal fictional shapes must be considered. The texts effectively explain their own formal rationale by virtue of the troubled, overt processes of apprehension that are foregrounded. Thus, when Higgins rhetorically asks his readers in the final volume of his autobiography, *The Whole Hog*, "Are not our feelings shapeless, sometimes shameless, uncontrollable, not ours at all?" (220), one has the same sense of the intangibility of human apprehension as when Dan Ruttle, narrator of *Scenes from a Receding Past*, insists that there are only "impressions" which "offer themselves, focus, slip away" (200). Throughout his work Higgins has sought to express some of the quality of this sense of being in the world. For instance, George O'Brien has astutely observed that the materials that form the subject matter of *Scenes*—memories, vignettes, moments, quotations, gossip, arcana, rage, pleasure, boredom—allow the author to "proceed in the direction of that nakedness which is more familiarly the painter's objective" (90–91), while Rüdiger Imhof views the "ruminating narratorial consciousness" of *Balcony of Europe* to be part of the novel's *raison d'être* (258–59), and Harry White draws our attention to Higgins's (in *Ronda Gorge & Other Precipices*) "fluid accumulation of images which convey the past rather than a static composite prose organized around a tangible plot" (212).

In the two novels that form the subject of our attention in this essay, a similar pattern emerges. *Lions* is comprised of a nominal central plot, historical comment and trivia, letters, dreams, extracts from his children's stories, anecdotes (both arbitrary and relevant), and a narrative voice that performs temporal leaps and plot transgressions, all in an effort to express the wandering narratorial consciousness with which one has grown familiar in the previous novels. *Bornholm*'s epistolary form, in turn, excludes the need for a primary interpretive narrator, and thus does not have the intermediary voice to impose shape on the letters. Higgins acknowledged that there might be a "lack of narrative progress" in the text, but believed that this was compensated for by the "attempts at picture making" (Letter to Swainson, 1982). Dermot Healy has similarly argued that "new fictional figures" in *Bornholm*—cities, dreams, sunlight, etc.—"offer a more earthy if desultory observation of a competing world" ("Towards *Bornholm*" 186), in place of the more formal characters of Higgins's previous works.

There is also a sense in which the novel represents an attempt to allow the complexity of the lives of the two letter-writers to express themselves in as unstructured a way as possible, subject only to the limits of the direct voice that speaks in the letters. A further complication lies in the fact that while nominally fictional, the novel is in fact composed of the letters exchanged between Anna Reiner, a Danish poet, and Higgins, between 1975 and 1980; Higgins insists that the letters are authentic, reprinted without revisions, and replete with "Elin's" pigeon English, to preserve the essence of Reiner's character.[4] Thus, while not technically a novel at all, it also becomes increasingly clear in *Bornholm* that the "real" is in fact fictional for the two letter-writers. Furthermore, the "novel" is almost entirely bereft of a central narratorial form and what structure there is emerges primarily from the intense nature of the emotional variations played out in the exchanges between the two writers, and in the process an extraordinarily effective textual-epistolary universe is created.

This sense of a self-contained textual universe is apparent in the two letter-writers, Fitzy's and Elin's, repeated references to life as a dream. Fitzy insists that he wants to visit Elin in Copenhagen, "before we disappear" (141), but for now, she "still exist[s], more or less" (143), unlike himself, who has "vanished to myself" (144). Elin replies, in her broken English, "[y]ou say you cannot understand why I am more real as a half-dream, less (and therefore uncalming) as seen" (162). Furthermore the sub-title to the final section, "The Dream is Dreaming Me," again emphasizes the sense of an almost phantasmagoric existence lived out by the characters in their virtual-textual universe. There is a sense, in *Bornholm*, of a unique space having been created, distinct from their actual lives, in which everything has a different texture, a different ontological density, or what Elin names, the "Oppersite Land" (87), in her "bogus Deutsch." The self-containment of the dream-world of letters becomes so tangible and richly nuanced that it ends up rendering the flesh-and-blood characters remote, so much so that Elin worries that she won't know who she meets when they meet in Dublin:

"it's all a bit museumlike, lived through so many times, turned into pictures, symbols, sort of icons one might say"⁵ (129). Life, as fiction, one might say.

The love-letters also reflect Elin's and Fitzy's respective responses to memory and language, both potent themes considering the spatial separation and the almost exclusive dependence on language to preserve a living texture for their love. Elin clearly distinguishes between the words she uses and the actuality of time spent together: "Not forgotten in words but in action. The sensual memory of you is going to disappear, replaced by reflections" (17). She knows that outside of the actuality, of her fading sensual memory, there are but "figments of imagination, monologues" (18). Initially, Elin responds to the barriers between them by pursuing her imaginative response:

> We don't know each other, no. We exited to a high degree each others' dreams. We don't know each other, we are dreaming. Everything depends on if we are clever enough to dream. And believe in our dreams. And realize our dreams so fervently we are able to. (21)

They plunge into a landscape of dreams wherein the constraints of time, language, and geography are diminished, though certainly not abandoned entirely. The dreaming proves to be unsustainable because the truth of their relationship must be registered. Elin pleads with Fitzy to confront this: "Please, my beloved let us save our dream by naming the reality, let us say awfull things so the rest can be true. The ghosts grow and grow when you never face them" (92). Fitzy responds to this plea by refusing to accept a distinction between the dreams and reality: "As to dream (perhaps the only word we cannot put quotation marks around) and "reality," whatever that may be, well they are for me one and the same" (93). The lines of communication carry for him a dream reality. "Doesn't a child," Fitzy asks, "who knows nothing, invent the whole world" (94)? The reality principle, however, must remain as a constituent part of the imagination and vice-versa in order for coherent dialogue to exist. Ultimately Fitzy falters: "It has been going on for some time. I am dreaming it, or it is dreaming me, for some time, particulars forgotten" (174). Reality dissolves, the pure dream remains and dialogue between the lovers ultimately ends, or at least the desire to articulate the nature of their affair ends.

Elin refuses to dissolve her reality principle into pure imaginative construction except in moments of extreme longing. She never loses sight of the rational, allowing herself to dream whilst constantly reminding herself that she is dreaming. She warns him: "I tell you Fitzy, I imagine you so you would die from it if you were here" (68). She knows that the actuality cannot compare to her vision of him. This distinction prevails in Elin's letters and the lack of a sensual life leads to her eventual estrangement. The "unreal correspondence" (146), cannot satisfy her as it can Fitzy:

> You never divide hope from reality, and you are not a happy person. I always divide hope from reality (try to) and am not a happy being. You refuse to see reality and I am hoping wrong hopes. This goes on: Wrong moves, failured gestures. Will it ever change? (153)

Ultimately, Elin's last letter does not even conclude the relationship, as meaning has long since been lost in a sea of imagination and language. The distinction between their differing positions also reflects a dialogue between the twin poles that exist in the novel: the "real" and the imagined. On the other hand, Fitzy appears to relish the imagined place, the transformed life, infused with the richest of imaginings, or as Dermot Healy has it: "At last Higgins has succeeded in giving himself the fictional life he was always seeking," but Elin's presence acts as a perpetual counter-balance so that Fitzy's "every word is interpreted, criticized, evaluated by another" ("Towards *Bornholm*" 186). Elin swiftly becomes acutely conscious that sensual existence can only be sustained for a limited period without human presence. The tone of her epistles frequently reflects her resignation, even if the desire for the sensual remains:

> I cannot say I miss you, because your living touch has shrivelled up in me, and you must touch again to bring me back to life again. (72)

> I hardly know what I am writing, just put words down, do not use the dictionary, just talking to you, touching my breasts in between . . . (76)

> To whisper in your mouth with no words. (77)

In language, the sensual is lost, and trapped as she is in a linguistic universe, this is a death-blow to the imagined life they have woven.

The two writers repeatedly comment on each other's letters and the novel thus becomes a self-conscious statement on the nature of fiction and the imaginative process. *Bornholm* is one of Higgins's most overtly self-reflexive novels because it directly confronts its own medium and in doing so interrogates the meaning of memory and the limits of language. Furthermore it foregrounds the troubled transformative process that is art. Elin and Fitzy create fictions forged from their imperfect memories, from linguistic abstraction, and they continually reflect on their different responses to the epistemological conditions of their observations and imaginings. The presumption of a fixed reality swiftly vanishes in the creation of the letters, and phenomenological concerns dominate thereafter; Elin does acknowledge the inadequacy of the reality principle in one of her letters: "Your memories of us are too full of 'unreliableness' but mostly more true than the reality" (65). Reality is thus conceived of as a collage of moving surfaces rather than a static empirically attainable actuality. The affair falters and dies because the "real," the sensual, is forsaken and replaced by a world comprising language, memory and imagination, but the metaphorical parallel extends to force the reader to re-consider the possibility of knowing the "real" in any fixed sense. The epistolary novel form reflects the primacy of experience without the overt formal constructs of linear narrative and narrated characterization. Elin and Fitzy instead emerge via their respective collages of recollection and expressions of love and loss, allowing the author to generate fictional ontologies that are not limited by time and space, by expectations of linearity, of sequence, or formal plotted elements; the resultant authentic human voices entice one to follow them beyond the usual plotted limits, so even though they reside (mostly separately) in different parts of Europe, their true residences are in the existential spaces they make for themselves, and momentarily for each other.

Like *Bornholm*, *Lions of the Grunewald* uses mainland Europe as its nominal backdrop; it is peopled by Dallan Weaver, an Irish writer, and his wife Nancy. Weaver conducts a dramatic extramarital affair which both acts as the primary narrative movement in the novel, and offers the opportunity to again explore familiar obsessions: love, loss, memory. Echoing Higgins's own time in Berlin during the late 1960s and 1970s, Weaver and Nancy reside in Berlin as guests of DILDO (*Deutsche Internationale Literatur Dienst*

Organisation) and mingle with persons real and imaginary, including Peter Handke, Max Frisch, Sir Kenneth Clarke and a host of others. The love-triangle traced out between Weaver, Nancy and his lover Lore is initially treated with much irreverence but gradually, as the sequential plot dissolves, the author's voice surfaces to reveal Higgins's familiar themes: love and its transience, the pain of the past, and ultimately, how one apprehends and bears such strangeness.

Higgins's epigrams to *Lions* are revealing. The first, taken from John Cheever's *Journals*, tells of when the lions escaped from the zoo during the last days of WWII. This, of course, echoes the zoo imagery prevalent throughout, but it also tells of nightmarish days of a "world that has outstripped our nightmares, our subconscious," the kind of days which the novel maps. A sense of desolation pervades all, extending even to the frantic coupling of two homosexual lovers in sub-zero snow, prior to one of them leaping into the uninviting, freezing Spree River. Everything ramifies, of course. Alice Munro's epigram from *The Progress of Love* also speaks of the obvious wrenches and slashing which accompanies the parting of lovers, predicting the marital chaos about to ensue. The final epigram, taken from Nabokov's *Speak Memory*, himself a habitual frequenter of Berlin, is especially telling: "In the evening there, in little *cul de sacs*, the soul seems to dissolve." Higgins's Weaver does indeed seem to dissolve when confronted with the impasse of naming the life he has lived. Berlin, fittingly, becomes a ghostly presence in his, and the narrator's consciousness. Eventually, Weaver effectively merges with Higgins's own voice. The dissolution is intensified by a disintegration of the linear narrative into a rush of half-memories, dreams and random observations. At the core of this life is Lore, with her teasing name and symbolic role as real, *and* metaphorical, expression of love.

Love is again an essential ingredient. A quality of impermanence is dominant, rather than any sentimental cry from the heart of lost love. Love itself, with its frightful joys and acute pains, is presented as the central motif of loss from which all else radiates. This is not to suggest that Lore is merely a functional image within which the author bemoans the loss of the past. Rather, love is presented as a way of seeing, so valuable and sacred that its loss is all the greater, or as Weaver claims, rephrasing Proust, "love is time and space the heart can catch" (198). Love is a state from which one can witness existence outside of the mad swirl of life. Time spent with Lore is, for Weaver, like "a morning outside of time" (196). As an extended epiphany, love becomes a means of comprehension, of consolation, a kind of imaginative intensity which allows him to redeem life from that state of ineffable confusion within which he is frequently lost.

Late in the novel, when Weaver, or by now Higgins's narratorial voice (the distinction grows increasingly unclear), appears to disintegrate as a plotted focal point, everything radiates from the memory of love, even the geography of Berlin:

> The other day I was thinking of you; or rather of *Nullgrab*, that quartered city you love so much, which amounts to the same thing. When I recall *Nullgrab* I remember you, or vice versa. Go quietly, the ghosts are listening. (274)

Past moments cannot be recalled unimpeded by the vastness of all else connected to them. The past is saturated with people, none more pervasive than old lovers who are forever marooned in the past, a point not lost on Weaver, echoing a familiar Higginsian refrain: "Is it even possible to think of somebody in the past? Are the memories of things better than the things themselves? Chateaubriand seemed to think so; and now he too belongs to that past" (274). One of Weaver's primary difficulties is the past, and yet he ultimately accepts its foibles with a kind of lyrical resignation that comes with clear comprehension of its mesmerizing transience. And yet, despite the onslaught of time, Weaver somehow retains the essence of Lore in his poetic imagination: "I say things but I may mean times. I say things and times but I may mean persons and places, or may be just thinking of you. Your name at the end of the world" (274). Love, for Higgins, is the key to the past, possibly the only one. It does not, of course, gain power over the unassailable power of the past but it does make it more manageable, more visible. Your *name* "at the end of the world," he tellingly writes. The tragedy of lost love rings through all of Higgins's long fiction, both as a lament for the loss of such a wonderful state and also as a celebration of that state as a way of seeing which, in its finest moments, vivifies the imagination, and rescues valuable remainders from the vanished past; such valuable remainders have always been at the center of his work.

Because he recognizes the visionary nature of being in love with Lore, Weaver likens their separation to death:

> So they sat together on the top step in the gloaming and sipped vodka and tasted the ice and fire and no doubt entertained (if that is the word) some considerations of those Final Things that must in time come to us all, to be recorded with all the ones who had gone before, all set down in the Great Book of Numbers. (235)

He strikes up a connection between death and the passing of love because love makes death remote and its departure is a chilling reminder of how quickly and mercilessly one hurtles to that final moment, and inherent in the realization of lost love are the implications for the consciousness which seems so dependent on love as a way of seeing, of being. None of Higgins's love "stories" end in joy, and it is the sense of futility that this failure lends to the works that helps to create the profound sense of impermanence at the center of all his work. These are no simple, tragic love stories. *Lions* tells not just of the passing of Weaver's one true love (his great love for Lore happens to coincide with the demise of his love for his wife, Nancy). For Weaver, it is the sense of life that love affords him that is so valuable: "It was another language of another world; you took me there. I couldn't follow you; but I followed you" (276). Love is a way of defeating the undefeatable, a way of arresting time, of intimately knowing a place and finally knowing how to rediscover the gleaming of one's past life. For Weaver, it appears that the key to imaginative existence is love, Higgins's potent, enduring metaphor for the imagined life, the poetic memory. I say metaphor but, of course, with Higgins the literal and the metaphorical slip into each other, change places, and force one to reconsider how such apparent fixities perpetually resonate across each other.

Throughout the novel, as elsewhere in Higgins, there is a sense that being in love is akin to a special faculty of mind, one that invites one to step beyond the habitual, a point echoed in one of the rejected epigrams to *Bornholm* by José Ortega y Gasset: "In loving we abandon the tranquility and permanence within ourselves and virtually migrate towards the object" (original proof copy of *Bornholm Night-Ferry*). In *Lions* (and later in *The Whole Hog* 180), rephrasing Proust, the narrator nudges us towards an understanding of his current mode of perception: ". . . love is time and space the heart can catch" (198). The escape from tranquility and permanence (the habitual), and the mesmeric, momentary apprehension of time and space that love affords Weaver (and Higgins's heroes in general), apart from valorizing love also establishes a powerful metaphorical motif that acts as a self-reflexive evocation of the imaginative life.

The specific nature of this imaginatively-glimpsed life that emerges in *Lions* necessitates a particular kind of fictional mode. While there is a central coherent plot that remains largely intact, there are many instances when Higgins's narrator digresses to trawl through Berlin's troubled history and inserts various historical events beside the microcosm of Weaver's own troubled life. Within the philosophical framework of the novel, this process justifies itself because the traditional demarcations between reality and illusion, fact and fiction, the past and present, are everywhere blurred, but the effect is dizzying and sometimes hazardous to the cohesion of the novel. Still, Higgins expresses his understanding of history very clearly in one phrase that acts as a refrain in the novel: "All days are different; all days are the same" (175). The apparent distinctions between the narrative threads (history, spatial designations, narrative types, sequential time) with which we usually order our experiences, are invalidated, at least in Weaver's imagining consciousness.

In a sense, the plotted events that comprise *Lions* are secondary, and yet deeply integrated with how the tale is told. Everything that happens is directed by the feasibility of the narrative form. Love, the most powerful image in the text, is likened to a way of seeing, a way of imaginative apprehension. Furthermore, the pastness of the tale means that the narrator must somehow create structures through which the past can be communicated. Like Joyce, Higgins crams his tale with topographical detail, allusions, historical references and real people, but unlike Joyce's Modernist example, *Lions* does not avail of a mythic order in an effort to allow a kind of coherent chaos to define the form of the text.

Many different techniques are availed of to articulate the mess of experience which must be both forced into coherent form, and simultaneously allowed to evade such coherence. Initially the narrator toys with overt self-reflexive play by using theatrical stage directions: "Quick curtains here to indicate the passage of time" (116). Such devices are more playful than disruptive. More technically familiar is the way that Nancy's character is constructed. As in *Balcony of Europe*, Nancy's character is partly revealed by certain key phrases that she repeatedly uses. This type of characterization results not in any meaningful revelation but in contributing to Higgins's wraith-like two-dimensional characters. Weaver is the only character who is fully realized in the novel. He is frequently liberated from chronological sequence when his imagination roams from Berlin to Russia (where he's never been) and to Dover and Hamburg. Anecdotes tumble forth from his imagination, sequential narration is abandoned as insufficient and the result, although disturbing, is an intelligible adventure through Weaver's troubled consciousness. As the novel progresses this becomes increasingly fragile and the third person past tense, sequential narrative of Part I grows more reliant on alternative methods. Although the plot is initially subverted by self-reflexive comments ("The truncated metropolis hereinafter designated *Nullgrab* is of course very much our own invention and figures and descriptions may be more aromatic than exact. An odour of pines pervades all" (12)), the straight sequential narrative remains intact until the end of Part I when the narrator frames a chapter around fragmentary dreams by both Nancy and Lore. Another chapter follows, which relates a tale about the Berlin poet Gottfried Benn, with little obvious connection to the plot. Part II develops into an increasingly anecdotal account and offers little in the way of direct significance to plot. Weaver's binding consciousness loses what few reservations he has, both in terms of his extra-marital affair and his digressive mind.

Part III confirms the radical disintegration of the sparse sequential narrative that existed at the beginning, coinciding with Lore and Weaver's separation. This is the time of the Munich Olympic slaughter but when Weaver tires of Munich, he recalls a trip to South Africa in detail. The central plot remains but is no longer the dominant ontological base, the digressions now forming the authoritative focus of the imagined world.

The final stages of the novel reveal Weaver's consciousness via his reminiscences, especially of his relationship with Lore, in the collage chapter of past moments, "The Other Day I Was Thinking of You," surely one of the finest pieces of writing in all of Higgins. Furthermore, the point of view of the narrator/author dissolves to be replaced by a series of letters and a short account of an imagined meeting between Günter Grass and Max Frisch. Finally, the voice that remains lingers in the knowledge that much of his life has evaporated. Near the end of this patchwork of memory, history, comedy and imaginative apprehension, the disconnected voice asks, "Of all that remains what residue is there, I ask you, trapped in vertiginous Time" (301)?

Higgins's sobering perspectives on time are supplemented by his commentary on dreams: "In dreams there is no time, no ages, just a seamless, tireless state of the sleeper's drifting fears. It had been a time of dire portents in Jo'burg . . . . To remember it or have it evoked in a nightmare was to make that heart bleed again" (258). Memory and the dream-state self-reflexively echo each other suggesting that the narrative structure clearly aspires to such a structure. Form and content rest easily together here. The widely-held desire for an ordered life, he suggests, is less important than the unsystematic way in which memory and the dream-state operate; thus so too must the fictions operate.

Much of Higgins's energy is directed at creating powerful images, almost visual in their bright intensity and these images seek to compensate for his abandonment of sequential narrative form. Dermot Healy recognizes this aspect in Higgins's writing: "The key to Higgins is the *image*—for him storytelling stopped there—If you told what was there visually the story would inevitably follow" ("A Travel Guide" B10). This accounts for the narrator's reluctance to flesh out authentic characters. We are cast a few morsels, probably "real," a few resonant phrases and a kind of life must emanate from there. The surface must somehow radiate meaning, as it must in life. There are no imposed symbolic frameworks or rigid characterization in Higgins's *Lions*, because such things belong to the inventions of artistic form and not to life. The challenge is, has always been after all, to allow the fiction to accommodate life.

Higgins's works are never comfortable fictions, they never seek to ingratiate themselves to a public in search of recognizable fictive conventions. Committed to the idea that all the mind apprehends is a fiction, the author has perpetually striven to articulate this position. That his fictional journey has frequently drifted into autobiography is indicative of his refusal to distinguish between art and life. *Lions of the Grunewald* and *Bornholm Night-Ferry* are both constructed according to this principle. Art is not simply a transformation of "reality," because, for Higgins, life is already story, perhaps lacking the complex ordering strategies of art, but story nonetheless. As Aidan Matthews has succinctly put it with reference to *Lions*: "So the fable becomes a fiction about fictions, about the fantasies of 30 years ago" (B12).

Higgins's life had been used as material for his art from the outset, but in *Lions* and *Bornholm* his life isn't simply plundered as material for fiction, it *is* that fiction. It is apparent that the author believes that the life he led all those years ago in Berlin and Copenhagen was as much a dream at the time as it is now. People and places merge with memory or Higgins's poetic imagination, to *suggest* a story rather than to tell it *as it was*. The life described is itself as near to a "story" as a life can get with its endless complexity and contradictions, all of which *appear* to evade order. The telling of events from one's life amounts to an act of possession, and in the act of possession life is transformed by the conventions of art. Higgins tries desperately to avoid this wilful possession. And by consciously losing a coherent narrative of his own life, he paradoxically claims it.

WORKS CITED

Higgins, Aidan. *Balcony of Europe*. London: Calder & Boyars, 1972.

—. *Felo de Se*. London: John Calder, 1960.

—. *Bornholm Night-Ferry*. London: Allison & Busby Ltd, 1983.

—. *Bornholm Night-Ferry* (original proof copy). McPherson Library Special Collection. University of Victoria, Canada.

—. *Flotsam & Jetsam*. London: Minerva, 1997.

—. *Helsingør Station & Other Departures*. London: Secker & Warburg, 1989.

—. *Images of Africa*. London: Calder & Boyars, 1971.

—. *Langrishe, Go Down*. London: Calder & Boyars, 1966.

—. Letter to Bill Swainson. 29 December 1980. McPherson Library Special Collection. University of Victoria, Canada.

—. Letter to Bill Swainson. 14 May 1981. McPherson Library Special Collection. University of Victoria, Canada.

—. *Lions of the Grunewald*. London: Secker & Warburg, 1993.

—. *Scenes from a Receding Past*. London: John Calder, 1977.

—. *The Whole Hog*. London: Secker & Warburg, 2000.

Healy, Dermot. "Towards *Bornholm Night-Ferry* and *Texts for the Air*: A Re-reading of Aidan Higgins." *Review of Contemporary Fiction* (Spring 1983): 181–192.

—. "A Travel Guide to the Imagination." *The Sunday Tribune* 23 April 1989: B10.

Imhof, Rüdiger. "Proust and Contemporary Irish Fiction." *The Internationalism of Irish Literature and Drama: Irish Literary Studies 41*. Ed. Joseph McMinn. Buckinghamshire: Colin Smythe, 1992: 255–260.

Matthews, Aidan. "A rush through the vagaries of Berlin life: Review of *Lions of the Grunewald*." *The Sunday Tribune* 21 November 1993: B12.

O'Brien, George. "Goodbye to All That." *The Irish Review* 7 (Autumn 1989): 89–92.

White, Harry. "Review of Aidan Higgins's *Helsingør Station & Ronda Gorge*." *Irish University Review* 20.1 (Spring 1990): 209–212.

NOTES

1. This quotation is a borrowed chapter title from *Lions of the Grunewald* (274).

2. In a conversation with the present author, July 2007, in Kinsale, Co. Cork.

3. Published variously in the *Review of Contemporary Fiction* 3.1 (1983), *Helsingør Station & Other Departures*, and in *Flotsam & Jetsam*.

4. Expressed in a letter to the present author on 8 October 2008.

5. Elin's *pigeon English* accounts for the grammatical tics and other idiosyncrasies hereafter in all quotations ascribed to her.

Select Bibliography

I. WORKS BY AIDAN HIGGINS

Books

As I was Riding Down Duval Boulevard with Pete La Salle. Dublin: Anam Press, 2003.

Balcony of Europe. London: Calder & Boyars, 1972; New York: Delacorte, 1972; Champaign, IL: Dalkey Archive Press, 2010.

A Bestiary. Champaign, IL: Dalkey Archive Press, 2004.

Bornholm Night-Ferry. London: Allison & Busby, 1983; Ireland: Brandon Books, 1983; London: Abacus, 1985.

Dog Days: A Sequel to Donkey's Years. London: Secker & Warburg, 1998.

Donkey's Years: Memories of a Life as Story Told. London: Secker & Warburg, 1995.

Felo de Se. London: John Calder, 1960; as *Killachter Meadow,* New York: Grove Press, 1961; as *Asylum and Other Stories,* London: John Calder, 1978; New York: Riverrun Press, 1979.

Flotsam & Jetsam. London: Minerva, 1997; Champaign, IL: Dalkey Archive Press, 2002.

Helsingør Station & Other Departures: Fictions and Autobiographies 1956-1989. London: Secker & Warburg, 1989.

Images of Africa: Diary (1956-60). London: Calder & Boyars, 1971.

Langrishe, Go Down. London: Calder & Boyars, 1966; New York: Grove Press, 1966; New York: Riverrun Press, 1980; London: Paladin, 1987; Champaign, IL: Dalkey Archive Press, 2004; Dublin: New Island, 2007.

Lions of the Grunewald. London: Secker & Warburg, 1993. Also as *Weaver's Women.* London: Secker & Warburg, 1993.

Ronda Gorge & Other Precipices: Travel Writings 1959–1989. London: Secker & Warburg, 1989.

Scenes from a Receding Past. London: John Calder, 1977; Dallas, TX: Riverrun Press, 1977.

The Whole Hog: A Sequel to Donkey's Years and Dog Days. London: Secker & Warburg, 2000.

Windy Arbours: Collected Criticism. Champaign, IL: Dalkey Archive Press, 2005.

Radio Plays

Assassin. 1973. In *Darkling Plain: Texts for the Air.* Ed. Daniel Jernigan. Champaign, IL: Dalkey Archive Press, 2010.

Boomtown, Texas, USA. 1990. In *Darkling Plain: Texts for the Air.* Ed. Daniel Jernigan. Champaign, IL: Dalkey Archive Press, 2010.

Discords of Good Humour. 1982. In *Darkling Plain: Texts for the Air.* Ed. Daniel Jernigan. Champaign, IL: Dalkey Archive Press, 2010.

Texts for the Air. 1983. In *Darkling Plain: Texts for the Air.* Ed. Daniel Jernigan. Champaign, IL: Dalkey Archive Press, 2010.

Uncontrollable Laughter. 1977. In *Darkling Plain: Texts for the Air.* Ed. Daniel Jernigan. Champaign, IL: Dalkey Archive Press, 2010.

Vanishing Heroes. 1983. In *Darkling Plain: Texts for the Air.* Ed. Daniel Jernigan. Champaign, IL: Dalkey Archive Press, 2010.

Winter is Coming. 1983. In *Darkling Plain: Texts for the Air.* Ed. Daniel Jernigan. Champaign, IL: Dalkey Archive Press, 2010.

Zoo Station. 1985. In *Darkling Plain: Texts for the Air.* Ed. Daniel Jernigan. Champaign, IL: Dalkey Archive Press, 2010.

Edited Anthologies

A Century of Short Stories. Ed. Aidan Higgins. London: Cape, 1977.

Colossal Gongorr and the Turks of Mars. By Carl, Julian and Elwin Higgins. Introduced and edited by Aidan Higgins. London: Jonathan Cape, 1979.

II. THEORETICAL STATEMENTS AND INTERVIEWS

Interviews

"Beckettwise and Unblooming." Interview with Aidan Higgins (with John Hall). *Guardian* (Manchester) 11 October 1971: 8.

"His Family and Other Animals." Interview with Aidan Higgins (with Boyd Tonkin). *The Independent* (London) 14 October 2000: 9.

Interview with Aidan Higgins (with Caroline Walsh). *The Irish Times* 15 October 1977: 12.

"Scenes from a Receding Past: Interview with Aidan Higgins." Interview with Aidan Higgins (with Helen Meany). *The Irish Times* 6 June 1995: 8.

"Writer in Profile: Aidan Higgins." Interview with Aidan Higgins. *RTE Guide* 5 February 1971: 13.

Essays, Reviews and Commentaries

"The Faceless Creator." *The Recorder: The Journal of the American Irish Historical Society* 8.1 (Spring 1995): 30–35. Rpt. in *Ireland of the Welcomes: New Irish Writing* Special Issue (1996): 16–19.

"Fresh Horrors." *The Irish Times* 3 December 1988: W9.

"Glancing Blows." *Books Ireland* October 1982: 174.

"The Heroe's Portion: Chaos or Anarchy in the Cultic Twoilet." *Review of Contemporary Fiction* (Spring 1983): 108–114.

"The Hidden Narrator." *Asylum Arts Review* 1.1 (Autumn 1995): 2–7.

Introduction. *Samuel Beckett: Photographs by John Minihan*. London: Secker & Warburg, 1995; New York: George Braziller, 1996. 1–21.

"Paradiddle and Paradigm." *Irish Review* 5 (Autumn 1988): 116–118.

"RTE Stills." Review of *A Portrait of the Artist as a Young Girl*. By John Quinn. *Books Ireland* May 1987: 85.

"Tired Lines; or Tales My Mother Told Me." *A Bash in the Tunnel: James Joyce by the Irish*. Ed. John Ryan. Brighton: Clifton Books, 1970. 55–60.

III. PERSONAL CORRESPONDENCES

Beckett, Samuel. Letter to Aidan Higgins concerning manuscript of "Killachter Meadow." 22 April 1958. *Review of Contemporary Fiction* (Spring 1983): 156–157.

IV. CRITICISM OF HIGGINS'S WORK

Arnold, Bruce. Review of *Langrishe, Go Down*. *Dublin Magazine* (Spring 1966): 79.

Baneham, Sam. "Aidan Higgins: A Political Dimension." *Review of Contemporary Fiction* 3.1 (1983): 168–174.

Banville, John. "Colony of Expatriates." *Hibernia* 6 October 1972: 18.

Beja, Morris. "Felons of Our Selves: The Fiction of Aidan Higgins." *Irish University Review* 3.2 (Autumn 1973): 163–178.

Boylan, Roger. "Reading Aidan Higgins." *Context: A Forum for Literary Arts and Culture* 20 (2007): 1–3.

Buckeye, Robert. "Form as the Extension of Content: 'their existence in my eyes.'" *Review of Contemporary Fiction* 3.1 (1983): 192–195.

Byrne, Jack. "Notes on Higgins's Ladies of Springfield House." *Review of Contemporary Fiction* 3.1 (1983): 195–210.

Cahalan, James M. "New Voices: The Contemporary Novel." *The Irish Novel: A Critical History*. New York: Twayne Publishers, 1988. 261–303.

Dallat, C. L. Review of *Flotsam & Jetsam*. *Times Literary Supplement* 21 March 1997: 23.

Dukes, Gerry. "Life with the lions." Review of *Lions of the Grunewald*. *The Irish Times* 13 November 1993: 9.

—. "Recycled living, required reading." Review of *Flotsam and Jetsam*. *The Irish Times* 22 February 1997.

Frehner, Ruth. *The Colonizers' Daughters: Gender in the Anglo-Irish Big House Novel*. Tübingen: Franacke, 1999.

Garfitt, Roger. "Constants in Contemporary Irish Fiction." *Two Decades of Irish Writing*. Ed. Douglas Dunn. Chester Springs, PA: Dufour Editions, 1975. 207–241.

Golden, Sean. "Parsing Love's *Complainte*: Aidan Higgins on the Need to Name." *Review of Contemporary Fiction* 3.1 (1983): 210–220.

Golden, Sean, and Peter Fallon, eds. *Soft Day: A Miscellany of Contemporary Irish Writing*. Notre Dame, IN: University of Notre Dame Press, 1980.

Healy, Dermot. "*Donkey's Years*: A Review." *Asylum Arts Review* 1.1 (Autumn 1995): 45–46.

—. "Towards *Bornholm Night-Ferry* and *Texts For the Air*: A Rereading of Aidan Higgins." *Review of Contemporary Fiction* 3.1 (1983): 181–192.

—. "A Travel Guide to the Imagination." *The Sunday Tribune* 23 April 1989: B10.

Imhof, Rüdiger. "*Bornholm Night-Ferry* and *Journal to Stella*: Aidan Higgins's Indebtedness to Jonathan Swift." *The Canadian Journal of Irish Studies* 10.2 (December 1984): 5–13.

—. "German Influences on John Banville and Aidan Higgins." *Literary Interrelations: Ireland, England and the World.* Ed. Wolfgang Zach and Heinz Kosok. Vol. 2. Tübingen: Gunter Narr Verlag, 1987. 335–347.

—. "How It Is on the Fringes of Irish Fiction." *Irish University Review* 22.1 (Spring/Summer 1992): 151–167.

—. "Post-Joycean Experiment in Recent Irish Fiction." *Ireland and France, A Bountiful Friendship: Literature, History and Ideas.* Ed. Barbara Hayley and Christopher Murray. Buckinghamshire: Colin Smythe, 1992. 124–136.

—. "Proust and Contemporary Irish Fiction." *The Internationalism of Irish Literature and Drama: Irish Literary Studies 41.* Ed. Joseph McMinn. Buckinghamshire: Colin Smythe, 1992. 255–260.

—. Review of *Lions of the Grunewald. Linenhall Review* 10.3 (1993): 23.

Imhof, Rüdiger, and Jürgen Kamm. "Coming to Grips with Aidan Higgins: 'Killachter Meadow'—An Analysis." *Études Irlandaises* 9 (December 1984): 145–160.

Kreilkamp, Vera. "Reinventing a Form: The Big House in Aidan Higgins's *Langrishe, Go Down.*" *The Canadian Journal of Irish Studies* 11.2 (1985): 27–38. Rpt. in *The Anglo-Irish Novel and the Big House.* Syracuse: NY: Syracuse University Press, 1998.

Liddy, James. "Notes on the Wandering Celt: Aidan Higgins's *Balcony of Europe.*" *Review of Contemporary Fiction* 3.1 (1983): 166–168.

Lubbers, Klaus. "*Balcony of Europe*: The Trend towards Internationalization in Recent Irish Fiction." *Literary Interrelations: Ireland, England and the World.* Ed. Wolfgang Zach and Heinz Kosok. Vol. 3. Tübingen: Gunter Narr Verlag, 1987. 235–247.

MacLaughlin, Brigid. "A Torrent of Nostalgia." *Sunday Independent* 2 July 1995: 10L.

Mahon, Derek. "An anatomy of melancholy." Review of *Dog Days*. *The Irish Times* 7 March 1998: 67.

—. "Tractatus." *The Hunt by Night*. Oxford: Oxford University Press, 1982. Also in *Selected Poems* (1991): 135.

Matthews, Aidan. "A rush through the vagaries of Berlin life: Review of *Lions of the Grunewald*." *The Sunday Tribune* 21 November 1993: B12.

McGonigle, Thomas. "51 Pauses After Reading Aidan Higgins." *Review of Contemporary Fiction* (Spring 1983): 175–180.

—. "Let the Dead Bury the Dead: A Prepared Slide From *St. Patrick's Day, Dublin, 1974*." *Review of Contemporary Fiction* 3.1 (1983): 221–224.

Melmoth, John. "Conjuring the Beast of Ballynagromoolia." *Times Literary Supplement* 24 November 1989: 1312.

Mullen, Michael. "Aidan Higgins: Figures in Landscapes." *Review of Contemporary Fiction* 3.1 (1983): 158–161.

Murphy, Neil. "Aidan Higgins." *The Review of Contemporary Fiction* 23.3 (2003): 49–83.

—. "Aidan Higgins: The Fragility of Form." *Irish Fiction and Postmodern Doubt: An Analysis of the Epistemological Crisis in Modern Irish Fiction*. Lewiston, NY: Edwin Mellen Press, 2004: 37–101.

—. "Dreams, Departures, Destinations: A Reassessment of the Work of Aidan Higgins." *Graph: A Journal of Literature & Ideas* 1 (1995): 64–71.

—. Review of *Lions of the Grunewald*. *Irish University Review* 25.1 (Spring/Summer 1995): 188–190.

O'Brien, George. "Consumed by Memories." Review of *Donkey's Years*. *The Irish Times* 10 June 1995: W9.

—. "Goodbye to All That." *The Irish Review* 7 (Autumn 1989): 89–92.

—. "On the Pig's Back." Review of *The Whole Hog*. *The Irish Times* 7 October 2000: 67.

O'Brien, John. "*Scenes From A Receding Past.*" *Review of Contemporary Fiction* 1983 (Spring): 164–166.

O'Neill, Patrick. "Aidan Higgins." *Contemporary Irish Novelists* [Studies in English and Comparative Literature]. Ed. Rüdiger Imhof. Tübingen: Gunter Narr Verlag, 1990. 93–107.

Proulx, Annie. "Drift and Mastery." Review of *Flotsam & Jetsam*. *The Washington Post* 16 June 2002: T07.

Rauchbauer, Otto. "Aidan Higgins, 'Killachter Meadow' und *Langrishe, Go Down* sowie Harold Pinters Fernsehfilm Langrishe, Go Down: Variationen eines Motivs." *A Yearbook of Studies in English Language and Literature* 3 (1986): 135–146.

Skelton, Robin. "Aidan Higgins and the Total Book." *Mosaic* 19 (1976): 27–37. Rpt. in *Celtic Contraries*. Syracuse, NY: Syracuse University Press, 1990. 211–223.

Wall, Eamonn. "Aidan Higgins's *Balcony of Europe*: Stephen Dedalus Hits the Road." *Colby Quarterly* (Winter 1995): 81–87.

Television-related

Langrishe, Go Down. Screenplay by Harold Pinter. Dir. David Jones. Perf. Judi Dench, Jeremy Irons, Harold Pinter, and Annette Crosbie. BBC2 Play of the Week, 1978.

Pinter, Harold. *Langrishe, Go Down* screenplay (1987). *Collected Screenplays 1*. London: Faber, 2000. 561–660.

Contributors' Notes

JOHN BANVILLE is the author of a number of novels including *The Book of Evidence, Shroud* and *The Sea*, which was awarded the Man Booker Prize in 2005.

MORRIS BEJA is Professor Emeritus at the Ohio State University. He works on twentieth-century British and American literature, the novel, Anglo-Irish literature, and film. He is the author of *Epiphany in the Modern Novel, Film and Literature, Joyce, the Artist Manqué, and Indeterminacy: Two Essays, James Joyce: A Literary Life*, and essays on twentieth-century British, Irish, and American fiction, and on film; editor of a scholarly edition of Virginia Woolf's *Mrs. Dalloway*, and of the *James Joyce Newestlatter*, and books on Orson Welles, James Joyce, Virginia Woolf, Samuel Beckett, and psychological fiction.

NEIL DONNELLY is a playwright whose plays for theatre include *The Station Master* (Edinburgh, 1974); *Upstarts* (Dublin, The Abbey Theatre, The Peacock stage, 1980); *Silver Dollar Boys* (Dublin, The Peacock, 1981); *Flying Home* (The Peacock, 1983); *Chalk Farm Blues* (The Peacock, 1984); *Boys of Summer* (Dublin, *The Gaiety Theatre*, 1985); *Blindfold* (Dublin, Team Theatre-in-Education, Dublin Theatre Festival 1986; *Goodbye Curraroe* (The Peacock Theatre, 1989); *The Reel McCoy* (The Peacock, 1989); *The Duty Master*

(1995); *Women Without Men* (Prosperous, Co. Kildare, 1995). He has been Writer-in-Association at The Abbey Theatre 1994/95, and with Mayo County Council in 1993 and was Harvey's Award winner in 1982. He is a member of Aosdana and lives in Co. Kildare.

Gerry Dukes was a lecturer in literature and Research Fellow at Mary Immaculate College, University of Limerick until 2006. He is now a freelance editor, critic and writer. He is a specialist in the work of James Joyce and Samuel Beckett. He has published an annotated edition of Beckett's post-war novellas and a copiously illustrated biography of the writer, both with Penguin. His most recent play, *Thesis*, (co-written with Paul Meade and David Parnell), has been produced in Ireland and Serbia. He is currently writing a study of Synge, Joyce, Beckett and modernist Irish writing.

Angela Frattarola is an Assistant Professor of English at Nanyang Technological University (Singapore), where she teaches classes in modernism, auditory technology, and twentieth-century literature. Her publications include "Listening for 'Found Sound' Samples in the Novels of Virginia Woolf," in the *Woolf Studies Annual*, and "The Phonograph and the Modernist Novel," forthcoming in *Mosaic: A Journal for the Interdisciplinary Study of Literature*.

Roberta Gefter Wondrich is a lecturer in English Literature at the University of Trieste, Italy. She holds a PhD in Anglophone literatures from the universities of Bologna and Trieste and she has specialized in the field of Irish contemporary fiction, on which she wrote a book (*Romanzi contemporanei d'Irlanda*, 2000) and several articles. She has also written on Shakespeare, Joyce, Isherwood and contemporary British fiction and she has translated D. H. Lawrence's

The Lost Girl and Kate O'Brien's *The Land of Spices* into Italian. She is currently working on a volume on the motif of the literary quest in some modern and contemporary Anglo-American texts.

DERMOT HEALY was born in Finea, County Westmeath, in 1947. His books include *Banished Misfortune* (stories), *Fighting with Shadows, A Goat's Song* and *Sudden Times* (novels) and *The Bend for Home* (memoir).

KEITH HOPPER teaches Literature and Film Studies for Oxford University's Department for Continuing Education. He is the author of *Flann O'Brien: A Portrait of the Artist as a Young Postmodernist* (Cork UP, 1995; revised edition 2009), and general editor of *Ireland into Film* (Cork UP, 2001–07)—a series of twelve books on the theme of literary adaptation. Recent and forthcoming publications include essays on Neil Jordan, Flann O'Brien, and W. B. Yeats.

DANIEL JERNIGAN is an assistant professor of English at Nanyang Technological University, Singapore. He studied at Purdue University, Indiana, receiving the PhD in 2002. His interests include drama and theatre studies, postmodernism, playwriting, and science studies. Dr. Jernigan's essays on Caryl Churchill and Tom Stoppard have been published in *Modern Drama, Comparative Drama*, and *Text and Presentation*. He is editor of *Drama and the Postmodern: Assessing the Limits of Metatheatre* (Cambria Press, 2008). He is also an aspiring playwright, whose plays have been produced in Singapore and Toronto and published in *The Massachusetts Review*. He is currently editing Aidan Higgins's radio plays for publication with Dalkey Archive Press.

PETER VAN DE KAMP teaches at the Institute of Technology, Tralee. A poet, translator, critic, anthologist and scholar, he has published 18 books including a biography of Flann O'Brien with Peter Costello, and has edited with Jacques Chuto et al. *The Collected Works of James Clarence Mangan*, and *The Selected Prose* and *Selected Poetry of James Clarence Mangan*, with Peter Liebregts a collection of essays on W. B. Yeats and politics (*Tumult of Images*) and with A. Norman Jeffares the recent series of anthologies, *Irish Literature: The Eighteenth Century* and *Irish Literature: The Nineteenth Century*.

MARTIN KLUGER, born 1948 in Berlin, is a German writer. His novels include *Abwesende Tiere* (2002), *Der Vogel, der spazieren ging* (2008) and the acclaimed *Die Gehilfin* (2006). He also writes for the cinema and television and lives in Berlin and Montevideo, Uruguay.

ROBERT LUMSDEN taught literature for several decades at the National University of Singapore and the National Institute of Education, Nanyang Technological University, Singapore. He holds a BA and an MA from University of Sussex, and a PhD from University of East Anglia. Dr. Lumsden has published articles and chapters in books on critical theory, poetry, modernism and practical criticism, and has co-edited, with Rajeev Patke, a collection of essays on the relation between critical theory and society titled *Institutions in Cultures: Theory and Practice* (Rodopi, 1996). His most recent book is *Reading Literature After Deconstruction* (Cambria Press, 2009). He has also published poetry and short fiction, and has recently completed a novel. His research interests include the tensions and connections existing between comedy, satire, and humor, and an account of various attempts to contain a sense of the numinous in literary language.

DEREK MAHON was born in Belfast in 1941. His poetry collections include *Night-Crossing* (1968); *Lives* (1972); *The Snow Party* (1975); *Poems 1962–1978* (1979); *Courtyards in Delft* (1981); *The Hunt By Night* (1982); *Antarctica* (Oldcastle, Co. Meath, Gallery Books, 1985); *Selected Poems* (Oldcastle, Co. Meath, The Gallery Press, 1990); *Selected Poems* (London & New York, Viking, and The Gallery Press, in association with Oxford UP, 1991), and more recently, *The Hudson Letter* (The Gallery Press, 1995, USA, Wake Forest UP, 1996); *Collected Poems* (The Gallery Press, 1999); *Harbour Lights* (The Gallery Press, 2005); and *Homage to Gaia* (The Gallery Press, 2008).

NEIL MURPHY is Associate Professor of contemporary literature at NTU, Singapore, and has previously taught at the University of Ulster and the American University of Beirut. He is the author of *Irish Fiction and Postmodern Doubt* (2004), and has co-edited two collections of essays, *British Asian Fiction: Framing the Contemporary* (2008) and *Literature and Ethics: Questions of Responsibility in Literary Studies* (2009). In addition he has published numerous articles and book chapters on contemporary Irish fiction, postmodernism, and theories of reading. He is currently writing a book on aesthetics and contemporary fiction.

GEORGE O'BRIEN was born in Ireland, educated at Ruskin College, Oxford, and the University of Warwick, and is Professor of English at Georgetown University, Washington D.C. Among his various publications are three volumes of memoirs, *The Village of Longing* (1987), *Dancehall Days* (1988) and *Out of Our Minds* (1994).

PATRICK O'NEILL is Professor of German, and Associate Dean (International), at Queen's University, Canada. He is the author of numerous journal articles and book chapters on German, English, and comparative literature, and on aspects of narratology and translation studies. He has also published nine books on Modern German and comparative literary studies, the most recent of which is *Polyglot Joyce: Fictions of Translation* (Toronto: University of Toronto Press, 2005).

ANNIE PROULX is a student of history, of human behaviour in changing circumstances, and of ruined landscapes. She writes fiction in Wyoming and New Mexico.

BERNARD SHARE's novel, *Transit,* is published by Dalkey Archive Press together with a reissue of *Inish*, which Spike Milligan, while failing to remember the name of the author, described as the funniest book he ever read. He (Share, not Milligan) has been an academic in Australia, edited CARA, the inflight magazine of Aer Lingus and was the founder editor of *Books Ireland*. The third edition of his *Slanguage, a dictionary of slang and colloquial English in Ireland*, appeared recently.

NEIL MURPHY has previously taught at the University of Ulster and the American University of Beirut, and is currently Associate Professor of Contemporary Literature at NTU, Singapore. He is the author of several books on Irish fiction and contemporary literature and has published numerous articles on contemporary Irish fiction, on postmodernism, and on Aidan Higgins. He is currently writing a book on contemporary fiction and aesthetics.

SELECTED DALKEY ARCHIVE PAPERBACKS

Petros Abatzoglou, *What Does Mrs. Freeman Want?*
Michal Ajvaz, *The Other City.*
Pierre Albert-Birot, *Grabinoulor.*
Yuz Aleshkovsky, *Kangaroo.*
Felipe Alfau, *Chromos.*
   Locos.
Ivan Ângelo, *The Celebration.*
   The Tower of Glass.
David Antin, *Talking.*
António Lobo Antunes, *Knowledge of Hell.*
Alain Arias-Misson, *Theatre of Incest.*
John Ashbery and James Schuyler, *A Nest of Ninnies.*
Heimrad Bäcker, *transcript.*
Djuna Barnes, *Ladies Almanack.*
   Ryder.
John Barth, *LETTERS.*
   Sabbatical.
Donald Barthelme, *The King.*
   Paradise.
Svetislav Basara, *Chinese Letter.*
Mark Binelli, *Sacco and Vanzetti Must Die!*
Andrei Bitov, *Pushkin House.*
Louis Paul Boon, *Chapel Road.*
   My Little War.
   Summer in Termuren.
Roger Boylan, *Killoyle.*
Ignácio de Loyola Brandão, *Anonymous Celebrity.*
   Teeth under the Sun.
   Zero.
Bonnie Bremser, *Troia: Mexican Memoirs.*
Christine Brooke-Rose, *Amalgamemnon.*
Brigid Brophy, *In Transit.*
Meredith Brosnan, *Mr. Dynamite.*
Gerald L. Bruns, *Modern Poetry and*
   the Idea of Language.
Evgeny Bunimovich and J. Kates, eds.,
   Contemporary Russian Poetry: An Anthology.
Gabrielle Burton, *Heartbreak Hotel.*
Michel Butor, *Degrees.*
   Mobile.
   Portrait of the Artist as a Young Ape.
G. Cabrera Infante, *Infante's Inferno.*
   Three Trapped Tigers.
Julieta Campos, *The Fear of Losing Eurydice.*
Anne Carson, *Eros the Bittersweet.*
Camilo José Cela, *Christ versus Arizona.*
   The Family of Pascual Duarte.
   The Hive.
Louis-Ferdinand Céline, *Castle to Castle.*
   Conversations with Professor Y.
   London Bridge.
   Normance.
   North.
   Rigadoon.
Hugo Charteris, *The Tide Is Right.*
Jerome Charyn, *The Tar Baby.*
Marc Cholodenko, *Mordechai Schamz.*
Emily Holmes Coleman, *The Shutter of Snow.*
Robert Coover, *A Night at the Movies.*
Stanley Crawford, *Log of the S.S. The Mrs Unguentine.*
   Some Instructions to My Wife.
Robert Creeley, *Collected Prose.*
René Crevel, *Putting My Foot in It.*
Ralph Cusack, *Cadenza.*
Susan Daitch, *L.C.*
   Storytown.
Nicholas Delbanco, *The Count of Concord.*
Nigel Dennis, *Cards of Identity.*
Peter Dimock, *A Short Rhetoric for Leaving the Family.*
Ariel Dorfman, *Konfidenz.*
Coleman Dowell, *The Houses of Children.*
   Island People.
   Too Much Flesh and Jabez.
Arkadii Dragomoshchenko, *Dust.*
Rikki Ducornet, *The Complete Butcher's Tales.*
   The Fountains of Neptune.
   The Jade Cabinet.
   The One Marvelous Thing.
   Phosphor in Dreamland.
   The Stain.
   The Word "Desire."
William Eastlake, *The Bamboo Bed.*
   Castle Keep.
   Lyric of the Circle Heart.
Jean Echenoz, *Chopin's Move.*
Stanley Elkin, *A Bad Man.*
   Boswell: A Modern Comedy.
   Criers and Kibitzers, Kibitzers and Criers.
   The Dick Gibson Show.
   The Franchiser.
   George Mills.
   The Living End.
   The MacGuffin.
   The Magic Kingdom.
   Mrs. Ted Bliss.
   The Rabbi of Lud.
   Van Gogh's Room at Arles.
Annie Ernaux, *Cleaned Out.*
Lauren Fairbanks, *Muzzle Thyself.*
   Sister Carrie.
Juan Filloy, *Op Oloop.*
Leslie A. Fiedler, *Love and Death in the American Novel.*

Gustave Flaubert, *Bouvard and Pécuchet.*
Kass Fleisher, *Talking out of School.*
Ford Madox Ford, *The March of Literature.*
Jon Fosse, *Melancholy.*
Max Frisch, *I'm Not Stiller.*
   Man in the Holocene.
Carlos Fuentes, *Christopher Unborn.*
   Distant Relations.
   Terra Nostra.
   Where the Air Is Clear.
Janice Galloway, *Foreign Parts.*
   The Trick Is to Keep Breathing.
William H. Gass, *Cartesian Sonata and Other Novellas.*
   Finding a Form.
   A Temple of Texts.
   The Tunnel.
   Willie Masters' Lonesome Wife.
Gérard Gavarry, *Hoppla! 1 2 3.*
Etienne Gilson, *The Arts of the Beautiful.*
   Forms and Substances in the Arts.
C. S. Giscombe, *Giscome Road.*
   Here.
   Prairie Style.
Douglas Glover, *Bad News of the Heart.*
   The Enamoured Knight.
Witold Gombrowicz, *A Kind of Testament.*
Karen Elizabeth Gordon, *The Red Shoes.*
Georgi Gospodinov, *Natural Novel.*
Juan Goytisolo, *Count Julian.*
   Juan the Landless.
   Makbara.
   Marks of Identity.
Patrick Grainville, *The Cave of Heaven.*
Henry Green, *Back.*
   Blindness.
   Concluding.
   Doting.
   Nothing.
Jiří Gruša, *The Questionnaire.*
Gabriel Gudding, *Rhode Island Notebook.*
John Hawkes, *Whistlejacket.*
Aleksandar Hemon, ed., *Best European Fiction 2010.*
Aidan Higgins, *A Bestiary.*
   Balcony of Europe.
   Bornholm Night-Ferry.
   Darkling Plain: Texts for the Air.
   Flotsam and Jetsam.
   Langrishe, Go Down.
   Scenes from a Receding Past.
   Windy Arbours.
Aldous Huxley, *Antic Hay.*
   Crome Yellow.
   Point Counter Point.
   Those Barren Leaves.
   Time Must Have a Stop.
Mikhail Iossel and Jeff Parker, eds., *Amerika:*
   Russian Writers View the United States.
Gert Jonke, *Geometric Regional Novel.*
   Homage to Czerny.
   The System of Vienna.
Jacques Jouet, *Mountain R.*
   Savage.
Charles Juliet, *Conversations with Samuel Beckett and*
   Bram van Velde.
Mieko Kanai, *The Word Book.*
Hugh Kenner, *The Counterfeiters.*
   Flaubert, Joyce and Beckett: The Stoic Comedians.
   Joyce's Voices.
Danilo Kiš, *Garden, Ashes.*
   A Tomb for Boris Davidovich.
Anita Konkka, *A Fool's Paradise.*
George Konrád, *The City Builder.*
Tadeusz Konwicki, *A Minor Apocalypse.*
   The Polish Complex.
Menis Koumandareas, *Koula.*
Elaine Kraf, *The Princess of 72nd Street.*
Jim Krusoe, *Iceland.*
Ewa Kuryluk, *Century 21.*
Eric Laurrent, *Do Not Touch.*
Violette Leduc, *La Bâtarde.*
Suzanne Jill Levine, *The Subversive Scribe:*
   Translating Latin American Fiction.
Deborah Levy, *Billy and Girl.*
   Pillow Talk in Europe and Other Places.
José Lezama Lima, *Paradiso.*
Rosa Liksom, *Dark Paradise.*
Osman Lins, *Avalovara.*
   The Queen of the Prisons of Greece.
Alf Mac Lochlainn, *The Corpus in the Library.*
   Out of Focus.
Ron Loewinsohn, *Magnetic Field(s).*
Brian Lynch, *The Winner of Sorrow.*
D. Keith Mano, *Take Five.*
Micheline Aharonian Marcom, *The Mirror in the Well.*
Ben Marcus, *The Age of Wire and String.*
Wallace Markfield, *Teitlebaum's Window.*
   To an Early Grave.
David Markson, *Reader's Block.*
   Springer's Progress.
   Wittgenstein's Mistress.
Carole Maso, *AVA.*

FOR A FULL LIST OF PUBLICATIONS, VISIT:
www.dalkeyarchive.com

SELECTED DALKEY ARCHIVE PAPERBACKS

LADISLAV MATEJKA AND KRYSTYNA POMORSKA, EDS.,
  *Readings in Russian Poetics: Formalist and
  Structuralist Views.*
HARRY MATHEWS,
  The Case of the Persevering Maltese: Collected Essays.
  Cigarettes.
  The Conversions.
  The Human Country: New and Collected Stories.
  The Journalist.
  My Life in CIA.
  Singular Pleasures.
  The Sinking of the Odradek Stadium.
  Tlooth.
  20 Lines a Day.
ROBERT L. MCLAUGHLIN, ED., *Innovations: An Anthology of
  Modern & Contemporary Fiction.*
HERMAN MELVILLE, *The Confidence-Man.*
AMANDA MICHALOPOULOU, *I'd Like.*
STEVEN MILLHAUSER, *The Barnum Museum.*
  In the Penny Arcade.
RALPH J. MILLS, JR., *Essays on Poetry.*
MOMUS, *The Book of Jokes.*
CHRISTINE MONTALBETTI, *Western.*
OLIVE MOORE, *Spleen.*
NICHOLAS MOSLEY, *Accident.*
  Assassins.
  Catastrophe Practice.
  Children of Darkness and Light.
  Experience and Religion.
  God's Hazard.
  The Hesperides Tree.
  Hopeful Monsters.
  Imago Bird.
  Impossible Object.
  Inventing God.
  Judith.
  Look at the Dark.
  Natalie Natalia.
  Paradoxes of Peace.
  Serpent.
  Time at War.
  The Uses of Slime Mould: Essays of Four Decades.
WARREN MOTTE,
  Fables of the Novel: French Fiction since 1990.
  Fiction Now: The French Novel in the 21st Century.
  Oulipo: A Primer of Potential Literature.
YVES NAVARRE, *Our Share of Time.*
  Sweet Tooth.
DOROTHY NELSON, *In Night's City.*
  Tar and Feathers.
WILFRIDO D. NOLLEDO, *But for the Lovers.*
FLANN O'BRIEN, *At Swim-Two-Birds.*
  At War.
  The Best of Myles.
  The Dalkey Archive.
  Further Cuttings.
  The Hard Life.
  The Poor Mouth.
  The Third Policeman.
CLAUDE OLLIER, *The Mise-en-Scène.*
PATRIK OUŘEDNÍK, *Europeana.*
FERNANDO DEL PASO, *News from the Empire.*
  Palinuro of Mexico.
ROBERT PINGET, *The Inquisitory.*
  Mahu or The Material.
  Trio.
MANUEL PUIG, *Betrayed by Rita Hayworth.*
  Heartbreak Tango.
RAYMOND QUENEAU, *The Last Days.*
  Odile.
  Pierrot Mon Ami.
  Saint Glinglin.
ANN QUIN, *Berg.*
  Passages.
  Three.
  Tripticks.
ISHMAEL REED, *The Free-Lance Pallbearers.*
  The Last Days of Louisiana Red.
  The Plays.
  Reckless Eyeballing.
  The Terrible Threes.
  The Terrible Twos.
  Yellow Back Radio Broke-Down.
JEAN RICARDOU, *Place Names.*
RAINER MARIA RILKE,
  The Notebooks of Malte Laurids Brigge.
JULIÁN RÍOS, *Larva: A Midsummer Night's Babel.*
  Poundemonium.
AUGUSTO ROA BASTOS, *I the Supreme.*
OLIVIER ROLIN, *Hotel Crystal.*
JACQUES ROUBAUD, *The Form of a City Changes Faster,
  Alas, Than the Human Heart.*
  The Great Fire of London.
  Hortense in Exile.
  Hortense Is Abducted.
  The Loop.
  The Plurality of Worlds of Lewis.
  The Princess Hoppy.
  Some Thing Black.
LEON S. ROUDIEZ, *French Fiction Revisited.*

VEDRANA RUDAN, *Night.*
STIG SÆTERBAKKEN, *Siamese.*
LYDIE SALVAYRE, *The Company of Ghosts.*
  Everyday Life.
  The Lecture.
  Portrait of the Writer as a Domesticated Animal.
  The Power of Flies.
LUIS RAFAEL SÁNCHEZ, *Macho Camacho's Beat.*
SEVERO SARDUY, *Cobra & Maitreya.*
NATHALIE SARRAUTE, *Do You Hear Them?*
  Martereau.
  The Planetarium.
ARNO SCHMIDT, *Collected Stories.*
  Nobodaddy's Children.
CHRISTINE SCHUTT, *Nightwork.*
GAIL SCOTT, *My Paris.*
DAMION SEARLS, *What We Were Doing and
  Where We Were Going.*
JUNE AKERS SEESE,
  Is This What Other Women Feel Too?
  What Waiting Really Means.
BERNARD SHARE, *Inish.*
  Transit.
AURELIE SHEEHAN, *Jack Kerouac Is Pregnant.*
VIKTOR SHKLOVSKY, *Knight's Move.*
  A Sentimental Journey: Memoirs 1917–1922.
  Energy of Delusion: A Book on Plot.
  Literature and Cinematography.
  Theory of Prose.
  Third Factory.
  Zoo, or Letters Not about Love.
JOSEF ŠKVORECKÝ, *The Engineer of Human Souls.*
CLAUDE SIMON, *The Invitation.*
GILBERT SORRENTINO, *Aberration of Starlight.*
  Blue Pastoral.
  Crystal Vision.
  Imaginative Qualities of Actual Things.
  Mulligan Stew.
  Pack of Lies.
  Red the Fiend.
  The Sky Changes.
  Something Said.
  Splendide-Hôtel.
  Steelwork.
  Under the Shadow.
W. M. SPACKMAN, *The Complete Fiction.*
ANDRZEJ STASIUK, *Fado.*
GERTRUDE STEIN, *Lucy Church Amiably.*
  The Making of Americans.
  A Novel of Thank You.
PIOTR SZEWC, *Annihilation.*
GONÇALO M. TAVARES, *Jerusalem.*
LUCIAN DAN TEODOROVICI, *Our Choice Presents . . .*
STEFAN THEMERSON, *Hobson's Island.*
  The Mystery of the Sardine.
  Tom Harris.
JEAN-PHILIPPE TOUSSAINT, *The Bathroom.*
  Camera.
  Monsieur.
  Running Away.
  Television.
DUMITRU TSEPENEAG, *Pigeon Post.*
  The Necessary Marriage.
  Vain Art of the Fugue.
ESTHER TUSQUETS, *Stranded.*
DUBRAVKA UGRESIC, *Lend Me Your Character.*
  Thank You for Not Reading.
MATI UNT, *Brecht at Night*
  Diary of a Blood Donor.
  Things in the Night.
ÁLVARO URIBE AND OLIVIA SEARS, EDS.,
  The Best of Contemporary Mexican Fiction.
ELOY URROZ, *The Obstacles.*
LUISA VALENZUELA, *He Who Searches.*
PAUL VERHAEGHEN, *Omega Minor.*
MARJA-LIISA VARTIO, *The Parson's Widow.*
BORIS VIAN, *Heartsnatcher.*
ORNELA VORPSI, *The Country Where No One Ever Dies.*
AUSTRYN WAINHOUSE, *Hedyphagetica.*
PAUL WEST, *Words for a Deaf Daughter & Gala.*
CURTIS WHITE, *America's Magic Mountain.*
  The Idea of Home.
  Memories of My Father Watching TV.
  *Monstrous Possibility: An Invitation to
  Literary Politics.*
  Requiem.
DIANE WILLIAMS, *Excitability: Selected Stories.*
  Romancer Erector.
DOUGLAS WOOLF, *Wall to Wall.*
  Ya! & John-Juan.
JAY WRIGHT, *Polynomials and Pollen.*
  The Presentable Art of Reading Absence.
PHILIP WYLIE, *Generation of Vipers.*
MARGUERITE YOUNG, *Angel in the Forest.*
  Miss MacIntosh, My Darling.
REYOUNG, *Unbabbling.*
ZORAN ŽIVKOVIĆ, *Hidden Camera.*
LOUIS ZUKOFSKY, *Collected Fiction.*
SCOTT ZWIREN, *God Head.*

FOR A FULL LIST OF PUBLICATIONS, VISIT:
www.dalkeyarchive.com